*Dayspring*s

Also by Margaret Silf

❧

LANDMARKS: An Ignatian Journey

TASTE AND SEE: Adventuring into Prayer

THE MILLER'S TALE (published by Avon Books)

Daysprings

Daily Readings for a Life with God

❦

MARGARET SILF

With illustrations by Roy Lovatt

DARTON · LONGMAN + TODD

First published in 1999 by
Darton, Longman and Todd Ltd
1 Spencer Court
140–142 Wandsworth High Street
London SW18 4JJ

ISBN 0–232–52350–9

A catalogue record for this book is available from the British Library.

Designed by Sandie Boccacci
Phototypeset in 10/13pt Bembo by Intype London Ltd
Printed and bound in Great Britain by
The Cromwell Press, Trowbridge, Wiltshire

AD
MAJOREM
DEI
GLORIAM

Contents

Table of liturgical dates

Year	*Sunday Cycle*	*Weekday Cycle*	*Ordinary time before Lent*	*Ordinary time after Pentecost*	*Year*
2000	B	II	Up to 7 March/Week 9	From 12 June/Week 10	2000
2001	C	I	Up to 27 Feb/Week 7	From 4 June/Week 9	2001
2002	A	II	Up to 12 Feb/Week 5	From 20 June/Week 7	2002
2003	B	I	Up to 4 Mar/Week 8	From 9 June/Week 10	2003
2004	C	II	Up to 24 Feb/Week 7	From 31 May/Week 9	2004
2005	A	I	Up to 8 Feb/Week 5	From 16 May/Week 7	2005
2006	B	II	Up to 28 Feb/Week 8	From 5 June/Week 9	2006
2007	C	I	Up to 20 Feb/Week 7	From 28 May/Week 8	2007
2008	A	II	Up to 5 Feb/Week 4	From 12 May/Week 6	2008
2009	B	I	Up to 24 Feb/Week 7	From 1 June/Week 9	2009
2010	C	II	Up to 16 Feb/Week 6	From 24 May/Week 8	2010
2011	A	I	Up to 8 Mar/Week 9	From 13 June/Week 11	2011
2012	B	II	Up to 21 Feb/Week 7	From 28 May/Week 8	2012
2013	C	I	Up to 12 Feb/Week 5	From 20 May/Week 7	2013
2014	A	II	Up to 4 Mar/Week 8	From 9 June/Week 10	2014
2015	B	I	Up to 17 Feb/Week 6	From 25 May/Week 8	2015
2016	C	II	Up to 9 Feb/Week 5	From 16 May/Week 7	2016
2017	A	I	Up to 28 Feb/Week 8	From 5 June/Week 9	2017
2018	B	II	Up to 13 Feb/Week 6	From 21 May/Week 7	2018
2019	C	I	Up to 5 Mar/Week 8	From 10 June/Week 10	2019
2020	A	II	Up to 25 Feb/Week 7	From 1 June/Week 9	2020

Introduction: Daysprings

Jesus spoke of his words entering our hearts as seed falls to the ground. Some of these seeds are smothered by the distractions and preoccupations that seem to take over our hearts like weeds. Some fall on our hard patches, solid with resentments or unresolved conflicts. Some are carried away on the winds of our busy-ness and our anxieties. Some, however, come to life, flower, and bring a whole new generation of heart-seeds into the soil of our lives and our world. These seeds, finding fertile soil, take root in our hearts and our experience and continue to grow and come to fullness through our days, weeks and years, transforming the very core of our being.

Yet how easily these life-giving words can slip away through over-burdened memories and fail to germinate. When I find this happening to me, it helps to remember the Samaritan woman of the gospel who met Jesus at Jacob's well (John 4:1–30). He was a complete stranger to her, yet he knew her heart and he told her her own story, in a way that she had never heard it told before. She listened to his words – the words of the one who is the Word – and then those words became a spring of living water welling up in her heart, flowing through her life and making it a place of joy and fruitfulness.

I believe that the words of Scripture hold that same promise for us today, two thousand years after that encounter at the well in Samaria. For us, too, they have the power to tell us our own story and to connect our personal life's experience to the story of redemption. We are invited first to *listen* to them, and then to *reflect* on what they might mean for us in the specific place and time and circumstances in which we are living our lives. Jacob's well is here and now, wherever we happen to find ourselves. The encounter with the Lord is today and every day, continually taking us by surprise and calling us forward to take one more step beyond ourselves and towards the kingdom. The living spring is ours to drink from, and ours to share with a thirsty world.

Daysprings is, perhaps, a little picnic basket to carry through the years. In this basket you will find a fragment of the living Word for every day, together with a short reflection which connects the words of Scripture to simple events, thoughts or encounters in our daily lives. Together, the words of Scripture and the words of the reflection offer you a space to spend a few moments of your own with the Lord each day. Sit with him awhile at the well. Receive the seed of life that he offers in his words. Welcome the living spring that he opens up within your heart. Let him gently suggest connections between his Word and your lived experience. And then take the joy and the vision you have discovered back to your own village, family, town, community, as the Samaritan woman took the good news back to her people.

If you are familiar with the lectionary readings used in the Anglican or Roman Catholic traditions, you will find that each daily text is taken from the readings for that day. The full references for these readings are provided on each page, though there may be occasional differences between the various lectionaries. The weekday readings and reflections cover a two-year liturgical cycle (Years I and II). You will find these in Parts 1, 2 and 3, for the seasons of Advent and Christmas, Lent and Easter, and the Weeks of Ordinary Time respectively. The Sunday readings follow a three-year liturgical cycle (Years A, B and C). You will find these in Part 4.

You may find the table of dates helpful in finding your place in the weekday and Sunday cycles and in locating the start and end of 'ordinary' time – bearing in mind of course that with God there is no such thing as 'ordinary time' or 'ordinary people'. In God, all time is sacred time and all of us are his sons and daughters.

Whether your tradition uses a set lectionary or not, *Daysprings* is an opportunity to be in prayerful communion with other Christians, as together we read and reflect on the Word which is God's gift to all of us, whatever our background. These fragments are small enough to carry with us through a busy life. Yet, because they are the Word of life, they are big enough to nourish our hungry hearts and still leave us with an overflow of love and grace to share with others.

I would like to thank all those who have in any way helped to put together this basket of fragments of Word and prayer, especially Morag Reeve, Helen Porter and Hannah Ward of Darton, Longman and Todd, Roy Lovatt for the illustrations, and all friends in North Staffordshire, for whom I originally wrote these daily reflections under the title 'Potter's Clay'.

May you *enjoy*, day by day, the bread of God's Word, grown from the seed of his love for you. May it nourish you and open up for you the living spring which is yours alone to discover, yet which flows from the heart of God, where we are all one in him.

PART 1: GOD BECOMES MAN

❧

Weekday readings and reflections for the seasons of Advent, Christmas and Epiphany

First Week of Advent ***(Weekday Cycle I)***

❦ Monday

O House of Jacob, come,
let us walk in the light of the Lord! (Isaiah 2:5)

I closed my book and turned out the light. It was then that I noticed the night sky, bright with starlight. As long as the light in my own room was burning, all I could see was my own room and its messy contents. But when I re-focused my gaze to what lay outside and beyond me, my vision was drawn out to a reality far beyond myself, and infinitely greater.

❦ Tuesday

They do no hurt, no harm,
on all my holy mountain,
for the country is filled with the knowledge of the Lord
as the waters swell the sea. (Isaiah 11:9–10)

The gently rising tide crept imperceptibly up the beach, gradually freeing stranded sea creatures and dried-up seaweeds from the desert wastes of ebb-tide, and what had at first seemed like a fear-inspiring invasion of the unknown, became a flood-tide of new life and grace and fruitfulness.

❦ Wednesday

We exult and we rejoice
that he has saved us;
for the hand of the Lord
rests on this mountain. (Isaiah 25:9–10)

The mountain of anxieties and resistances in my heart and in my life seemed unsurmountable, until, in the quiet of prayer, you rested your hand of blessing upon it. From then on, however harsh the terrain, it became the mountain where I had met *you*, and a place of joy and gratitude.

Thursday

Open to me the gates of holiness:
I will enter and give thanks. (Psalm 118:19)

You open the gates of your presence to us in the separateness and silence of our prayer, but when we go *through* those gates, we find ourselves in the heart of the hurts and the needs of our brothers and sisters.

Friday

The deaf, that day,
will hear the words of a book
and, after shadows and darkness,
the eyes of the blind will see. (Isaiah 29:18)

I didn't hear the sound of your crying, because I was tuned in to my own regrets. I didn't see your hand outstretched in need, because my eyes were blinded by my own resentments. Forgive me, friend, and let me try again.

Saturday

When the Lord has given you the bread of suffering and the water of distress, he who is your teacher will hide no longer, and you will see your teacher with your own eyes . . . He will send rain for the seed you sow in the ground, and the bread that the ground provides will be rich and nourishing. (Isaiah 30:20, 23)

The bread that springs from the seeds of our sorrow will sustain us more truly and more completely than the fairy cakes of our fleeting pleasures.

The week's readings

Monday	Isaiah 2:1–5; Psalm 122(121); Matthew 8:5–11
Tuesday	Isaiah 11:1–10; Psalm 72(71); Luke 10:21–4
Wednesday	Isaiah 25:6–10; Psalm 23(22); Matthew 15:29–37
Thursday	Isaiah 26:1–6; Psalm 118(117); Matthew 7:21, 24–7
Friday	Isaiah 29:17–24; Psalm 27(26); Matthew 9:27–31
Saturday	Isaiah 30:19–21, 23–6; Psalm 147(146); Matthew 9:35 – 10:1, 6–8

First Week of Advent *(Weekday Cycle II)*

❦ Monday

> *'I tell you that many will come from east and west to take their places with Abraham and Isaac and Jacob at the feast in the kingdom of heaven.'* (Matthew 8:11)

The dinner guests were carefully screened to avoid social embarrassment. The conversation was suitably polite and the atmosphere a little chilled. Down the road at the hostel the men shivered as they wrapped thankful hands round bowls of hot soup; friendly banter warmed up the raw night air. It was a feast, because love sat among them.

❦ Tuesday

> *'Happy the eyes that see what you see, for I tell you that many prophets and kings wanted to see what you see and never saw it; to hear what you hear, and never heard it.'* (Luke 10:23–4)

When we catch a glimpse of you in a baby's first grasp or an old man's memories, in the first crocus or the last autumn rose, we see what no book can contain or human wisdom can reveal.

❦ Wednesday

> *'See, this is our God*
> *in whom we hoped for salvation;*
> *the Lord is the one in whom we hoped.'* (Isaiah 25:9)

A tremour of joy always ran through Jennie's heart as she assisted at a birth. Every newborn child seemed to be a carrier of the unspoken hopes of all humanity. In a little speck of life, a hope for a better future. How much more powerful then, the hope that is born in you, the bringer of eternal life?

❧ Thursday

'It is not those who say to me "Lord, Lord", who will enter the kingdom of heaven, but the person who does the will of my Father in heaven.' (Matthew 7:21)

My prayer ended, so I thought, with a heartfelt promise to you to mend that strained relationship. The real prayer began when I saw her coming towards me in the street and faced up to my desire to avoid the meeting.

❧ Friday

The Lord is my light and my help;
whom shall I fear?
The Lord is the stronghold of my life;
before whom shall I shrink? (Psalm 27:1)

When I stand in the full light of the noonday sun I do not worry about whether my torch battery might fail. Then, Lord, knowing you to be the ground of my being, may I let go of the many lesser matters that pull me down into anxiety?

❧ Saturday

Then moonlight will be bright as sunlight and sunlight itself will be seven times brighter – like the light of seven days in one – on the day the Lord dresses the wound of his people and heals the bruises his blows have left. (Isaiah 30:26)

In your hands we see the silver gleam of the surgeon's knife, cutting the cancers from our hearts, but in your eyes we see the golden light of a healer's love, releasing us from pain into wholeness.

The week's readings

Monday	Isaiah 2:1–5; Psalm 122(121); Matthew 8:5–11
Tuesday	Isaiah 11:1–10; Psalm 72(71); Luke 10:21–4
Wednesday	Isaiah 25:6–10; Psalm 23(22); Matthew 15:29–37
Thursday	Isaiah 26:1–6; Psalm 118(117); Matthew 7:21, 24–7
Friday	Isaiah 29:17–24; Psalm 27(26); Matthew 9:27–31
Saturday	Isaiah 30:19–21, 23–6; Psalm 147(146); Matthew 9:35 – 10:1, 6–8

Second Week of Advent *(Weekday Cycle I)*

❦ Monday

Some men appeared, carrying on a bed a paralysed man whom they were trying to bring in and lay down in front of Jesus. But as the crowd made it impossible to find a way of getting him in, they went up on to the flat roof and lowered him and his stretcher down through the tiles into the middle of the gathering, in front of Jesus. (Luke 5:18–19)

With hindsight I can see that it was often when life 'let me down' that I found myself closest to you and your saving touch.

❦ Tuesday

A voice cries, 'Prepare in the wilderness a way for the Lord.
Make a straight highway for our God across the desert.' (Isaiah 40:3)

In the gardens of my life my path meanders round every delightful distraction, but my *deserts* lead me *straight to you.*

❦ Wednesday

Those who hope in the Lord renew their strength,
they put out wings like eagles.
They run and do not grow weary,
walk and never tire. (Isaiah 40:31)

When I am doing those things that satisfy my heart's deepest desires, I discover that they generate new energy within me that leaves me enough to spare to fuel the necessary tasks that I would rather not do at all.

❦ Thursday

For I, the Lord, your God,
I am holding you by the right hand;
I tell you, 'Do not be afraid,
I will help you.' (Isaiah 41:13)

Nick came alongside his little brother Jamie and gripped his hand, as they made their way along the exposed mountain path. It didn't make the path any less slippery, but it gave Jamie the confidence and courage to step forward without fear.

❧ Friday

Thus says the Lord, your redeemer, the Holy One of Israel:
I, the Lord, your God, teach you what is good for you,
I lead you in the way that you must go. (Isaiah 48:17)

In a world where every demand and pressure seems to *drive* us, may we know your love that *meets* us where we are, and *leads* us gently forwards towards our own deepest truth in you.

❧ Saturday

Then the prophet Elijah arose like a fire,
his word flaming like a torch. (Ecclesiasticus 48:1)

Your word, too, Lord, touches our lives like a torch, which burns away our masks and pretences, yet kindles the steady candle of your leading-love in our hearts.

The week's readings

Monday	Isaiah 35:1–10; Psalm 85(84); Luke 5:17–26
Tuesday	Isaiah 40:1–11; Psalm 96(95); Matthew 18:12–14
Wednesday	Isaiah 40:25–31; Psalm 103(102); Matthew 11:28–30
Thursday	Isaiah 41:13–20; Psalm 145(144); Matthew 11:11–15
Friday	Isaiah 48:17–19; Psalm 1; Matthew 11:16–19
Saturday	Ecclesiasticus 48:1–4, 9–11; Psalm 80(79); Matthew 17:10–13

Second Week of Advent *(Weekday Cycle II)*

❦ Monday

> *Let the wilderness and the dry-lands exult,*
> *let the wasteland rejoice and bloom.* (Isaiah 35:1)

There is an inner desert, where my branches fade and fail in the heat of the sun and my leaves wither. It is there that my roots reach down, in their great need, for the untapped well of the ground water, which alone can bring to life the hidden seeds in my heart.

❦ Tuesday

> *A voice cries: 'Prepare in the wilderness a way for the Lord.*
> *Make a straight highway for our God across the desert.'* (Isaiah 40:3)

When the Berlin Wall came down, most of it was crushed, to produce what turned out to be the finest quality road-making material. The road-blocks of oppression can be turned into the stepping-stones of peace.

❦ Wednesday

> *'Shoulder my yoke and learn from me, for I am gentle and humble in heart, and you will find rest for your souls. Yes, my yoke is easy and my burden light.'* (Matthew 11:29–30)

The Arab woman stooped, raised the heavy jug, full with the day's water supply, carefully onto her head, and walked back to the village, steadily and deliberately. The burden of her life would not be lifted, nor would it become lighter; but she would carry it with ease and confidence, because she had learned to walk her life's journey in perfect balance.

❦ Thursday

For I, the Lord, your God,
I am holding you by the right hand;
I tell you, 'Do not be afraid,
I will help you.' (Isaiah 41:13)

Everyone could hear the hysterical sobbing amid the crowd of Christmas shoppers, but no one could quite see where it was coming from. Then the child's mother made her way through the mass of people, gently, but with firm determination. She reached out to take hold of her toddler's hand. At once the sobbing stopped, and all was well.

❦ Friday

Jesus spoke to the crowds: 'What description can I find for this generation? It is like children shouting to each other as they sit in the market place:
"We played the pipes for you and you wouldn't dance;
We sang dirges, and you wouldn't be mourners."' (Matthew 11:16–17)

I notice that my most desolate moods descend when the world won't dance to my tune, or cry over my little troubles, and that I feel most at peace when I am so absorbed in the music, or the sorrow, of another, that I forget to think about my own.

❦ Saturday

Give us life that we may call upon your name. (Psalm 79:18)

We do not call upon your name in order that you might give us life. Rather, it is your gift of life, welling up inside us, that makes us able to call out to you, the source of everything we are.

The week's readings

Monday	Isaiah 35:1–10; Psalm 85(84); Luke 5:17–26
Tuesday	Isaiah 40:1–11; Psalm 96(95); Matthew 18:12–14
Wednesday	Isaiah 40:25–31; Psalm 103(102); Matthew 11:28–30
Thursday	Isaiah 41:13–20; Psalm 145(144); Matthew 11:11–15
Friday	Isaiah 48:17–19; Psalm 1; Matthew 11:16–19
Saturday	Ecclesiasticus 48:1–4, 9–11; Psalm 80(79); Matthew 17:10–13

Third Week of Advent *(Weekday Cycle I)*

❦ Monday

The Lord is good and upright.
He shows the path to those who stray,
he guides the humble in the right path;
he teaches his way to the poor. (Psalm 25:8–9)

The map was no use. The directions I had been given made no sense when I was lost. Then a friendly companion came alongside: 'I'll come with you and show you the way,' he said. And I knew that I had met you, my Lord and guide, in the maze of my life, and that your way of leading me is to walk the way with me.

❦ Tuesday

The Lord is close to the broken-hearted;
those whose spirit is crushed he will save. (Psalm 34:18)

You change the broken fragments of our lives into eucharistic bread, and the crushed grapes of our sorrow into eucharistic wine. Bless us, Lord, even as life breaks and crushes us, and give us to each other.

❦ Wednesday

Send victory like a dew, you heavens,
and let the clouds rain it down. (Isaiah 45:8)

The only victory that is worthy of a human heart is a victory that leaves gentleness and fruitful growth in its wake, not grief and mourning.

❦ Thursday

The mountains may depart,
the hills be shaken,
but my love for you will never leave you. (Isaiah 54:10)

The earthquakes of our experience re-arrange the landscape of our lives, and the changing scenes give us ever new possibilities to seek you and find you.

☙ Friday

It is the Lord God who speaks, who gathers the outcasts of Israel. (Isaiah 56:8)

You draw to yourself the ones we push to the outside edges. You listen to the ones without a voice. You turn us inside out, to show us who we really are.

The week's readings

Monday	Numbers 24:2–7, 15–17; Psalm 25(24); Matthew 21:23–7
Tuesday	Zephaniah 3:1–2, 9–13; Psalm 34(33); Matthew 21:28–32
Wednesday	Isaiah 45:6–8, 18, 21–6; Psalm 85(84); Luke 7:19–23
Thursday	Isaiah 54:1–10; Psalm 30(29); Luke 7:24–30
Friday	Isaiah 56:1–3, 6–8; Psalm 67(66); John 5:33–6

For readings and reflections from 17 December, see Last Week of Advent/Days Approaching Christmas.

Third Week of Advent *(Weekday Cycle II)*

❧ Monday

'I see him – but not in the present,
I behold him – but not close at hand:
a star from Jacob takes the leadership,
a sceptre arises from Israel.' (Numbers 24:17)

We see you, darkly, through the eyes of our faith in you. You see us, brightly, through the eyes of your faith in us to become the people you have created us to be.

❧ Tuesday

Look towards him and be radiant;
let your faces not be abashed. (Psalm 34:5)

Only when I gaze into your light am I able to forget the long dark shadow that stretches out behind me.

❧ Wednesday

The Lord will make us prosper
and our earth shall yield its fruit.
Justice shall march before him
and peace shall follow his steps.
(Psalm 85:12–13)

Dare we walk the ways that our hearts know to be true and just, and trust God for the peace that he promises will follow?

❧ Thursday

His anger lasts but a moment; his favour through life.
At night there are tears, but joy comes with dawn. (Psalm 30:5)

Your love for us, and your presence alongside us, are the permanent reality. Only the shadows of our passing frustrations obscure it from our sight, as rainclouds obscure a clear blue sky.

❧ Friday

O God, be gracious and bless us
and let your face shed its light upon us.
So will your ways always be known upon earth
and all nations learn your saving help. (Psalm 67:1–2)

In the dark of our despair we weep for our life's losses. In the dawning of grace and trust we discover the pearl we had never dared to hope could ever be ours.

The week's readings

Monday	Numbers 24:2–7, 15–17; Psalm 25(24); Matthew 21:23–7
Tuesday	Zephaniah 3:1–2, 9–13; Psalm 34(33); Matthew 21:28–32
Wednesday	Isaiah 45:6–8, 18, 21–6; Psalm 85(84); Luke 7:19–23
Thursday	Isaiah 54:1–10; Psalm 30(29); Luke 7:24–30
Friday	Isaiah 56:1–3, 6–8; Psalm 67(66); John 5:33–6

For readings and reflections from 17 December, see Last Week of Advent/Days Approaching Christmas.

Last Week of Advent/Days Approaching Christmas (Weekday Cycles I and II)

✠ 17 December

> *May the mountains bring forth peace for the people, and the hills, justice.* (Psalm 72:3)

The most fertile soil in the area had had its ancient origins in a volcanic eruption that had brought devastation in its wake. So too, Lord, our worst upheavals are often the source of our richest growth.

✠ 18 December

> *The angel of the Lord appeared to him in a dream and said, 'Joseph son of David, do not be afraid to take Mary home as your wife, because she has conceived what is in her by the Holy Spirit.'* (Matthew 1:20)

It frightens us too, Lord, and it can frighten those around us, when your seed starts to grow in our hearts. Give us the courage to embrace our deepest truths and take them home.

✠ 19 December

> *'He will . . . turn the hearts of fathers towards their children and the disobedient back to the wisdom that the virtuous have, preparing for the Lord a people fit for him.'* (Luke 1:17)

Turning back to you will always challenge us to turn back to each other. There cannot be the one without the other.

❧ 20 December

'I am the handmaid of the Lord,' said Mary, 'let what you have said be done to me.' (Luke 1:38)

She gave you the blank cheque of her life. You cashed it in. You took everything she had, and more, and left her grieving at the foot of the cross. And then you returned her capital with so much interest that all the world could live on it from that day forward.

❧ 21 December

'Blessed is she who believed that the promise made her by the Lord would be fulfilled.' (Luke 1:45)

Ben paused for a moment's rest after planting his spring bulbs. There was only a bare patch of earth to mark all his efforts. But he *knew* what would be there in the springtime. That knowledge – beyond sight and reason – transformed his labour and transfigured the bare earth into a place of faith and blessing.

❧ 22 December

When Hannah had weaned Samuel she took him to the temple of the Lord . . . She said . . . 'This is the child I prayed for, and the Lord granted me what I asked him. Now I make him over to the Lord for the whole of his life. He is made over to the Lord.'
There she left him, for the Lord. (1 Samuel 1:24, 27–8)

The test of the purity of my prayer is this: when you give me what I ask of you, can I immediately let it go again? And can I do so with joy?

❧ 23 December

Lord, make me know your ways.
Lord, teach me your paths.
Make me walk in your truth, and teach me. (Psalm 25:4)

You do not call us to study your truth, or to understand it, explain it or teach it. You call us to *walk* in it until we know every contour of its landscape, to be at home in it, and to risk each day's journey entirely to its leading. You call us to a knowledge that will be imprinted on the soles of our feet and etched in the hollows of our hearts.

The Feast of Christmas

❦ 24 December

'God, who from on high will bring the rising Sun to visit us,
to give light to those who live
in darkness and the shadow of death,
and to guide our feet
into the way of peace.' (Luke 1:78–9)

To be in your presence is to become gradually bathed in your light, as surely as to stand in the dawn is to see the darkness melt into the daylight. We can do nothing to bring your light to our hearts; we can only wait and trust in your promise of its coming.

❦ 25 December

As for Mary, she treasured all these things
and pondered them in her heart (Luke 2:19)

We can store our heart's treasure in dusty albums in cupboards that we seldom visit, or we can let it be our daily companion, growing with us and forging past memories into future hope.

The week's readings

17 December	Genesis 49:2, 8–10; Psalm 72(71); Matthew 1:1–17
18 December	Jeremiah 23:5–8; Psalm 72(71); Matthew 1:18–24
19 December	Judges 13:2–7, 24–5; Psalm 71(70); Luke 1:5–25
20 December	Isaiah 7:10–14; Psalm 24(23); Luke 1:26–38
21 December	Song of Songs 2:8–14; Psalm 33(32); Luke 1:39–45
22 December	1 Samuel 1:24–8; 1 Samuel 2:1, 4–8; Luke 1:46–56
23 December	Malachi 3:1–4, 23–4; Psalm 25(24); Luke 1:57–66
24 December	2 Samuel 7:1–5, 8–11, 6; Psalm 89(88); Luke 1:67–79

A shoot springs from the stock of Jesse,
A scion thrusts from his roots (Isaiah 11.1)

On this day new life grows from a fallen creation. In your birth our broken lives become the cradle of grace.

Days Following Christmas *(Weekday Cycles I and II)*

❦ 29 December

Simeon took the child Jesus into his arms and blessed God; and he said:
'Now, Master, you can let your servant go in peace,
just as you promised;
because my eyes have seen [your] salvation.' (Luke 2:29)

We recognise you when we take you to ourselves and touch your reality, and that happens when we take each other to ourselves and bless the Christ who is at once both hidden and revealed in our brothers and sisters. Such moments are blessed. They open the doors to the peace that passes understanding.

❦ 30 December

When they had done everything the Law of the Lord required, they went back to Galilee, to their own town of Nazareth. Meanwhile the child grew to maturity, and he was filled with wisdom, and God's favour was with him. (Luke 2:39–40)

It is not enough simply to do what your Law commands us. You ask us not merely to obey, but to *grow.*

❦ 31 December

Let the heavens rejoice and earth be glad,
let the sea and all within it thunder praise,
let the land and all it bears rejoice,
all the trees of the wood shout for joy
at the presence of the Lord for he comes,
he comes to rule the earth. (Psalm 96:11–13)

In the last hours of the dying year our hearts and our homes break out in celebration, to welcome the new. The winter trees are gestating the coming springtime, and you, Lord, are coming to claim us as your own.

❦ 1 January

May the Lord bless you and keep you.
May the Lord let his face shine on you and be gracious to you.

May the Lord uncover his face to you and bring you peace. (Numbers 6:24–6)

A new year and another mile of the journey. Three hundred and sixty-five new chances to watch the sun rise on God's surprises along the way.

❧ 2 January

You are anointed with truth, not with a lie,
and as it has taught you, so you must stay in him.
Live in Christ. (1 John 2:27)

The touch of your truth on our hearts is the reason why every falsehood within us leaves us feeling exiled from our real home in you.

The week's readings

29 December	1 John 2:3–11; Psalm 96(95); Luke 2:22–35
30 December	1 John 2:12–17; Psalm 96(95); Luke 2:36–40
31 December	1 John 2:18–21; Psalm 96(95); John 1:1–18
1 January	Numbers 6:22–7; Psalm 67(66); Galatians 4:4–7; Luke 2:16–21
2 January	1 John 2:22–8; Psalm 98(97); John 1:19–28

For readings and reflections for the period 25–28 December inclusive, see Part 4.

❦ 3 January

You know that God is righteous –
then you must recognise that everyone whose life is righteous
has been begotten by him. (1 John 2:29)

Clarry was the most cantankerous old lady in the nursing home. Everyone kept out of her way. But one day she caught me unawares and insisted on showing me her album of photos of the many stray cats she had once rescued and looked after. It was Clarry who taught me that God scatters his seeds even in the most neglected weed-beds and grows his greetings in the most unlikely corners.

❦ 4 January

As John stood there with two of his disciples, Jesus passed, and John stared hard at him and said, 'Look, there is the lamb of God.' (John 1:35–6)

Let us be people who do not seek to hold our friends' attention but rather to redirect it towards *you*.

❦ 5 January

Philip found Nathaniel and said to him, 'We have found the one Moses wrote about in the Law, the one about whom the prophets wrote: he is Jesus son of Joseph, from Nazareth.' 'From Nazareth?' said Nathaniel, 'Can anything good come from that place?' 'Come and see,' replied Philip. (John 1:45–6)

We would never refuse to unwrap a gift because we don't like the colour of the wrapping paper. Why, then, do we so often refuse to get to know our neighbours, for no better reason?

❦ 6 January

John said, 'Someone is following me, someone who is more powerful than I am, and I am not fit to kneel down and undo the strap of his sandals. I have baptised you with water, but he will baptise you with the Holy Spirit.' (Mark 1:7–8)

We are the builders of a roadway, the cables along which the good news can pass, the bowls in which the feast can be offered. The One who follows is the One who leads, the Reality that makes sense of our pale shadows.

❦ 7 January

[At the wedding at Cana] Jesus said to the servants, 'Fill the jars with water,' and they filled them to the brim. 'Draw some out now,' he told them, 'and take it to the steward.' They did this; the steward tasted the water, and it had turned into wine. (John 2:7–9)

The miracle of transformation begins in the empty spaces of our hearts, where you turn the water of our experience into the wine of your grace. The miracle is fulfilled and recognised when the love you have poured into us to fill our needs has been poured out again to meet the needs of others.

The week's readings

3 January	1 John 2:29 – 3:6; Psalm 98(97); John 1:29–34
4 January	1 John 3:7–10; Psalm 98(97); John 1:35–42
5 January	1 John 3:11–21; Psalm 100(99); John 1:43–51
6 January	1 John 5:5–13; Psalm 147; Mark 1:6–11
7 January	1 John 5:14–21; Psalm 149; John 2:1–12

For readings and reflection for the Feast of Epiphany, see Part 4.

Week Following the Epiphany *(Weekday Cycle I)*

✠ Monday

Jesus' fame spread throughout Syria, and those who were suffering from disease and painful complaints of one kind or another, the possessed, epileptics, the paralysed, were all brought to him and he cured them. (Matthew 4:24)

Dare we open up to you the *dis*-ease of our hearts, Lord? The sick sorrow of regret, and the pain of unhealed memories, our obsessions and compulsions and the fears that cripple us? Dare we open up these wounds to the healer's touch?

✠ Tuesday

Jesus took the five loaves and the two fish, raised his eyes to heaven and said the blessing; then he broke the loaves and handed them to his disciples to distribute among the people. He also shared out the two fish among them all. (Mark 6:41)

We may prepare the food with care and express our thanks to you in all sincerity, but until we share it with our brothers and sisters the meal has no meaning and the miracle no power.

✠ Wednesday

Jesus spoke to them, and said, 'Courage! It is I! Do not be afraid.' Then he got into the boat with them, and the wind dropped. (Mark 6:50–1)

You calm our life's storms, not by changing our circumstances, but by entering into them with us and changing our fear into trust.

✠ Thursday

A man who does not love the brother that he can see cannot love God, whom he has never seen. (1 John 4:20)

My heart may melt with compassion when I see the plight of refugees on the other side of the world, but if I can't find the time to attend to the needs of the people next door, I am failing to live in love.

❦ Friday

Jesus' reputation continued to grow, and large crowds would gather to hear him and to have their sickness cured, but he would always go off to some place where he could be alone and pray. (Luke 5:15–16)

Prayer is not the icing on the cake, but the flour and the yeast that makes our living bread, from which everything else we do is nourished and sustained.

❦ Saturday

John replied . . . 'I myself am not the Christ; I am the one who has been sent in front of him . . . He must grow greater, I must grow smaller.' (John 3:28, 30)

I am always pleased to see the postman, but when he walks back down the path again and fades into the distance, I am holding the real purpose of his visit – the good news he has brought me.

The week's readings

Monday	1 John 3:22 – 4:6; Psalm 2; Matthew 4:12–17, 23–5
Tuesday	1 John 4:7–10; Psalm 72(71); Mark 6:34–44
Wednesday	1 John 4:11–18; Psalm 72(71); Mark 6:45–52
Thursday	1 John 4:19 – 5:4; Psalm 72(71); Luke 4:14–22
Friday	1 John 5:5–13; Psalm 147; Luke 5:12–16
Saturday	1 John 5:14–21; Psalm 149; John 3:22–30

Week Following the Epiphany (Weekday Cycle II)

Monday

It is not every spirit, my dear people, that you can trust;
test them, to see if they come from God. (1 John 4:1)

We can tell where a movement in our hearts or an influence in our lives is coming from by noticing where it is leading us. What comes from God will always tend to draw the good out of our bad and the best out of our good. What is destructive within us or around us will always tend to diminish our good into poor and our bad into worst.

Tuesday

It was getting very late, and his disciples came up to Jesus and said, 'This is a lonely place and it is getting very late, so send them away, and they can go to the farms and villages round about, to buy themselves something to eat.' Jesus replied, 'Give them something to eat yourselves.' (Mark 6:35–7)

'Why don't you save the millions of starving children in the world?' I asked you.
'Why don't you slip round to see if the old lady next door is warm enough?' you replied.

Wednesday

'In love there can be no fear,
but fear is driven out by perfect love:
because to fear is to expect punishment,
and anyone who is afraid still is imperfect in love.' (1 John 4:18)

We walk through our lives constantly looking backwards over our shoulders in fear of the expected pain and aggravation. How much more safely we would move if we focused our gaze on the love that draws us forward.

Thursday

Unrolling the scroll he found the place where it is written:
The spirit of the Lord has been given to me,
for he has anointed me.

He has sent me to bring the good news to the poor,
to proclaim liberty to captives
and to the blind new sight,
to set the downtrodden free,
to proclaim the Lord's year of favour' . . . Then he began to speak to them: 'This text is being fulfilled today even as you listen.' (Luke 4:17–22)

For two thousand years we have waited for your Coming, and every day we have missed it, because we were expecting it tomorrow.

❦ Friday

Jesus' reputation continued to grow, and large crowds would gather to hear him and to have their sickness cured, but he would always go off to some place where he could be alone and pray. (Luke 5:15–16)

When I need you most, Lord, you sometimes seem so far away. It is then, perhaps, that you are in your lonely place, drawing from your Father the strength for both of us.

❦ Saturday

'He must grow greater,
I must grow smaller.' (John 3:30)

The smaller I become, the less I weigh, the less I am bound by the gravitational pull of my own self-centredness, and the more freely my soul can fly to you.

The week's readings

Monday	1 John 3:22 – 4:6; Psalm 2; Matthew 4:12–17, 23–5
Tuesday	1 John 4:7–10; Psalm 72(71); Mark 6:34–44
Wednesday	1 John 4:11–18; Psalm 72(71); Mark 6:45–52
Thursday	1 John 4:19 – 5:4; Psalm 72(71); Luke 4:14–22
Friday	1 John 5:5–13; Psalm 147; Luke 5:12–16
Saturday	1 John 5:14–21; Psalm 149; John 3:22–30

PART 2: FROM DEATH TO LIFE

❦

Weekday readings and reflections for the seasons of Lent, Holy Week and Eastertide

The First Days of Lent *(Weekday Cycles I and II)*

✠ Ash Wednesday

Turn to the Lord your God again
for he is all tenderness and compassion,
slow to anger, rich in graciousness, and ready to relent. (Joel 2:13)

Not a society for saints, but a meeting place for the broken: a hospital church. A community that acknowledges its needs and surrenders itself to healing. How many of us first came to God through a door marked '*Accident and Emergency*?' And how gently we were received, how lovingly tended. No recriminations, no interrogations. Simply his overwhelming desire for us, that we might be whole again.

✠ Thursday

'I set before you life or death, blessing or curse.
Choose life!' (Deuteronomy 30:19)

Sinking behind the clouded horizon of a stress-filled day, we may glimpse a beautiful sunset. Right at the heart of shabby supermarket consumerism, eager, generous hands drop their contributions into the charity box. And a child's trusting smile survives our grumblings. Little pointers, showing the direction to Life.

✠ Friday

To break unjust fetters and undo the things of the yoke, to share your bread with the hungry and shelter the homeless poor, to clothe the man you see to be naked, and not to turn from your own kin. (Isaiah 58:6–7)

I may spend my life visiting the prisoners. I may write a hundred letters to my MP. I may study every book on liberation theology. But if, my friend, I hold you captive in my resentful memories, my heart remains a stone.

❧ Saturday

> *If you do away with the yoke,*
> *the clenched fist, the wicked word,*
> *if you give your bread to the hungry and relief to the oppressed,*
> *your light will rise in the darkness*
> *and your shadows become like noon.* (Isaiah 58:9–10)

The grieving father of the victim of a terrorist bombing murmurs: 'I forgive them.' A clenched fist relaxes in shocked amazement and lets the gun fall. And a strange new light flickers through the darkened city.

The week's readings

Ash Wednesday	Joel 2:12–18; Psalm 51(50); 2 Corinthians 5:20 – 6:2; Matthew 6:1–6, 16–18
Thursday	Deuteronomy 30:15–20; Psalm 1; Luke 9:22–5
Friday	Isaiah 58:1–9; Psalm 51(50); Matthew 9:14–15
Saturday	Isaiah 58:9–14; Psalm 86(85); Luke 5:27–32

First Week of Lent (Weekday Cycle I)

❦ Monday

'I was hungry, and you never gave me food.' (Matthew 25:42)

We heard that you were hungry and we called a conference to discuss food vouchers.
Father, forgive!
You looked lost in our neighbourhood, and we closed ranks.
Father, forgive!
You were dirty and dishevelled, and we complained that our new shoes were hurting.
Father, forgive!
There was a rumour that you might have AIDS, and we took our child away from your child's school.
Father, forgive!
We heard that you were in prison, and we decided that it was probably your own fault.
Father, forgive!

❦ Tuesday

The Lord is close to the broken-hearted;
Those whose spirit is crushed, he will save. (Psalm 34:18)

The March winds play havoc with the newly sprung daffodils. I bend to gather those that have been snapped off in the night before their buds had a chance to open, to bring them into the warmth and let them open up their beauty. And a gentle voice whispers in the wind: 'If you care enough to do this for them, how much more surely will I do the same for you?'

❦ Wednesday

The crowds got even bigger and Jesus addressed them. 'This is a wicked generation; it is asking for a sign. The only sign it will be given is the sign of Jonah.' (Luke 11:29)

Jonah couldn't cope with your challenge, Lord. And so he fled, right into the heart of the storm. We know the storm, and we know the flights of panic. And we know how it feels when the whale brings us back on the very same beach from which we were running away. Bring us through the storms of faithlessness, back to the beaches of surrender.

❦ Thursday

> *Jesus said to his disciples: 'Ask, and it will be given to you; search, and you will find; knock, and the door will be opened to you.'* (Matthew 7:7)

As the tree's branches grow in their desire to reach for light, and its roots grow in their delving for water, so my heart grows in its desire for you, its creator, and I find you in the process of my seeking.

❦ Friday

> *My soul is longing for the Lord,*
> *more than watchmen for daybreak.* (Psalm 130:6)

The nights were long, as my mother lay dying. But then, at dawn, she would often fall into a fitful sleep. I listened each night for the first single bird call before the dawn chorus proper began, and I watched for the first flush of sunrise over the garden. And then I would go out for half an hour among the roses. I met you there, Lord, among the roses, and you received all the sorrows and the longings of the night into your new-dawning love.

❦ Saturday

> *'You have learnt how it was said: You must love your neighbour and hate your enemy. But I say this to you: love your enemies and pray for those that persecute you.'* (Matthew 5:43–4)

As my friend walked away from me in anger, I realised, in grief, that I had lost her love because I had failed to heed your command to let my love be all-inclusive; I had excluded from my loving everything that caused me pain.

The week's readings

Monday	Leviticus 19:1–2, 11–18; Psalm 19(18); Matthew 25:31–46
Tuesday	Isaiah 55:10–11; Psalm 34(33); Matthew 6:7–15
Wednesday	Jonah 3:1–10; Psalm 51(50); Luke 11:29–32
Thursday	Esther 4:17; Psalm 138(137); Matthew 7:7–12
Friday	Ezekiel 18:21–8; Psalm 130(129); Matthew 5:20–6
Saturday	Deuteronomy 26:16–19; Psalm 119(118); Matthew 5:43–8

First Week of Lent (Weekday Cycle II)

⁂ Monday

The precepts of the Lord are right,
they gladden the heart.
The command of the Lord is clear,
it gives light to the eyes. (Psalm 19:8)

When I follow my own will, I may experience pleasure and see the world through rose-tinted spectacles. But when I follow *your* will for me, I experience joy, and I see the world in its true colours, and in the unclouded clarity of your light.

⁂ Tuesday

I sought the Lord and he answered me,
from all my terrors he set me free. (Psalm 34:4)

I had a problem. I asked you for the solution. You answered by releasing me from the anxiety that was gripping me, and then, for the first time, I was free to understand the real nature of the problem, and there was space in my mind for the solution.

⁂ Wednesday

God saw their efforts to renounce their evil behaviour. And God relented: he did not inflict on them the disaster which he had threatened. (Jonah 3:10)

Miriam was trembling with suppressed anger as she dismissed the class after challenging them about their selfish behaviour. Most of them walked past her, heads in the air, eyes defiant. But as Malcolm shuffled past, she noticed the tears gathering in his eyes. He looked up at her, distressed; her face softened into gentleness, and he read forgiveness in her gaze.

❧ Thursday

Your love, O Lord, is eternal,
discard not the work of your hands. (Psalm 138:8)

Our potter, of infinite patience and love, when we are displeasing to you, do not cast us aside, but take the clay of our hearts and mould it as you would have it be, until it bears your imprint. Your remoulding will hurt, but it will not destroy.

❧ Friday

'You have learnt how it was said to our ancestors: you must not kill, and if anyone does kill he must answer for it before the court. But I say this to you; anyone who is angry with his brother will answer for it before the court; if a man calls his brother "Fool" he will answer for it before the Sanhedrin; and if a man calls him "Renegade" he will answer for it in hell fire.' (Matthew 5:21–2)

I noticed how my angry retort had caused my colleague to shrivel and shrink. And I realised, too late, that in the warmth of a kinder and more generous word she could have grown and blossomed.

❧ Saturday

'You must therefore be perfect, just as your heavenly Father is perfect.' (Matthew 5:48)

Called to perfection, to completness, to wholeness, until all our fragmented parts are drawn together and all our brokenness is healed, and we are one in him and in his peace.

The week's readings

Monday	Leviticus 19:1–2, 11–18; Psalm 19(18); Matthew 25:31–46
Tuesday	Isaiah 55:10–11; Psalm 34(33); Matthew 6:7–15
Wednesday	Jonah 3:1–10; Psalm 51(50); Luke 11:29–32
Thursday	Esther 4:17; Psalm 138(137); Matthew 7:7–12
Friday	Ezekiel 18:21–8; Psalm 130(129); Matthew 5:20–6
Saturday	Deuteronomy 26:16–19; Psalm 119(118); Matthew 5:43–8

Second Week of Lent (Weekday Cycle I)

☙ Monday

'Give, and there will be gifts for you: a full measure, pressed down, shaken together, and running over, will be poured into your lap.' (Luke 6:38)

Our containers are far too small for the fullness of grace. We have two choices: either we turn aside from the supply and settle for what we have; or we let it overflow, and flood the world around us.

☙ Tuesday

'The greatest among you must be your servant. Anyone who exalts himself will be humbled, and anyone who humbles himself will be exalted.' (Matthew 23:12)

Who might merit the title today of this century's greatest Christian? A picture comes to mind of a small, grey-haired, vulnerable woman, called Teresa, going about her daily work in the dusty streets of Calcutta. No status in the Church. No status in the world. No money, no family, no power. Just an ordinary servant-saint.

☙ Wednesday

'Can you drink the cup that I am going to drink?' (Matthew 20:22)

Sometimes we have to swallow very hard, when the bitter words are flung at us, or the hurtful comments or the unjust accusations. And we remember a lonely man in a dark garden, who struggled with the bitter cup. 'Share my dying in the darkness,' he calls to us, 'and you will share my resurrection at dawn.'

☙ Thursday

'A blessing on the man who puts his trust in the Lord, with the Lord for his hope.
He is like a tree by the waterside that thrusts its roots to the stream:
When the heat comes it feels no alarm, its foliage stays green;
It has no worries in a year of drought, and never ceases to bear fruit.' (Jeremiah 17:7–8)

With every prayer, our roots reach deeper, searching for the ground water. With every act of kindness, our branches stretch a little further to the sky, become a little greener. Root and branch. Darkness and light. Praying and living. Our wholeness and our fullness.

❧ Friday

> *'Here comes the man of dreams,' they said to one another. 'Come on, let us kill him and throw him into some well; we can say that a wild beast devoured him. Then we shall see what becomes of his dreams.'* (Genesis 37:20)

Dreams are like soap bubbles – so easy to make, so easy to break. A child's dreams, especially, are so vulnerable to the cold winds of disapproval, from parents, teachers, friends. Walk beside us, Lord, and breathe your new life into our broken dreams. Let your spirit turn our deepest dreams to prayers.

❧ Saturday

> *'While he was still a long way off, his father saw him and was moved with pity. He ran to the boy, clasped him in his arms and kissed him tenderly.'* (Luke 15:20)

They found the runaway teenager in Singapore. A row over a football match, and he had taken himself halfway across the world on his father's credit card. That's what you could *really* call a family row. Easy to imagine what we might have to say to the lad, if he were ours, when he dares to come back – and perhaps not too difficult, either, to imagine the surge of joy and the heartfelt welcome at the airport when we receive him safely home.

The week's readings

Monday	Daniel 9:4–10; Psalm 79(78); Luke 6:36–8
Tuesday	Isaiah 1:10, 16–20; Psalm 50(49); Matthew 23:1–12
Wednesday	Jeremiah 18:18–20; Psalm 31(30); Matthew 20:17–28
Thursday	Jeremiah 17:5–10; Psalm 1; Luke 16:19–31
Friday	Genesis 37:3–4, 12–13, 17–28; Psalm 105(104); Matthew 21:33–43, 45–6
Saturday	Micah 7:14–15, 18–20; Psalm 103(102); Luke 15:1–3, 11–32

Second Week of Lent (Weekday Cycle II)

❦ Monday

'The amount you measure out is the amount you will be given back.' (Luke 6:38)

The living pool receives the streams from the mountains and lets them flow freely onwards to the sea. The stagnant pool receives the inflowing but has no outflow. The living water gives growth and life. The stagnant water diminishes into death.

❦ Tuesday

'Cease to do evil.
Learn to do good,
search for justice,
help the oppressed.' (Isaiah 1:16–17)

After the drink-driving conviction Jim had to stop driving immediately. It took him rather longer to learn to live free of his addiction. And then, very gradually, to discover how to channel his energies into helping those people he had harmed.

❦ Wednesday

Jesus answered: 'Can you drink the cup that I am going to drink?' They replied, 'We can.' 'Very well,' he said, 'you shall drink my cup.' (Matthew 20:22)

Your cup has many flavours, Lord: the cup of loneliness; the cup of fear; the cup of poverty; the cup of terror. But always, because your lips have touched it, it is a cup of blessing.

❧ Thursday

Happy indeed is the man
who follows not the counsel of the wicked;
nor lingers in the way of sinners,
nor sits in the company of scorners,
but whose delight is the law of the Lord. (Psalm 1:1–2)

It seemed churlish, at the time, when Jean kept refusing to stay with her friends while they watched the forbidden videos. She came close to losing their friendship, until they began to sense that she was the one person in their group to whom they could turn when the things they had seen on the screen started to take hold of their real lives.

❧ Friday

'It was the stone rejected by the builders that became the keystone.' (Matthew 21:42)

Catherine was turned down in all her job applications, because of her debilitating handicap. Then her application for a disability allowance was rejected on the grounds that her handicap was not sufficiently debilitating. Trapped in this cycle, she turned to you. She learned to pray, until her whole life became a prayer, and many people came to her, seeking peace, and wisdom, and *you*.

❧ Saturday

The Pharisees and the scribes complained: 'This man', they said, 'welcomes sinners and eats with them.' (Luke 15:1)

We may learn to *tolerate* those who offend us, but you show us how to *welcome* them. We may bring ourselves to send them a sandwich, but you call us to seek them out and share the table with them.

The week's readings

Monday	Daniel 9:4–10; Psalm 79(78); Luke 6:36–8
Tuesday	Isaiah 1:10, 16–20; Psalm 50(49); Matthew 23:1–12
Wednesday	Jeremiah 18:18–20; Psalm 31(30); Matthew 20:17–28
Thursday	Jeremiah 17:5–10; Psalm 1; Luke 16:19–31
Friday	Genesis 37:3–4, 12–13, 17–28; Psalm 105(104); Matthew 21:33–43, 45–6
Saturday	Micah 7:14–15, 18–20; Psalm 103(102); Luke 15:1–3, 11–32

Third Week of Lent *(Weekday Cycle I)*

✠ Monday

Like the deer that yearns for running streams,
So my soul is yearning for you, my God. (Psalm 42:1)

August in Jerusalem. The Arab family received us with overwhelming hospitality out of the fierce heat of the midday sun. The children circled around us, and their mother set a jug of pure, clear, cold water before us. We drank, deeply, thankfully, and that draught of cold water, offered in love, satisfied deeper longings than mere thirst.

✠ Tuesday

Peter went up to Jesus and said: 'Lord, how often must I forgive my brother if he wrongs me? As often as seven times?' Jesus answered, 'Not seven, I tell you, but seventy times seven.' (Matthew 18:21)

The difference between seven and seventy times seven is the distance between time and eternity, the bridge from conditional to unconditional love and the way from humanity to God.

✠ Wednesday

Jesus said to his disciples 'Do not imagine that I have come to abolish the Law or the Prophets. I have come not to abolish but to complete them.' (Matthew 5:17)

I expected you to throw away the old me and start again from scratch to make me new. But you are simply making me ever more completely what I truly am.

✠ Thursday

'Listen to my voice, then I will be your God and you shall be my people. Follow right to the end the way that I have marked out for you.' (Jeremiah 7:23)

The crest of every hill revealed another, higher, more distant peak ahead, and there was no end to the track marked out by the irregular stone cairns. We were frequently disheartened, but we knew that the cairns pointed the way – the only way – to the perfect view, the vision, at the end of the journey.

❦ Friday

'I will heal their disloyalty, I will love them with all my heart, for my anger has turned from them. I will fall like dew on Israel.' (Hosea 14:5–6)

Dew is gentle. Dew falls silently, while we sleep, softening our hard crusts so that grace might penetrate our hearts.

❦ Saturday

Let us set ourselves to know the Lord;
that he will come is as certain as the dawn,
he will come to us as showers come,
like spring rains watering the earth. (Hosea 6:3)

Ever so gradually the frozen earth thaws and the furrows start to crumble. The March sun gleams pale; clouds race; rain soaks and softens, and our heart-seed wakes from its winter dreaming.

The week's readings

Monday	2 Kings 5:1–15; Psalms 42, 43(41, 42); Luke 4:24–30
Tuesday	Daniel 3:25, 34–43; Psalm 25(24); Matthew 18:21–35
Wednesday	Deuteronomy 4:1, 5–9; Psalm 147; Matthew 5:17–19
Thursday	Jeremiah 7:23–8; Psalm 95(94); Luke 11:14–23
Friday	Hosea 14:2–10, Psalm 81(80); Mark 12:28–34
Saturday	Hosea 5:15 – 6:6; Psalm 51(50); Luke 18:9–14

Third Week of Lent *(Weekday Cycle II)*

❦ Monday

O send forth your light and your truth;
let these be my guide.
Let them bring me to your holy mountain,
to the place where you dwell. (Psalm 43:3)

The winter sea was as black as the starless night, as I stood on the deck of the ferry. A map would be useless in such a place, I thought. Then, for a brief moment, the sweeping beam from a distant lighthouse cut through the darkness. We were still far away from the harbour, but the direction was clear.

❦ Tuesday

Azariah stood in the heat of the fire, and he began to pray:
Oh, do not abandon us for ever,
for the sake of your name;
do not repudiate your covenant. (Daniel 3:25, 34)

Every day you send us some reminder, small or great, concealed or obvious, that you are keeping your covenant promise to be always with us. And those reminders are what make it possible for us to stay faithful to *our* covenant promises to walk with *you.*

❦ Wednesday

'I tell you solemnly, till heaven and earth disappear, not one dot, not one little stroke, shall disappear from the Law until its purpose is achieved.' (Matthew 5:18)

For as long as the river flows, it must respect the limits of its banks, if its stream is not to become a destroying flood. This is the law of its journey, until the journey ends and it is poured into the ocean, and the river banks have served their purpose.

❧ Thursday

'He who is not with me is against me; and he who does not gather with me scatters.' (Luke 11:23)

Every moment of my life gives me a choice of how to spend that moment's energy: gathering or scattering; with you, or against you.

❧ Friday

I will fall like dew on Israel.
He shall bloom like the lily,
and thrust out roots like the poplar,
his shoots will spread far. (Hosea 14:6–7)

The short time of my morning prayer, and the peace it gives me, seems to evaporate into the bustle of the day, as rapidly as the dew disappears from the grass-blades at sunrise. Yet its effects penetrate every moment of that day, nourishing its roots, and enabling its fruitfulness.

❧ Saturday

Let us set ourselves to know the Lord;
that he will come is as certain as the dawn,
he will come to us as showers come,
like spring rains watering the earth. (Hosea 6:3)

Barbara stopped off at the church on her way to work, and knelt down before the altar, gazing at the East window, opening up her troubled heart in prayer. On the other side of town, Rahim stopped work for a moment, in response to the silent prayer-call in his heart. He turned his inner eyes to the East, and called out to the God of his fathers. Two strangers, two faiths, two human hearts set in the direction of the Lord, and certain of his coming.

The week's readings

Monday	2 Kings 5:1–15; Psalms 42, 43(41, 42); Luke 4:24–30
Tuesday	Daniel 3:25, 34–43; Psalm 25(24); Matthew 18:21–35
Wednesday	Deuteronomy 4:1, 5–9; Psalm 147; Matthew 5:17–19
Thursday	Jeremiah 7:23–8; Psalm 95(94); Luke 11:14–23
Friday	Hosea 14:2–10; Psalm 81(80); Mark 12:28–34
Saturday	Hosea 5:15 – 6:6; Psalm 51(50); Luke 18:9–14

Fourth Week of Lent *(Weekday Cycle I)*

❧ Monday

At night there are tears, but joy comes with dawn . . .
You have changed my mourning into dancing. (Psalm 30:5, 11)

Today I can feel gratitude, even for the desert times and the pain and the heartache in the years that have passed. I can feel it sincerely, because the pain, as well as the joy, has brought me to this place where I stand today: a good place, a place of promise, that I am learning to trust.

❧ Tuesday

Wherever the river flows, all living creatures teeming in it will live. Fish will be plentiful, for wherever the water goes it brings health, and life teems wherever the river flows. (Ezekiel 47:9)

When love begins to flow through the current of our lives, the whole landscape of living starts to change. There is a springtime on our river banks, and springtime leads to harvest. We notice a new flower that we hadn't seen before; we hear the meanings of silence and read the unspoken signals in our friends' faces. A tiny seed. A teeming harvest.

❧ Wednesday

'Does a woman forget her baby at the breast,
or fail to cherish the son of her womb?
Yet even if these forget, I will never forget you.' (Isaiah 49:15)

The wounded eyes of the abused child open again, and trust flickers there momentarily. There is a loving that is more powerful even than all the hurting. Can this thing be?

❧ Thursday

Jesus said to the Jews: 'How can you believe, since you look to one another for approval and are not concerned with the approval that comes from the one God?' (John 5:44)

When I was a child I lived under the constant need to please others. As I grew up, I more often chose to please myself. Only now do I begin to realise that all you ask of me is that I should let myself become what you created me to be.

❧ Friday

'Can it be true the authorities have made up their minds that he is the Christ? Yet we all know where he comes from, but when the Christ appears no one will know where he comes from.' (John 10:26–7)

The last thing we expected was to find you sitting at the next desk, standing behind us in the supermarket queue, alongside us in the traffic jam. We had our eyes fixed to the telescope and we failed to see the grass growing at our feet.

❧ Saturday

When the guards went back, the chief priests and Pharisees asked them: 'Why did you not bring him?' The guards answered. 'Nobody has ever talked like this man.' (John 7:45–6)

The author of all our being speaks with authority. We recognise his voice, at the centre of our reality. The centre that cannot fail to respond, whatever the cost.

The week's readings

Monday	Isaiah 65:17–21; Psalm 30(29); John 4:43–54
Tuesday	Ezekiel 47:1–9, 12; Psalm 46(45); John 5:1–3, 5–16
Wednesday	Isaiah 49:8–15; Psalm 145(144); John 5:17–30
Thursday	Exodus 32:7–14; Psalm 106(105); John 5:31–47
Friday	Wisdom 2:1, 12–22; Psalm 34(33); John 7:1–2, 10, 25–30
Saturday	Jeremiah 11:18–20; Psalm 7; John 7:40–52

Fourth Week of Lent *(Weekday Cycle II)*

Monday

For me you have changed my mourning into dancing;
O Lord my God, I will thank you forever. (Psalm 30:11–12)

Maureen could have cried as she coaxed her small son to leave her at the start of his first day at school. The fledgling fell so reluctantly out of the safety of the nest, because he had not yet tasted the joys of flight.

Tuesday

Wherever the river flows, all living creatures teeming in it will live. Fish will be plentiful, for wherever the water goes it brings health, and life teems wherever the river flows. Along the river, on either bank, will grow every kind of fruit tree. With leaves that never wither and fruit that never fails; they will bear new fruit every month, because this water comes from the sanctuary. (Ezekiel 47:9–10, 12)

Your living water is no unsteady trickle, but an unstoppable river, flowing and overflowing with the abundance of life for ourselves and for all who walk along our river-banks.

Wednesday

'Does a woman forget her baby at the breast,
or fail to cherish the son of her womb?
Yet even if these forget, I will never forget you.' (Isaiah 49:15)

Claire tried to pick up the pieces after her teenage pregnancy and the adoption of her baby. But for thirty years she yearned to know the child she had given up. At last her lifelong search ended in a long-delayed reunion, and in a joy once lost but never forgotten.

❧ Thursday

'You have never heard his voice,
you have never seen his shape,
and his word finds no home in you
because you do not believe
in the one he has sent.' (John 5:37–8)

But those who *do* believe, hear his voice across marketplace and factory floor and playground, and see his shape in every human shape there is.

❧ Friday

'Can it be true the authorities have made up their minds that he is the Christ? Yet we all know where he comes from, but when the Christ appears no one will know where he comes from.' Then, as Jesus taught in the Temple, he cried out: 'Yes, you know me and you know where I come from. Yet I have not come of myself.' (John 7:26–8)

My stranger-friend, I know you so well, yet I don't know you at all. I know that part of you that shares my life and comes from my home town. But there is a secret unkown source of you that comes from far beyond us both.

❧ Saturday

Some said 'He is the Christ,' but others said: 'Would the Christ be from Galilee?' . . . The Pharisees answered . . . 'Prophets do not come out of Galilee!' (John 7:40–2, 52)

Why do we expect our Mother Teresas to be in India, and not on the streets of our own neighbourhood, when you have taught us to expect to find you where we are?

The week's readings

Monday	Isaiah 65:17–21; Psalm 30(29); John 4:43–54
Tuesday	Ezekiel 47:1–9, 12; Psalm 46(45); John 5:1–3, 5–16
Wednesday	Isaiah 49:8–15; Psalm 145(144); John 5:17–30
Thursday	Exodus 32:7–14; Psalm 106(105); John 5:31–47
Friday	Wisdom 2:1, 12–22; Psalm 34(33); John 7:1–2, 10, 25–30
Saturday	Jeremiah 11:18–20; Psalm 7; John 7:40–52

Fifth Week of Lent (Weekday Cycle I)

❧ Monday

'I am the light of the world; anyone who follows me will not be walking in the dark; he will have the light of life.' (John 8:12)

When my heart is light, I go into my room and light a candle; I close my eyes and I come to you in prayer. When my heart is heavy, and my hope goes dark, I struggle to manage without you, until I stumble and fall and finally open my eyes to find your hand upon me and a flicker of candlelight reflected in your eyes.

❧ Tuesday

He looked down from heaven to the earth
that he might hear the groans of the prisoners
and free those condemned to die. (Psalm 101:19, 20)

You hang high above us, to reach us in our depths. You are bound and nailed, so that we might become free. You are silenced into death, so that our cries might reach the Father.

❧ Wednesday

'If you make my word your home you will indeed be my disciples,
you will learn the truth,
and the truth will make you free.' (John 8:31–2)

Your word falls as a seed into our hearts. Your seed holds the secret of our deepest truth. And your truth becomes the blossoming of our eternal freedom.

❧ Thursday

'I will make you father of a multitude of nations. I will make you most fruitful.' (Genesis 17:6)

When your word takes root in our hearts, our lives become an outgrowth of your truth, releasing the seeds of your kingdom into the waiting soil around us.

❧ Friday

In my anguish I called to the Lord;
I cried to my God for help.
From his temple he heard my voice;
my cry came to his ears. (Psalm 18:6)

In our emptiest spaces God has the most room to live and move and work his miracles.

❧ Saturday

'It is better for one man to die for the people, than for the whole nation to be destroyed.' (John 11:50)

We made our own preparations for your entry to Jerusalem. We loaded our own guilt onto the back of the waiting scapegoat. It was the new girl, the quiet one, who got caught by the headmistress when we ran away. It was the colleague from the other department who was blamed for the mistakes we made. We believed it when they told us that the foreigners were taking our jobs and the homeless littering our streets. And then, when it was too late, there was blood on our hands.

The week's readings

Monday	Daniel 13:1–9,15–17, 19–30, 30–62; Psalm 23(22); John 8:12–20
Tuesday	Numbers 21:4–9; Psalm 102(101); John 8:21–30
Wednesday	Daniel 3:14–20, 24–5, 28; Daniel 3:52–6; John 8:31–42
Thursday	Genesis 17:3–9; Psalm 105(104); John 8:51–9
Friday	Jeremiah 20:10–13; Psalm 18(17); John 10:31–42
Saturday	Ezekiel 37:21–8; Jeremiah 31:10–13; John 11:45–57

Fifth Week of Lent *(Weekday Cycle II)*

✠ Monday

'If there is one of you who has not sinned, let him be the first to throw a stone at her.' (John 8:7)

Lord, take the stones that we throw at each other in judgement, and turn them into bread that we share with each other in love.

✠ Tuesday

'He who sent me is with me
and he has not left me to myself.' (John 8:29)

Sometimes all I want is to be left to myself. But when I am, I soon discover that 'myself' is far too small a place to live in.

✠ Wednesday

'If you make my word your home you will indeed be my disciples,
you will learn the truth,
and the truth will make you free.' (John 8:31–2)

To make one small choice without fear of loss or hope of gain is to make a choice in freedom and to cast a vote for truth. And every vote will be counted.

✠ Thursday

Jesus replied: 'I tell you most solemnly, before Abraham ever was, I AM.' (John 8:58)

To *be* who we truly *are*, fully and joyfully, here and now, is to *be* eternally, joined to the One who for ever *is*.

❧ Friday

In my anguish I called to the Lord;
I cried to my God for help.
From his temple he heard my voice;
my cry came to his ears. (Psalm 18:6)

We never allow our 999 lines to be jammed by less important conversations. So, too, our cries to God override all our lesser concerns and carry us straight to his heart.

❧ Saturday

Caiaphas, the high priest of that year, said: 'You don't seem to have grasped the situation at all; you fail to see that it is better for one man to die for the people, than for the whole nation to be destroyed.' (John 11:49–50)

'Better to sacrifice a small minority group of single parents, or unwelcome asylum-seekers, for the greater good of the majority.' The words of the year's leaders, to a nation about to sell its soul.

The week's readings

Monday	Daniel 13:1–9, 15–17, 19–30, 30–62; Psalm 23(22); John 8:1–11
Tuesday	Numbers 21:4–9; Psalm 102(101); John 8:21–30
Wednesday	Daniel 3:14–20, 24–5, 28; Daniel 3:52–6; John 8:31–42
Thursday	Genesis 17:3–9; Psalm 105(104); John 8:51–9
Friday	Jeremiah 20:10–13; Psalm 18(17); John 10:31–42
Saturday	Ezekiel 37:21–8; Jeremiah 31:10–13; John 11:45–57

Holy Week *(Weekday Cycles I and II)*

✠ Monday

Mary brought in a pound of very costly ointment, pure nard, and with it anointed the feet of Jesus, wiping them with her hair; the house was full of the scent of the ointment. (John 12:3)

We pour out our grieving and rejoicing, mingled, over your feet. In a moment of intimate connection, we let your aching heart touch ours. A costly moment, for us and for you. A moment that releases a new fragrance of possibility.

✠ Tuesday

Peter said to him: 'Why can't I follow you now? I will lay down my life for you.' 'Lay down your life for me?' answered Jesus. 'I tell you most solemnly, before the cock crows you will have disowned me three times.' (John 13:37–8)

You receive our eager gestures and intentions, knowing at once both the sincerity of our desires and the weakness of our wills. You know that our faithfulness will barely make it through the night. Yet you keep on loving us, beyond the cockcrow.

✠ Wednesday

While they were eating Jesus said 'I tell you solemnly, one of you is about to betray me.' They were greatly distressed and started asking him in turn, 'Not I, Lord, surely?' He answered 'Someone who has dipped his hand into the dish with me, will betray me . . .' Judas who was to betray him, asked in his turn, 'Not I, Rabbi, surely?' (Matthew 26:20–5)

I dip my hand into your dish each week, Lord, and I come to your table faithfully, a believer in an unbelieving world . . . Not I, Lord . . . surely?

❦ Holy Thursday

> *'Never!' said Peter. 'You shall never wash my feet.' Jesus replied, 'If I do not wash you, you can have nothing in common with me.' 'Then, Lord,' said Simon Peter, 'not only my feet, but my hands and my head as well!'* (John 13:8–9)

We cannot give to others what we have not been willing to receive ourselves. Give us the grace, Lord, to let you bathe us in your love, so that we may give that same love to each other.

❦ Good Friday

> *One of the soldiers pierced his side with a lance; and immediately there came out blood and water.* (John 19:34)

The stony Lenten path leads us to the point of nothingness, where God himself is to be destroyed. And in the moment of destruction, the stream of Life is released, to flow for ever from the Son of Man to the people of God.

❦ Holy Saturday/Passover

> *Joseph of Arimathaea went to Pilate and asked for the body of Jesus. He then took it down, wrapped it in a shroud and put him in a tomb which was hewn in stone in which no one had yet been laid. It was Preparation Day and the sabbath was imminent.* (Luke 23:52–4)

This day, caught between eternal death and everlasting life, holds all our bleakness in its hours. We offer you all that in us that clings to the tomb and cowers in the darkness of the hewn stone. The Preparation journey lasts a lifetime, but the sabbath is at hand.

The week's readings

Monday	Isaiah 42:1–7; Psalm 27(26); John 12:1–11
Tuesday	Isaiah 49:1–6; Psalm 71(70); John 13:21–33, 36–8
Wednesday	Isaiah 50:4–9; Psalm 69(68); Matthew 26:14–25
Thursday	Exodus 12:1–8, 11–14; Psalm 116(115), John 13:1–15
Good Friday	Isaiah 52:13 – 53:12; Psalm 31(30); John 18:1 – 19:42
Holy Saturday	No liturgical readings

Octave of Easter (Weekday Cycle I)

✠ Monday

While they were on their way, some of the guard went off into the city to tell the chief priests all that had happened. These held a meeting with the elders and, after some discussion, handed a considerable sum of money to the soldiers with these instructions, 'This is what you must say, "His disciples came during the night and stole him away while we were asleep." ' (Matthew 28:11–13)

My lies may cost me dearly, but the truth will set me free.

✠ Tuesday

Jesus said, 'Mary!' She knew him then and said to him in Hebrew, 'Rabbuni!' – which means Master. (John 20:16)

Our teachers never told us this, Lord. Our books and courses never mentioned it. They taught us much *about* you. But we needed to hear you speak our name, before we could *know* you, and, in that knowledge, know ourselves. And when you spoke our name, our response was easy and inevitable, and uttered in our own familiar language.

✠ Wednesday

Now while he was with them at table, he took the bread and said the blessing; then he broke it and handed it to them. And then their eyes were opened and they recognised him. (Luke 24:30–1)

Out of all the anguish and the turbulence of our present moment and our present struggles, a familiar gesture, instantly recognised, slices through the confusion with a brilliant shaft of light. Moments of clarity, restoring our certainty that your presence, like the sun, is always there, and only the clouds come and go.

✠ Thursday

'Why are you so agitated, and why are these doubts rising in your hearts? Look at my hands and feet; yes, it is I indeed. Touch me and see for yourselves; a ghost has no flesh and bones as you can see I have.' (Luke 24:38–40)

A ghost might have been easier to cope with – more easily dismissed as a trick of the imagination. But instead you ask for our real, embodied, full-blooded response to your indestructible Reality, energising every particle of your creation.

✠ Friday

The disciples came on in the boat, towing the net and the fish; they were only about a hundred yards from land . . . Jesus said to them, 'Come and have breakfast.' None of the disciples was bold enough to ask, 'Who are you?' They knew quite well it was the Lord. (John 21:12)

There is still a hundred yards of water between me and the impossible invitation. My mind tells my heart to look before I leap, but my heart knows quite well who is cooking my breakfast.

✠ Saturday

Mary of Magdala went to those who had been his companions and who were mourning and in tears, and told them. (Mark 16:10)

What we have seen, we must tell. For there is a world full of mourning, aching for the touch of joy.

The week's readings

Monday	Acts 2:14, 22–32; Psalm 16(15); Matthew 28:8–15
Tuesday	Acts 2:36–41; Psalm 33(32); John 20:11–18
Wednesday	Acts 3:1–10; Psalm 105(104); Luke 24:13–35
Thursday	Acts 3:11–26; Psalm 8; Luke 24:35–48
Friday	Acts 4:1–12; Psalm 118(117); John 21:1–14
Saturday	Acts 4:13–21; Psalm 118(117); Mark 16:9–15

Octave of Easter *(Weekday Cycle II)*

Monday

I saw the Lord before me always,
for with him at my right hand, nothing can shake me.
So my heart was glad and my tongue cried out with joy. (Acts 2:25–6)

However deeply I delve into the story of my life, I can find no situation that hasn't been prefigured by the story of *your* living and dying. It makes meaning in my chaos; it brings steadiness in my storms and joy to my journeying.

Tuesday

Mary stayed outside near the tomb, weeping . . . Jesus said: 'Woman, why are you weeping? Who are you looking for?' Supposing him to be the gardener, she said: 'Sir, if you have taken him away, tell me where you have put him, and I will go and remove him.' Jesus said: 'Mary!' She knew him then and said to him in Hebrew, 'Rabbuni!' – which means Master. (John 20:11–16)

When our eyes are blinded by our tears and our ears are closed up in sadness, we often draw the curtains on our lives and we miss the daybreak when it dawns. At times like that only your touch can tear apart the veil that comes between us.

Wednesday

Peter said [to the crippled beggar at the Temple gate] 'I have neither silver nor gold, but I will give you what I have: in the name of Jesus Christ the Nazarene, walk!' (Acts 3:6)

The two friends rarely exchanged material gifts. There was no need. Instead, they exchanged an unpossessive, unconditional love, through which each gave the other the empowerment to become his true self, fully alive.

❧ Thursday

They were still talking about all this when Jesus himself stood among them and said to them, 'Peace be with you!' In a state of alarm and fright, they thought they were seeing a ghost. But he said 'Why are you so agitated, and why are these doubts rising in your hearts? Look at my hands and feet; yes, it is I indeed. Touch me and see for yourselves; a ghost has no flesh and bones as you can see I have.' And as he said this he showed them his hands and feet. Their joy was so great that they still could not believe it, and they stood there dumbfounded. (Luke 24:36–41)

And today, no less than when you lived and died on earth, your Spirit dwells in the solid flesh and bones of *our* bodies, and you show us *your* wounds when you show us those of our sisters and brothers.

❧ Friday

It was light by now and there stood Jesus on the shore, though the disciples did not realise that it was Jesus. Jesus called out: 'Have you caught anything friends?' And when they answered 'No' he said, 'Throw the net out to starboard and you'll find something.' So they dropped the net and there were so many fish that they could not haul it in. (John 21:4–6)

We stubbornly go on dredging the depths of our own spent resources to scratch a meagre meal, while you wait for us to turn round and recognise the feast you have prepared for us, on *your* side of our hearts.

❧ Saturday

He said to them, 'Go out to the whole world; proclaim the Good News to all creation.' (Mark 16:15)

When every creature breathes unpolluted air, and every fish swims in uncontaminated water, we too shall be whole: creatures and Creator eternally reconnected.

The week's readings

Monday	Acts 2:14, 22–32; Psalm 16(15); Matthew 28:8–15
Tuesday	Acts 2:36–41; Psalm 33(32); John 20:11–18
Wednesday	Acts 3:1–10; Psalm 105(104); Luke 24:13–35
Thursday	Acts 3:11–26; Psalm 8; Luke 24:35–48
Friday	Acts 4:1–12; Psalm 118(117); John 21:1–14
Saturday	Acts 4:13–21; Psalm 118(117); Mark 16:9–15

Second Week of Easter (Weekday Cycle I)

✠ Monday

'Unless a person is born through water and the Spirit, he cannot enter the kingdom of God: what is born of the flesh is flesh; what is born of the Spirit is spirit.' (John 3:5–6)

The seed of our immortal nature lies unfulfilled in the earth of our lives, until your Spirit awakens it to the promise of your eternal springtime.

✠ Tuesday

'The wind blows where it pleases; you hear its sound, but you cannot tell where it comes from or where it is going. That is how it is with all who are born of the Spirit.' (John 3:8)

I hear the rustling of my life's leaves, and the creaking of its branches. I feel the hardness of its fears and the warmth of its loving. Yet everything that is me is brought to life by the secret, silent, invisible sap of your Spirit, rising from beyond me, raising me to beyond myself.

✠ Wednesday

'For God sent his Son into the world, not to condemn the world, but so that through him the world might be saved.' (John 3:17)

You are not waiting to judge us for our failures in loving. You are waiting to fill us with your own capacity to love.

✠ Thursday

When the officials brought the apostles in to face the Sanhedrin, the high priest demanded an explanation. 'We gave you a formal warning,' he said, 'not to preach in his name, and what have you done? You have filled Jerusalem with your teaching.' (Acts 5:27–8)

Those who ran away and hid, those who denied you and abandoned you and crouched in the upper room, afraid of the authorities, have been filled with your risen presence, and all Jerusalem cannot contain their courage and their joy.

❧ Friday

'Leave these men alone and let them go. If this enterprise, this movement of theirs, is of human origin, it will break up of its own accord; but if it does in fact come from God you will not only be unable to destroy them, but you might find yourselves fighting against God.' (Acts 5:38–9)

The enterprise they feared is ours today, and nothing can destroy it. Nothing can subvert the living God.

❧ Saturday

In the evening the disciples went down to the shore of the lake and got into a boat to make for Capernaum on the other side of the lake. It was getting dark by now and Jesus had still not rejoined them. The wind was strong and the sea was getting rough. They had rowed three or four miles when they saw Jesus walking on the lake and coming towards the boat. This frightened them, but he said: 'It is I. Do not be afraid.' (John 6:16–20)

We have known the darkness of the lake, and the fear of the storm-swell beneath our boat. Where are you, Lord, when we row against the wind, and why, when you come to our frightened hearts, do we so often fail to hear your assurance, 'It is I. Do not be afraid'?

The week's readings

Monday	Acts 4:23–31; Psalm 2; John 3:1–8
Tuesday	Acts 4:32–7; Psalm 93(92); John 3:7–15
Wednesday	Acts 5:17–26; Psalm 34(33); John 3:16–21
Thursday	Acts 5:27–33; Psalm 34(33); John 3:31–6
Friday	Acts 5:34–42; Psalm 27(26); John 6:1–15
Saturday	Acts 6:1–7; Psalm 33(32); John 6:16–21

Second Week of Easter (Weekday Cycle II)

⁂ Monday

> *As they prayed, the house where they were assembled rocked; they were all filled with the Holy Spirit and began to proclaim the word of God boldly.* (Acts 4:31)

We build up our defences, like a city in an earthquake zone, but we know we are defenceless before the power of your Spirit. We trust that you will turn our helplessness into your strength and our fear into your courage.

⁂ Tuesday

> *'The wind blows where it pleases; you hear its sound, but you cannot tell where it comes from or where it is going. That is how it is with all who are born of the Spirit.'* (John 3:8)

We know, yet we know not, where we came from or where we are going. We only know that we are making the journey with you, and, like the migrating geese, we must trust the inner compass you have planted in our hearts.

⁂ Wednesday

> *'And indeed, everybody who does wrong hates the light and avoids it,*
> *for fear his actions should be exposed;*
> *but the man who lives by the truth comes out into the light,*
> *so that it may be plainly seen that what he does is done in God.'* (John 3:20–1)

When we find the courage to come out of the darkness and face the truth about who we really are, we discover an unexpected bonus: the light also reveals to us the hurts and needs of our sisters and brothers.

⁂ Thursday

> *'He who is born of the earth*
> *is earthly himself and speaks in an earthly way.*
> *He who comes from heaven*
> *bears witness to the things he has seen and heard.'* (John 3:31)

I come to you in prayer with mud on my feet, bringing my earth-self with my earth-bound hopes and needs. You send me back to earth with a grain of heaven in my heart, to be sown back into the earth of my today.

❧ Friday

Looking up, Jesus saw the crowds approaching and said to Philip: 'Where can we buy some bread for these people to eat?' . . . Philip answered, 'Two hundred denarii would only buy enough to give them a small piece each.' One of his disciples, Andrew, Simon Peter's brother, said, 'There is a small boy here with five barley loaves and two small fish, but what is that among so many?' (John 6:5–9)

Our 'much' provides almost nothing.
Your 'almost nothing' provides a feast.

❧ Saturday

It was getting dark by now and Jesus had still not rejoined them. The wind was strong and the sea was getting rough. They had rowed three or four miles when they saw Jesus walking on the lake and coming towards the boat. This frightened them, but he said: 'It is I. Do not be afraid.' They were for taking him into the boat, but in no time it reached the shore at the place they were making for. (John 6:17–21)

In our need, we are so concerned to bring you on board our little boat that we forget that you hold all the power of the oceans in your hands.

The week's readings

Monday	Acts 4:23–31; Psalm 2; John 3:1–8
Tuesday	Acts 4:32–7; Psalm 93(92); John 3:7–15
Wednesday	Acts 5:17–26; Psalm 34(33); John 3:16–21
Thursday	Acts 5:27–33; Psalm 34(33); John 3:31–6
Friday	Acts 5:34–42; Psalm 27(26); John 6:1–15
Saturday	Acts 6:1–7; Psalm 33(32); John 6:16–21

Third Week of Easter *(Weekday Cycle I)*

✠ Monday

Then they said to him, 'What must we do if we are to do the works that God wants?' Jesus gave them this answer, 'This is working for God: you must believe in the one he has sent.' (John 6:28–9)

How much energy we expend in working out what to do for you and how to do it! If we would only rest in our believing and trust you to open up each new step before us, how much more fruitful our lives might be.

✠ Tuesday

'I am the bread of life. He who comes to me will never be hungry; he who believes in me will never thirst.' (John 6:35)

For years I tried to live on the surface satisfactions and the sweetmeats of existence. Until I became painfully aware of the aching hunger at the centre of my being. And gratefully, needfully, I stretched out my hands for the life-giving bread that alone could fill me, and that you never cease to offer.

✠ Wednesday

Saul then worked for the total destruction of the Church; he went from house to house arresting both men and women and sending them to prison. (Acts 8:3)

Nothing we can do, not the full sum of the worst that we can perpetrate, can place us beyond the ranging beam of grace.

✠ Thursday

Jesus said to the Jews: 'No one can come to me unless he is drawn by the Father who sent me, and I will raise him up at the last day. It is written in the prophets: They will all be taught by God, and to hear the teaching of the Father, and learn from it, is to come to me.' (John 6:44–5)

Like iron filings we are drawn by your magnetic power. And the more we discover of your magnetism, the more powerfully it draws us home to you.

❦ Friday

Suddenly, while Saul was travelling to Damascus and just before he reached the city, there came a light from heaven all round him. He fell to the ground, and then he heard a voice saying, 'Saul, Saul, why are you persecuting me?' 'Who are you, Lord?' he asked, and the voice answered, 'I am Jesus and you are persecuting me. Get up now and go into the city, and you will be told what you will have to do.' (Acts 9:3–7)

When your light pierces our darkness, it reveals not your condemnation, but first your questioning, then your challenge, and finally your guidance and empowerment.

❦ Saturday

After hearing his doctrine, many of the followers of Jesus said, 'This is intolerable language. How can anyone accept it?' . . . Then Jesus said to the Twelve, 'What about you, do you want to go away too?' Simon Peter answered, 'Lord, who shall we go to? You have the message of eternal life, and we believe; we know that you are the Holy One of God.' (John 6:60, 67–9)

Our faith sometimes leads us into impossible corners and down impassable tracks. It seems like the end of the road. A Calvary moment. You ask us, gently: 'Are you going to turn aside?' And your very gentleness renews our inner certainty that yours is the only Way through the impossible.

The week's readings

Monday	Acts 6:8–15; Psalm 119(118); John 6:22–9
Tuesday	Acts 7:51 – 8:1; Psalm 31(30); John 6:30–5
Wednesday	Acts 8:1–8; Psalm 66(65); John 6:35–40
Thursday	Acts 8:26–40; Psalm 66(65); John 6:44–51
Friday	Acts 9:1–20; Psalm 117(116); John 6:52–9
Saturday	Acts 9:31–42; Psalm 116(115); John 6:60–9

Third Week of Easter *(Weekday Cycle II)*

✠ Monday

'Do not work for food that cannot last,
but work for food that endures to eternal life.' (John 6:27)

I stopped beside a colleague's desk, and noticed the photographs of his two children propped up proudly against his files. 'That's to remind me why I'm really here,' he told me. 'When I'm tempted to pack it all in, I look at them and I know I'm working for something much more precious than a salary.' And I knew that my colleague was working for hope, working for love.

✠ Tuesday

The Jews said to Jesus: 'What sign will you give to show us that we should believe in you? What work will you do? Our fathers had manna to eat in the desert.' (John 6:30–1)

'Prove that you love me,' he said to her. 'Do what *I* want.' It was the end of their friendship. She found someone to whom she could *give* her love, where it was not demanded.

✠ Wednesday

'I have come from heaven,
not to do my own will,
but to do the will of the one who sent me.' (John 6:38)

In the still silent centre of prayer we are touched by the power of your will, your desire for our wholeness. Then we are sent out to the outer edges of our lives and our world, to carry your desire out, from the dark of prayer into the light of action.

✠ Thursday

'No one can come to me
unless he is drawn by the Father who sent me.' (John 6:44)

Jake tipped the iron filings out onto the sheet of paper, as the science teacher had told him to do. They lay there, quite lifeless and pointless. Then he gently drew the magnet across the paper and watched as they all moved towards the power so much greater than themselves, following the deepest laws of their nature.

❧ Friday

Suddenly, while Saul was travelling to Damascus and just before he reached the city, there came a light from heaven all round him. He fell to the ground, and then he heard a voice saying, 'Saul, Saul, why are you persecuting me?' (Acts 9:3–4)

Gemma's nerves had been stretched to breaking point, yet she knew there was no excuse for the way she had turned on her little son and made him the focus of all her frustration. It was nearly midnight when she went to bed, still seething with resentment. Something drew her into the nursery as she passed. The nightlight was still burning. Its glow fell like a ray from heaven across the child's tear-stained face. 'Gemma,' she seemed to hear her heart reproach her, 'why are you being so untrue to yourself?'

❧ Saturday

After this, many of his disciples left him and stopped going with him . . . Then Jesus said to the Twelve, 'What about you, do you want to go away too?' Simon Peter answered, 'Lord, who shall we go to? You have the message of eternal life, and we believe; we know that you are the Holy One of God.' (John 6:66–8)

Once we have met ourselves, in you, stripped of all our masks and our defences, there can be no way back. To turn away again would be to violate the very heart of our own reality.

The week's readings

Monday	Acts 6:8–15; Psalm 119(118); John 6:22–9
Tuesday	Acts 7:51 – 8:1; Psalm 31(30); John 6:30–5
Wednesday	Acts 8:1–8; Psalm 66(65); John 6:35–40
Thursday	Acts 8:26–40; Psalm 66(65); John 6:44–51
Friday	Acts 9:1–20; Psalm 117(116); John 6:52–9
Saturday	Acts 9:31–42; Psalm 116(115); John 6:60–9

Fourth Week of Easter (Weekday Cycle I)

Monday

'I have come so that they may have life
and have it to the full.' (John 10:10)

Dare we entrust ourselves to the empty spaces we must cross, to discover the fullness that is waiting for us, even now, right where we are?

Tuesday

The Jews gathered round him and said, 'How much longer are you going to keep us in suspense? If you are the Christ, tell us plainly.' Jesus replied: 'I have told you, but you do not believe.' (John 10:24–5)

A clear, unambiguous sign from God would change the world, like a universal change of government. But the Christ brings us something more permanent and more true: a change of heart.

Wednesday

'Whoever believes in me
believes not in me
but in the one who sent me,
and whoever sees me,
sees the one who sent me.' (John 12:44–5)

I read the letter from my friend over and over again. It bridged the miles between us. A word from her, and I felt we were once more sharing our life's journey. How much more surely does *your* Word, incarnate in your Son, bring me into your living presence?

Thursday

'I tell you most solemnly,
whoever welcomes the one I send welcomes me,
and whoever welcomes me welcomes the one who sent me.' (John 13:20)

The lone parent was new to the district. After the service was over, she left the church alone, with her boisterous toddler. The regular congregation wondered who she was, but nobody took the trouble to find out. Strange, that you should be unwelcome in your own House.

❦ Friday

Thomas said, 'Lord, we do not know where you are going, so how can we know the way?' Jesus said: 'I am the Way, the Truth and the Life.' (John 14:6)

I don't need to know the way; I am on a journey where everyone I meet is my destination, for in everyone I meet, I meet You.

❦ Saturday

Philip said: 'Lord, let us see the Father and then we shall be satisfied.' 'Have I been with you all this time, Philip,' said Jesus to him, 'and you still do not know me? To have seen me is to have seen the Father.' (John 14:8–9)

I hold a fallen berry in my hand. It contains the complete genetic code of the tree from which it sprang. The berry will grow into the tree and the tree will yield the berry. When I touch the berry, I touch the meaning of the tree.

The week's readings

Monday	Acts 11:1–18; Psalms 42, 43(41, 42); John 10:1–10
Tuesday	Acts 11:19–26; Psalm 87(86); John 10:22–30
Wednesday	Acts 12:24 – 13:5; Psalm 67(66); John 12:44–50
Thursday	Acts 13:13–25; Psalm 87(86); John 13:16–20
Friday	Acts 13:26–33; Psalm 2; John 14:1–6
Saturday	Acts 13:44–52; Psalm 98(97); John 14:7–14

Fourth Week of Easter (Weekday Cycle II)

❦ Monday

My soul is thirsting for God,
the God of my life;
when can I enter and see the face of God? (Psalm 43:2)

The whole being of the crocus was concentrated on its thirst for the food and water that was nourishing its hidden secret. All through the winter it pushed determinedly, blindly, towards its still unknown fulfilment, until, on a cold March morning, it spread its flower to the full glory of the springtime sunshine.

❦ Tuesday

In you all find their home. (Psalm 87:7)

There were some unlikely bedfellows in the Animal Rescue Centre. In the wild they would have been implacable enemies, or predators one upon the other. But in their pain and their helplessness they lay side by side, drawn together by the loving care that ministered to them.

❦ Wednesday

O God, be gracious and bless us
and let your face shed its light upon us.
So will your ways be known upon earth
and all nations lean upon your saving help. (Psalm 67:1–2)

Let your light shine upon us, Lord, as upon reflecting cats' eyes that mark the road for other dark-night travellers to find their way.

❦ Thursday

'Whoever welcomes the one I send welcomes me,
and whoever welcomes me welcomes the one who sent me.' (John 13:20)

A warm Irish voice spoke out of the huddled, homeless figure by the wall. 'Can you spare a few pence for a cup of tea?' he asked. Behind him rose the full majesty of Liverpool Cathedral. And behind the cathedral rose the spreading glory of the sunset sky. The church joined him for tea that afternoon, and the world shared his sandwich and the heavens spread the table for him. What a small price to pay for a heavenly banquet.

✠ Friday

> *'Do not let your hearts be troubled.*
> *Trust in God still, and trust in me.'* (John 14:1)

Alison climbed with laboured steps and painful breaths. At the end of all the climbing, she knew that she would stand on the roof of the world and see the full glory of the mountains. Her trust in that vision made every hardship worthwhile.

✠ Saturday

> *'I have made you a light for the nations,*
> *so that my salvation may reach the ends of the earth.'* (Acts 13:47)

When I blow out my prayer candle, the wisps of smoke float off into every remote corner of the house. Prayer begins for real when the light goes out – out into the dark places.

The week's readings

Monday	Acts 11:1–18; Psalms 42, 43(41, 42); John 10:1–10
Tuesday	Acts 11:19–26; Psalm 87(86); John 10:22–30
Wednesday	Acts 12:24 – 13:5; Psalm 67(66); John 12:44–50
Thursday	Acts 13:13–25; Psalm 87(86); John 13:16–20
Friday	Acts 13:26–33; Psalm 2; John 14:1–6
Saturday	Acts 13:44–52; Psalm 98(97); John 14:7–14

Fifth Week of Easter (Weekday Cycle I)

✠ Monday

'If anyone loves me he will keep my word
and my Father will love him,
and we shall come to him and make our home with him.' (John 14:23)

The results of living lovingly are beyond anything we can imagine. When our hearts are open to each other, we discover that we have opened our hearts to you, and you will not hesitate to make your home there.

✠ Tuesday

'Peace I bequeath to you,
my own peace I give you,
a peace the world cannot give, this is my gift to you.
Do not let your hearts be troubled or afraid.' (John 14:27)

When we live in your peace, the conflicts of our lives – both inside and outside ourselves – don't go away. Instead you draw us into the still centre at the heart of the storm, where healing can begin.

✠ Wednesday

'I am the vine, you are the branches.
Whoever remains in me, with me in him, bears fruit in plenty,
for cut off from me you can do nothing.' (John 15:5)

The wood is carpeted with bluebells. Every May they flood my heart with their joyful exuberance of blue. Year in, year out, their fragile bulbs break out again into the fullness of their living. Yet how dispiriting is the sight of a jug of bluebells, plucked at dawn and, by midday, drooping sadly down to premature death.

✠ Thursday

'Remain in my love.
If you keep my commandments you will remain in my love,
just as I have kept my Father's commandments and remain in his love.

I have told you this so that my own joy may be in you
and your joy be complete.' (John 15:9–11)

To keep your commandments is to obey the deepest dictates of my heart as a stream obeys its deepest impulse when it courses down towards the ocean, watering the land as it flows.

⁂ Friday

'You do not choose me, no, I chose you;
and I commissioned you to go out and to bear fruit,
fruit that will last.' (John 15:16)

The mother watched patiently as her child made his options. Choosing subjects, choosing a job, choosing friends. He was sure that he was in control, yet she had made the choice that made all other choices possible: the choice to give him life.

⁂ Saturday

'If they persecuted me, they will persecute you too;
if they kept my word, they will keep your word as well.' (John 15:20)

When we run up against the rock face, let us remember that you ran up against it too. You were broken against it, so that the seeds of eternal life might be released. Seeds that settle and take root in the rocks of persecution, breaking down the hardness, bringing life.

The week's readings

Monday	Acts 14:5–18; Psalm 115(113b); John 14:21–6
Tuesday	Acts 14:19–28; Psalm 145(144); John 14:27–31
Wednesday	Acts 15:1–6; Psalm 122(121); John 15:1–8
Thursday	Acts 15:7–21; Psalm 96(95); John 15:9–11
Friday	Acts 15:22–31; Psalm 57(56); John 15:12–17
Saturday	Acts 16:1–10; Psalm 100(99); John 15:18–21

Fifth Week of Easter *(Weekday Cycle II)*

✠ Monday

May you be blessed by the Lord,
the maker of heaven and earth.
The heavens belong to the Lord,
but the earth he has given to men. (Psalm 115:15–16)

We feel pangs of hurt and sadness if we realise that a gift we have given in love is neglected, or used carelessly, or even wilfully damaged. How do *you* feel, Lord, when you see how we treat your gift to us of this earth, our home?

✠ Tuesday

'Peace I bequeath to you,
my own peace I give you,
a peace the world cannot give, this is my gift to you.
Do not let your hearts be troubled or afraid.' (John 14:27)

As long as I stay in the battle zone of my own conflicting wants and fears, there is constant warfare in my heart. But when you draw me down into the deepest longing of my being, the tumult ceases, there is no more competition, and my heart feels whole again.

✠ Wednesday

'I am the vine, you are the branches.
Whoever remains in me, with me in him, bears fruit in plenty,
for cut off from me you can do nothing.' (John 15:5)

When we have all gained our personal independence and established our own little kingdoms, then we will have finally completed the fragmentation of your creation and the destruction of ourselves and of each other . . .

✠ Thursday

'Remain in my love.
If you keep my commandments you will remain in my love,
just as I have kept my Father's commandments and remain in his love.

I have told you this so that my own joy may be in you
and your joy be complete.' (John 15:9–11)

. . . Yet there is another way. We can reverse the process of destructive fragmentation; we do so every time we reach out to each other in love, and every time we reach out to you in prayer. It is then that the independence we so cherished starts to become the wholeness that we long for.

❦ Friday

'You do not choose me, no, I chose you;
and I commissioned you to go out and to bear fruit,
fruit that will last.' (John 15:16)

I watched the bee hovering over the fragrant petals before choosing the one on which to land. It was a choice made out of the sheer joy of the moment, but also a choice made in perfect accord with the natural laws of pollination and fruitfulness. May your choosing of us, and our response to your choosing, also be made in joy and for fruitfulness.

❦ Saturday

'If you belonged to the world,
the world would love you as its own;
but because my choice withdrew you from the world,
therefore the world hates you.' (John 15:19)

Oscar Romero fell to the ground in the very act of celebrating Mass, fearlessly proclaiming your love with his last breaths. The greater the power of the light, the more powerfully it will provoke the powers of darkness, until all darkness shall be dispelled and only the Light remains, eternally.

The week's readings

Monday	Acts 14:5–18; Psalm 115(113b); John 14:21–6
Tuesday	Acts 14:19–28; Psalm 145(144); John 14:27–31
Wednesday	Acts 15:1–6; Psalm 122(121); John 15:1–8
Thursday	Acts 15:7–21; Psalm 96(95); John 15:9–11
Friday	Acts 15:22–31; Psalm 57(56); John 15:12–17
Saturday	Acts 16:1–10; Psalm 100(99); John 15:18–21

Sixth Week of Easter *(Weekday Cycle I)*

✠ Monday

Jesus said to his disciples: 'When the Advocate comes, whom I shall send to you from the Father, the Spirit of truth who issues from the Father, he will be my witness. And you too will be witnesses, because you have been with me from the outset.' (John 15:26–7)

The Spirit is your witness, giving us evidence, in our own lived experience, of your Reality. Shall our lives, too, provide such living evidence to others?

✠ Tuesday

Jesus said to his disciples: 'Now I am going to the one who sent me. Not one of you has asked, "Where are you going?" Yet you are sad at heart because I have told you this. Still I must tell you the truth: it is for your own good that I am going, because unless I go the Advocate will not come to you.' (John 16:5–7)

In the dark times of our prayer you seem to have withdrawn far beyond the reach of our minds and senses. Yet the darkness reveals the stars, and the cloud that receives you holds the promise of an unimaginable new dawning of power and love.

✠ Wednesday

'In fact he is not far from any of us, since it is in him that we live, and move, and exist.' (Acts 17:27–8)

The tiny oak leaves are just beginning to unfurl, and waking up to springtime. If I could tell them about the vast network of branch and trunk and root that holds them in being, they would never believe me. An obvious reality for me – an impossible leap of imagination for them. How far am I, then, from understanding the sources of your love that hold me in being?

✠ Thursday – Ascension Day

Then he took them out as far as the outskirts of Bethany, and lifting up his hands he blessed them. Now as he blessed them, he withdrew from them and was carried to heaven. They worshipped him and then went back to Jerusalem full of joy. (Luke 24:50–3)

As the train was about to depart, he held her close and assured her of his love. As it drew away from the station, he waved his blessing upon her. Her heart was aching, but she cherished the parting embrace deep in her heart. It planted joy into the heartache, and trust into the promise of his return.

❦ Friday

> *'A woman in childbirth suffers, because her time has come; but when she has given birth to the child she forgets the suffering in her joy that a child has been born into the world. So it is with you: you are sad now, but I shall see you again, and your hearts will be full of joy.'* (John 16:21–2)

The final stage of labour seemed to last for hours. I started to think, 'This child isn't ever going to be born,' but my common sense knew better. When I start to wonder whether your kingdom will ever come, I remember the moment when the midwife placed my daughter in my arms. And I believe.

❦ Saturday

> *'Ask and you will receive, and so your joy will be complete.'* (John 16:24)

I asked for food and you taught me how to fish. I asked for security and you gave me the freedom to live without fear. I asked for happiness, and you gave me joy. I come to you with the leaves and petals of my desires, but you satisfy their roots.

The week's readings

Monday	Acts 16:11–15; Psalm 149; John 15:26 – 16:4
Tuesday	Acts 16:22–34; Psalm 138(137); John 16:5–11
Wednesday	Acts 17:15, 22 – 18:1; Psalm 148; John 16:12–15
Thursday	Acts 1:1–11; Psalm 47(46); Ephesians 1:17–23; Luke 24:46–53
Friday	Acts 18:9–18; Psalm 47(46); John 16:20–3
Saturday	Acts 18:23–8; Psalm 47(46); John 16:23–8

Sixth Week of Easter *(Weekday Cycle II)*

✠ Monday

> *'They will expel you from the synagogues, and indeed the hour is coming when anyone who kills you will think he is doing a holy duty for God. They will do these things because they have never known either the Father or myself.'* (John 16:2–3)

The gulf between Barbara and her son widened daily as their quarrel over his girlfriend deepened. Barbara refused to have the girl in the house or to hear anything good about her. 'If you *knew* her you wouldn't react like this,' he protested. But Barbara didn't *want* to know.

✠ Tuesday

> *Late that night Paul and Silas were praying and singing God's praises, while the other prisoners listened. Suddenly there was an earthquake that shook the prison to its foundations. All the doors flew open and the chains fell from all the prisoners.* (Acts 16:25–6)

The earth-shaking force of our lives' worst experiences can bring about the radical remaking that prepares us for our lives' most powerful growth and opens up the doors of our hearts to your redeeming liberation.

✠ Wednesday

> *Jesus said to his disciples: 'I still have many things to say to you but they would be too much for you now. But when the Spirit of truth comes, he will lead you to the complete truth.'* (John 16:12–13)

We stop short of the truth for many reasons: out of fear of the consequences to ourselves from all that it might reveal, or out of love that seeks to shelter each other from hurting. Before we can face the completeness of your truth, we need you to free us fully from our fears and to open us fully to your love that heals all hurting.

✠ Thursday – Ascension Day

> *'And know that I am with you always;*
> *yes, to the end of time.'* (Matthew 28:20)

With us always . . . even then, when we are walking away from you . . .
especially then, when we are sure we can manage without you . . .

and precisely then, when we feel you have given up on us . . .
With us always, and closer to us than we are to ourselves.

❧ Friday

> *'You are sad now, but I shall see you again, and your hearts will be full of joy, and that joy no one shall take from you.'* (John 16:22)

We may gather happiness painlessly, like blackberries at the roadside, easily reached. But joy is a more elusive fruit, and often lies beyond a barrier of thorns, and on the other side of sorrow.

❧ Saturday

> *'Ask and you will receive, and so your joy will be complete.'* (John 16:24)

When we reveal our needs to you, we are bringing you the empty spaces of our hearts, for your filling. Unless we open our empty hands, how can you fill them with our daily bread?

The week's readings

Monday	Acts 16:11–15; Psalm 149; John 15:26 – 16:4
Tuesday	Acts 16:22–34; Psalm 138(137); John 16:5–11
Wednesday	Acts 17:15, 22 – 18:1; Psalm 148; John 16:12–15
Thursday	Acts 1:1–11; Psalm 47(46); Ephesians 1:17–23; Matthew 28:16–20
Friday	Acts 18:9–18; Psalm 47(46); John 16:20–3
Saturday	Acts 18:23–8; Psalm 47(46); John 16:23–8

Seventh Week of Easter *(Weekday Cycle I)*

✠ Monday

> *'I have told you all this so that you may find peace in me. In the world you will have trouble, but be brave; I have conquered the world.'* (John 16:33)

The more comfortable we feel in our believing and the practice of our faith, the more likely we are to be drifting away from you. Give us rather the peace that takes us past the comfort, through disturbance, into courage, towards the truth.

✠ Tuesday

> *You poured down, O God, a generous rain:*
> *when your people were starved you gave them new life.* (Psalm 68:9)

Not just watering-cans, to keep us going through the hard times, but generous, soaking, saturating grace that brings life out of our most deeply buried roots.

✠ Wednesday

> *'I am not asking you to remove them from the world, but to protect them from the evil one. They do not belong to the world any more than I belong to the world. Consecrate them in the truth; your word is truth. As you sent me into the world, I have sent them into the world, and for their sake I consecrate myself, so that they too may be consecrated in truth.'* (John 17:15–19)

Consecration . . . not a life taken out of the world, but a life commissioned to enter far more deeply *into* the world, carrying your truth and your love. Consecration . . . a call and a commission for every believer.

✠ Thursday

> *'Father, may they be one in us, as you are in me and I am in you.'* (John 17:21)

Paul is blind. Tomorrow he leaves for a holiday in Italy with his sighted brother-in-law, Jim. Jim speaks no Italian, but Paul is fluent in the language. They joke as they pack: 'I'll be his tongue, and he'll be my eyes,' says Paul. Lord, may our unity in you lead us to a fullness that is infinitely greater than the sum of our separate selves.

Friday

'I tell you most solemnly, when you were young, you put on your own belt and walked where you liked, but when you grow old you will stretch out your hands, and somebody else will put a belt round you and take you where you would rather not go.' (John 21:18)

When I began my journey of faith, I felt strong and sure and I thought I knew where I was going. But the further I travelled, the more I became aware of my ever-growing helplessness and inadequacy, and my absolute need of you.

Saturday

There were many other things that Jesus did; if all were written down, the world itself, I suppose, would not hold all the books that would have to be written. (John 21:25)

And if each of us were to tell of all the ways the Lord has touched our lives and our hearts, the world itself could not contain all our stories.

The week's readings

Monday	Acts 19:1–8; Psalm 68(67); John 16:29–33
Tuesday	Acts 20:17–27; Psalm 68(67); John 17:1–11
Wednesday	Acts 20:28–38; Psalm 68(67); John 17:11–19
Thursday	Acts 22:30; 23:6–11; Psalm 16(15); John 17:20–6
Friday	Acts 25:13–21; Psalm 103(102); John 21:15–19
Saturday	Acts 28:16–20, 30–1; Psalm 11(10); John 21:20–5

Seventh Week of Easter (Weekday Cycle II)

⁂ Monday

'I have told you all this so that you may find peace in me. In the world you will have trouble, but be brave; I have conquered the world.' (John 16:33)

Armchair believing may provide a comfortable sanctuary amid life's storms, but our faith becomes authentic when it is sharpened on the cutting edge of challenge, struggle and opposition.

⁂ Tuesday

'Eternal life is this:
to know you, the only true God,
and Jesus Christ whom you have sent.' (John 17:3)

If we stand in the street and gaze at some distant landmark, we can be sure of attracting a crowd of curious observers, following our gaze. Surely, then, our earthly lives can become signposts to others, showing the way towards your eternal life, if we know you, and let our gaze be focused on you and not upon ourselves.

⁂ Wednesday

'I am not asking you to remove them from the world, but to protect them from the evil one.' (John 17:15)

When the storms blow against me, my instinctive prayer is to ask you to transplant me to a safer, more welcoming place. You answer my prayer by leaving me where I am, in the eye of the storm, but by strengthening and deepening the roots of my life, down to their true centre in you.

⁂ Thursday

Jesus raised his eyes to heaven and said:
'Holy Father, I pray not only for these,
but for those also
who through their words will believe in me,
May they all be one.' (John 17:20)

Two thousand years ago you stood among your first disciples, and prayed for *us*. And today your Spirit lives in our hearts and echoes that prayer back to you, its source.

✠ Friday

> *Then he said to him a third time: 'Simon, son of John, do you love me?' Peter said, 'Lord, you know everything; you know I love you.' Jesus said to him: 'Feed my sheep.'* (John 21:7)

The test of our loving is always in the warmth of our giving.

✠ Saturday

> *There were many other things that Jesus did; if all were written down, the world itself, I suppose, would not hold all the books that would have to be written.* (John 21:25)

Your gospel is written indelibly, uniquely, on every believer's heart, and all creation is too small to contain its living presence.

The week's readings

Monday	Acts 19:1–8; Psalm 68(67); John 16:29–33
Tuesday	Acts 20:17–27; Psalm 68(67); John 17:1–11
Wednesday	Acts 20:28–38; Psalm 68(67); John 17:11–19
Thursday	Acts 22:30; 23:6–11; Psalm 16(15); John 17:20–6
Friday	Acts 25:13–21; Psalm 103(102); John 21:15–19
Saturday	Acts 28:16–20, 30–1; Psalm 11(10); John 21:20–5

PART 3: CREATION CALLED HOME TO GOD

❧

Weekday readings and reflections for the weeks of Ordinary Time

First Week of Ordinary Time (Weekday Cycle I)

❧ Monday

As Jesus was walking along by the Sea of Galilee he saw Simon and his brother Andrew casting a net in the lake – for they were fishermen. And Jesus said to them, 'Follow me and I will make you into fishers of men.' (Mark 1:16–18)

Every loving relationship I form with those I meet is a thread in the net you are weaving, with which to draw your people home. Let me be sure to keep them all in good repair.

❧ Tuesday

The people were so astonished that they started asking each other what it all meant. 'Here is a teaching that is new,' they said, 'and with authority behind it.' (Mark 1:27)

Sandra surprised everyone in her prayer group by the power and authority with which she spoke of her faith. She spoke your Word with authority, because she knew you, its author, as her own friend and guide.

❧ Wednesday

In the morning, long before dawn, he got up and left the house, and went off to a lonely place and prayed there. Simon and his companions set out to search for him, and when they found him they said: 'Everybody is looking for you.' (Mark 1:35–7)

David stopped for ten minutes in a quiet corner of the car park, before going into work, just to let your peace settle in his heart and listen to the murmur of your love. Punctually, at nine o'clock, he went up to the office, and into an explosion of phone calls, messages and problems, but confident that ten minutes in your silence would take him safely through the demands of ten hours at his desk.

❧ Thursday

Every day, as long as this 'today' lasts, keep encouraging one another. (Hebrews 3:13)

The kind word, spoken into the moment of stress, tells me that you believe in me. It does more than that: it reassures me that I can believe in myself.

❦ Friday

He was preaching the word to them when some people came bringing him a paralytic carried by four men, but as the crowd made it impossible to get the man to him, they stripped the roof over the place where Jesus was; and when they had made an opening, they lowered the stretcher on which the paralytic lay. (Mark 2:3–4)

When I acknowledge my own helplessness, and let you carry me, then new possibilities open up in the midst of impossibility, and healing can begin.

❦ Saturday

The word of God is something alive and active; it cuts like any double-edged sword, but more finely. (Hebrews 4:12)

The two-edged blade of your Spirit slices through my being, Lord, like the blade of a master sculptor, ruthlessly stripping me of all that hinders my growth in you, yet tenderly revealing the shape and form of who I really am.

The week's readings

Monday	Hebrews 1:1–6; Psalm 97(96); Mark 1:14–20
Tuesday	Hebrews 2:5–12; Psalm 8; Mark 1:21–8
Wednesday	Hebrews 2:14–18; Psalm 105(104); Mark 1:29–39
Thursday	Hebrews 3:7–14 Psalm 95(94); Mark 1:40–5
Friday	Hebrews 4:1–5, 11; Psalm 78(77); Mark 2:1–12
Saturday	Hebrews 4:12–16; Psalm 19(18); Mark 2:13–17

First Week of Ordinary Time (Weekday Cycle II)

✠ Monday

And Jesus said to them, 'Follow me and I will make you into fishers of men.' (Mark 1:18)

When we look at the nets that our own life's story has woven, we see the holes of our sin and failure, linked together by the threads of our faith and our hope. Yet you use us as we are, our faith and our failure, our holes and our hopes, to make us into those who fish for your kingdom.

✠ Tuesday

'Here is a teaching that is new', they said, 'and with authority behind it: he gives orders even to unclean spirits and they obey him.' (Mark 1:27)

The fears and the temptations that haunt us in our darkness are banished by the touch of your authority as surely as a baby's night-time terrors are dispelled when his mother switches on the light and takes him in her arms.

✠ Wednesday

In the morning, long before dawn, he got up and left the house, and went off to a lonely place and prayed there. Simon and his companions set out in search of him, and when they found him they said: 'Everybody is looking for you.' (Mark 1:35–7)

The solitude and silence of Kate's time of prayer was abruptly interrupted by an insistent knocking at the door. Her neighbour was in trouble and needed urgent help. 'I'll come at once', she said, and she knew that her prayer had not been ended but made incarnate.

✠ Thursday

When the Philistines heard the noise of the shouting, they said: 'What can this great shouting in the Hebrew camp mean?' And they realised that the ark of the Lord had come into the camp. At this the Philistines were afraid, and they said: 'God has come to the camp.' (1 Samuel 4:6–7)

If, in the middle of my worst struggles, I can stop and remember 'God is with me in this battlefield', then the warring factions in my heart shrink back, afraid, knowing themselves to be powerless in your presence.

❦ Friday

'These will be the rights of the king who is to reign over you . . . he will take the best of your manservants and maidservants, of your cattle and your donkeys, and make them work for him. He will tithe your flocks, and you yourselves will become his slaves. When that day comes, you will cry out on account of the king you have chosen for yourselves, but on that day God will not answer you.' (1 Samuel 8:11, 16–18)

As soon as I allow anything less than you, Lord, to rule my heart, it will drain me of all my energy and my resources and make me its slave. Only in my surrender to you will I be free, but you will never force my choice.

❦ Saturday

As he was walking on Jesus saw Levi the son of Alphaeus, sitting by the customs house, and he said to him 'Follow me.' (Mark 2:14)

If we follow you, Lord, we will find ourselves walking alongside people we have spent a lifetime trying to avoid, and we will forget why we ever wanted to avoid them.

The week's readings

Monday	1 Samuel 1:1–8; Psalm 116(115); Mark 1:14–20
Tuesday	1 Samuel 1:9–20; 1 Samuel 2:1, 4–8; Mark 1:21–8
Wednesday	1 Samuel 3:1–10, 19–20; Psalm 40(39); Mark 1:29–39
Thursday	1 Samuel 4:1–11; Psalm 44(43); Mark 1:40–5
Friday	1 Samuel 8:4–7, 10–22; Psalm 89(88); Mark 2:1–12
Saturday	1 Samuel 9:1–14, 17–19; 10:1; Psalm 21(20); Mark 2:13–17

Second Week of Ordinary Time *(Weekday Cycle I)*

❦ Monday

During his life on earth, he offered up prayer and entreaty, aloud and in silent tears, to the one who had the power to save him out of death . . . Although he was Son, he learnt to obey through suffering. (Hebrews 5:7)

Sister Maria had faithfully recited the Divine Office through every day of her adult life. Then one morning she couldn't: her heart was too heavy and her spirits too low. She laid the book aside, and let her desperate tears fall freely. They burned her eyes, even as they taught her a new depth of prayer.

❦ Tuesday

We, now we have found safety, should have a strong encouragement to take a firm grip on the hope that is held out to us. Here we have an anchor for our soul, as sure as it is firm, and reaching right through beyond the veil where Jesus has entered before us. (Hebrews 6:18–20)

The slenderest thread of your life, surrendered on Calvary, becomes a cable of love, strong enough to draw us from death to life – the only anchor that doesn't hold us fixed to the seabed of our fallenness – the only anchor we can trust.

❦ Wednesday

A prince from the day of your birth
on the holy mountains;
from the womb before the daybreak I begot you. (Psalm 110:3)

Only an hour ago this tiny creature had been hidden in the womb, and now her mother gazed at the newborn in sheer wonder. In this small bundle of humanity every possibility lay dormant, like a new day at its dawning, pregnant with mystery and promise.

❦ Thursday

He has his place at the right of the throne of divine majesty in the heavens, and he is the minister of the sanctuary and of the true Tent of Meeting which the Lord, and not any man, set up. (Hebrews 8:1–2)

You dwell eternally with the Father, but the tent of your living presence is also pitched in every believing heart, so that God-with-us may travel through an unbelieving world.

❦ Friday

I will put my laws into their minds and write them on their hearts.
Then I will be their God and they shall be my people . . .
They will all know me, the least no less than the greatest. (Hebrews 8:10–11)

You write your truth in our hearts in a Word so simple that a child may take hold of it, yet so profound that it eludes our highest understanding.

❦ Saturday

The blood of Christ, who offered himself as the perfect sacrifice to God through the eternal Spirit, can purify our inner self from dead actions, so that we do our service to the living God. (Hebrews 9:14)

The glory of the summer roses had faded into a tangle of windswept autumn twigs. Jake cut back the dead wood and piled it onto the fire. This was not a time to regret the summer past, but to turn his attention to the needs of next springtime's growth.

The week's readings

Monday	Hebrews 5:1–10; Psalm 110(109); Mark 2:18–22
Tuesday	Hebrews 6:10–20; Psalm 111(110); Mark 2:23–8
Wednesday	Hebrews 7:1–3, 15–17; Psalm 110(109); Mark 3:1–6
Thursday	Hebrews 7:25 – 8:6; Psalm 40(39); Mark 3:7–12
Friday	Hebrews 8:6–13; Psalm 85(84); Mark 3:13–19
Saturday	Hebrews 9:2–3, 11–14; Psalm 47(46); Mark 3:20–1

Second Week of Ordinary Time (Weekday Cycle II)

☙ Monday

'Nobody puts new wine into old wineskins; if he does, the wine will burst the skins, and the wine is lost and the skins too. No! New wine, fresh skins!' (Mark 2:22)

Derek came in to school early to tidy the classroom and prepare his classes for the day. Before the children arrived, he wiped the board clean of yesterday's work, to make space for a new day's discoveries. And as he did so, he mentally let go of his preoccupation with his own inadequacies. Yesterday's failures would be no fit container for tomorrow's fruits.

☙ Tuesday

The Lord said to Samuel, 'Take no notice of his appearance or his height for I have rejected him; God does not see as man sees; man looks at appearances but the Lord looks at the heart.' (1 Samuel 16:7)

Marjorie took home a bouquet of the most expensive blooms from the flower show. Christine bought herself a dozen daffodil bulbs. The appearance is for today, but the heart belongs to tomorrow

☙ Wednesday

Jesus went into the synagogue, and there was a man there who had a withered hand . . . Jesus said to the man, 'Stretch out your hand.' He stretched it out and his hand was better. (Mark 3:1, 5)

When I am feeling low I nurse my sorrows like a broken arm, and wrap myself in self-pity. I only know of one cure: to stretch out my hands and my heart towards another person who is feeling worse.

☙ Thursday

You have kept an account of my wanderings;
you have kept a record of my tears. (Psalm 56:8)

Little James didn't need to tell his mother about all the catalogue of sorrows the day had brought. He felt her arms tighten around him, and he *knew* that she knew and understood.

❦ Friday

Jesus went up into the hills and summoned those he wanted. So they came to him and he appointed twelve; they were to be his companions and to be sent out to preach, with power to cast out devils. (Mark 3:13–15)

If we would carry his Word to the world and heal with his power, we must first become his companions, in the hill country of our prayer.

❦ Saturday

Jesus went home, and such a crowd collected that they could not even have a meal. When his relatives heard of this they set out to take charge of him, convinced he was out of his mind. (Mark 3:20–1)

A goldfinch strayed into the garden one day. The sparrows were bewildered. Their bewilderment turned to hostility. They turned against the goldfinch and drove him away, for the ordinary cannot tolerate for long the presence of the extraordinary.

The week's readings

Monday	1 Samuel 15:16–23; Psalm 50(49); Mark 2:18–22
Tuesday	1 Samuel 16:1–13; Psalm 88(87); Mark 2:23–8
Wednesday	1 Samuel 17:32–3, 37, 40–51; Psalm 144(143); Mark 3:1–6
Thursday	1 Samuel 18:6–9; 19:1–7; Psalm 56(55); Mark 3:7–12
Friday	1 Samuel 24:3–21; Psalm 57(56); Mark 3:13–19
Saturday	2 Samuel 1:1–4, 11–12, 17, 19, 23–7; Psalm 80(79); Mark 3:20–1

Third Week of Ordinary Time *(Weekday Cycle I)*

✠ Monday

Christ offers himself only once to take the faults of many on himself, and when he appears a second time, it will not be to deal with sin but to reward with salvation those who are waiting for him. (Hebrews 9:27–8)

The story of our faith journey does not end in judgement, but in joy!

✠ Tuesday

Jesus replied: 'Who are my mother and my brothers?' And looking round at those sitting in a circle about him, he said, 'Here are my mother and my brothers. Anyone who does the will of God, that person is my brother and sister and mother.' (Mark 3:33–5)

In our kinship with each other, our loneliness ends, but our responsibility begins.

✠ Wednesday

All the priests stand at their duties every day, offering over and over again the same sacrifices which are quite incapable of taking sins away. Jesus, on the other hand, has offered one single sacrifice for sins. (Hebrews 10:11–12)

Claudia had been faithful in all her religious observances since she was a child, but it seemed to make no difference to her life. It was only in the extremity of a crisis, when prayer was the last thing on her mind, that a new kind of peace broke through into her helplessness, taking her heart by surprise and making the efforts of her mind and will redundant.

✠ Thursday

'Would you bring in a lamp to put it under a tub or under the bed? Surely you will put it on the lampstand? For there is nothing hidden but it must be disclosed, nothing kept secret except to be brought to light.' (Mark 4:21–2)

We carry the Light of the world in our hearts, yet so often we keep it confined to a single hour on Sunday, when it so longs to spill out over every moment of every day.

❦ Friday

You happily accepted being stripped of your belongings, knowing that you owned something that was better and lasting. (Hebrews 10:34)

The treasure at the centre of our being needs no defences because it is indestructible. It is the treasure that we only discover when we have nothing left to lose.

❦ Saturday

All these [Abraham, Sarah, Isaac, Jacob] died in faith, before receiving any of the things that had been promised, but they saw them in the far distance and welcomed them, recognising that they were only strangers and nomads on earth. (Hebrews 11:13)

Mother Teresa did not abolish poverty, nor did Anne Frank set her people free. But their journeys in trust, towards the distant star of truth and love, carried the whole human family with them.

The week's readings

Monday	Hebrews 9:15, 24–8; Psalm 98(97); Mark 3:22–30
Tuesday	Hebrews 10:1–10; Psalm 40(39); Mark 3:31–5
Wednesday	Hebrews 10:11–18; Psalm 110(109); Mark 4:1–20
Thursday	Hebrews 10:19–25; Psalm 24(23); Mark 4:21–5
Friday	Hebrews 10:32–9; Psalm 37(36); Mark 4:26–34
Saturday	Hebrews 11:1–2, 8–19; Luke 1:69–75; Mark 4:35–41

Third Week of Ordinary Time *(Weekday Cycle II)*

Monday

'No one can make his way into a strong man's house and burgle his property unless he has tied up the strong man first. Only then can he burgle his house.' (Mark 3:27)

When I stifle and suppress the strongest yearnings of my heart, then the lesser idols of my life can take control. But when your sovereign Spirit reigns unhindered, the occupying forces shrink and withdraw.

Tuesday

Jesus replied: 'Who are my mother and my brothers?' And looking round at those sitting in a circle about him, he said, 'Here are my mother and my brothers. Anyone who does the will of God, that person is my brother and sister and mother.' (Mark 3:33–5)

We belong to the biggest family on earth. We are responsible for the loving-care of a million siblings, and they for us.

Wednesday

'Go and tell my servant David, "Thus the Lord speaks: Are you the man to build me a house to dwell in? I have never stayed in a house from the day I brought the Israelites out of Egypt until today, but have always led a wanderer's life in a tent." ' (2 Samuel 7:5–6)

When we try to contain you in our own constructions, we are as far removed from your reality as a set of china geese, fixed to a living-room wall, is removed from the reality of the flight of wild geese that sweep the skies on their migration journey.

Thursday

I will not enter the house where I live
nor go to the bed where I rest.
I will give no sleep to my eyes,
to my eyelids will give no slumber
till I find a place for the Lord. (Psalm 132:3–5)

A day that passes without contact with you is a day when I feel exiled from my innermost home; a night without your blessing is a night without my deepest rest.

❧ Friday

'This is what the kingdom of God is like. A man throws seed on the land. Night and day, while he sleeps, when he is awake, the seed is sprouting and growing; how, he does not know. Of its own accord the land produces first the shoot, then the ear, then the full grain in the ear.' (Mark 4:26–9)

Nothing can prevent the secret, silent growth of your seed in our hearts, unless we cover it over and flatten it down with the weight of our own imagined wisdom.

❧ Saturday

David's anger flared up against the man [who had stolen the poor man's ewe lamb]. 'As the Lord lives,' he said to Nathan, 'the man who did this deserves to die! He must make fourfold restitution for the lamb, for doing such a thing and showing no compassion.' Then Nathan said to David, 'You are the man.' (2 Samuel 12:5–7)

It had been a heavy day in court for Justice John: several cases of benefit fraud, a couple of car thefts and a man who had fiddled his expense claims. 'They had it coming to them,' he thought to himself, complacently, as he picked up his phone and called his stockbroker. With his privileged inside knowledge about the coming takeover bid, now was the right moment to make a killing on those share dealings.

The week's readings

Monday	2 Samuel 5:1–7, 10; Psalm 89(88); Mark 3:22–30
Tuesday	2 Samuel 6:12–15, 17–19; Psalm 24(23); Mark 3:31–5
Wednesday	2 Samuel 7:4–17; Psalm 89(88); Mark 4:1–20
Thursday	2 Samuel 7:18–19, 24–9; Psalm 132(131); Mark 4:21–5
Friday	2 Samuel 11:1–10, 13–17; Psalm 51(50); Mark 4:26–34
Saturday	2 Samuel 12:1–7, 10–17; Psalm 51(50); Mark 4:35–41

Fourth Week of Ordinary Time (Weekday Cycle I)

❧ Monday

> *'What is your name?' Jesus asked the Gerasene demoniac.*
> *'My name is legion,' he answered, 'for there are many of us.'* (Mark 5:9)

Adam is known by many names: his children call him 'Dad' and his pupils call him 'Sir'; his friends call him generous and his family call him extravagant; he calls himself angry and tender, and frightened and bold, confused and confident; he changes his names as often as he changes his mood. His true name, the name of his wholeness, is only known to you.

❧ Tuesday

> *There was a woman who had suffered from a haemorrhage for twelve years . . . she had heard about Jesus and she came up behind him through the crowd and touched his cloak . . . and the source of the bleeding dried up instantly, and she felt in herself that she was cured of her complaint.* (Mark 5:25–9)

When life has drained us to the point of helpless desperation, your touch can heal. You heal us by touching those hurting places that are draining our energy. You heal us by turning *draining* back into *inflowing*.

❧ Wednesday

> *Jesus said to them, 'A prophet is only despised in his own country, among his own relations and in his own house,' and he could work no miracle there . . . He was amazed at their lack of faith.* (Mark 6:4–6)

Dare we invite the Lord to come into our church community today? Would he find, among us, his own, the faith that makes miracles possible?

❧ Thursday

> *Then he summoned the Twelve and began to send them out in pairs, giving them authority over unclean spirits. And he instructed them to take nothing for the journey except a staff – no bread, no haversack, no coppers for their purses.* (Mark 6:7–9)

We enter life, and we leave it, with nothing in our hands, and we make our life's central journey with just the staff of your love and your grace to lean upon, and to remind us that we cannot take a single step without you.

❦ Friday

> *Continue to love each other like brothers, and remember always to welcome strangers, for by doing this, some people have entertained angels without knowing it.* (Hebrews 13:1–2)

If we receive everyone who crosses our threshold as if they were an angel, we might be surprised to find how many of them react as if they were.

❦ Saturday

> *The apostles rejoined Jesus and told him all they had done and taught. Then he said to them, 'You must come away to some lonely place all by yourselves and rest for a while.'* (Mark 6:30–1)

Our work and our ministries, that we find so necessary and all-important, can lead us round and round in ever-decreasing circles, until we come to that still point, at the centre, where you say 'Stop! And rest with me a while!'

The week's readings

Monday	Hebrews 11:32–40; Psalm 31(30); Mark 5:1–20
Tuesday	Hebrews 12:1–4; Psalm 22(21); Mark 5:21–43
Wednesday	Hebrews 12:4–7, 11–15; Psalm 103(102); Mark 6:1–6
Thursday	Hebrews 12:18–19, 21–4; Psalm 48(47); Mark 6:7–13
Friday	Hebrews 13:1–8; Psalm 27(26); Mark 6:14–29
Saturday	Hebrews 13:15–17, 20–1; Psalm 23(22); Mark 6:30–4

Fourth Week of Ordinary Time (Weekday Cycle II)

❦ Monday

A man with an unclean spirit came out from the tombs towards Jesus. The man lived in the tombs and no one could secure him any more, even with a chain, because he had often been secured with fetters and chains but had snapped the chains and broken the fetters, and no one had the strength to control him. (Mark 5:2–5)

There are parts of me that I have buried so deeply that even *I* can no longer recognise them. There are aspects of my personality that I keep firmly fastened down with the chains of all my energy, for fear of what they might do if they broke loose. But when the volcano erupts, and the chains snap and my very worst breaks out, I find you standing there, to recognise, to heal, and to lead me to freedom.

❦ Tuesday

Taking with him the child's father and mother and his own companions, he went into the place where the child lay. And taking the child by the hand he said to her, 'Talitha, kum!' which means, 'Little girl, get up.' (Mark 5:40–1)

When you call us into the fullness of life, it is no solitary calling, but a miracle that affects everyone we love and everyone you love; your word, spoken to one, is spoken for all.

❦ Wednesday

When David saw the angel who was ravaging the people, he spoke to the Lord. 'It was I who sinned,' he said, 'I who did this wicked thing. But these, this flock, what have they done? Let your hand lie heavy on me then, and on my family.' (2 Samuel 24:17)

When our hands strike out against another's helplessness, the dark moment will remain as a heavy shadow across an injured life, dimming the light for all around us.

❦ Thursday

Then he summoned the Twelve and began to send them out in pairs, giving them authority over unclean spirits. And he instructed them to take nothing for the journey except a staff – no bread, no haversack, no coppers for their purses. (Mark 6:7–9)

No human currency can purchase the encounter with God, and no human haversack can carry it. Only in our journeying will we discover it, when we are least expecting it.

❧ Friday

> *Herod was afraid of John, knowing him to be a good and holy man, and gave him his protection. When he had heard him speak he was greatly perplexed, and yet he liked to listen to him.* (Mark 6:20)

The fear of the Lord: that in us that recognises our own darkness revealed by your Light; the mystery that confounds our understanding yet irresistibly attracts us.

❧ Saturday

> *'Since you have asked for this,' the Lord said to Solomon, 'and not asked for a long life for yourself or riches or the lives of your enemies, but have asked for a discerning judgement for yourself, here and now I do what you ask. I give you a heart wise and shrewd as none before you has had and none will have after you. What you have not asked I shall give you too: such riches and glory as no other king ever had.'* (1 Kings 3:10–13)

If I ask you for happiness, health, success, security, I am really asking you to enter into my kingdom. If I ask for wisdom and love, I am asking you to draw *me* into *yours*.

The week's readings

Monday	2 Samuel 15:13–14, 30; 16:5–13; Psalm 3; Mark 5:1–20
Tuesday	2 Samuel 18:9–10, 14, 24–5, 30 – 19:3; Psalm 86(85); Mark 5:21–43
Wednesday	2 Samuel 24:2, 9–17; Psalm 33(32); Mark 6:1–6
Thursday	1 Kings 2:1–4, 10–12; 1 Chronicles 29:10–12; Mark 6:7–13
Friday	Ecclesiasticus 47:2–11; Psalm 18(17); Mark 6:14–29
Saturday	1 Kings 3:4–13; Psalm 119(118); Mark 6:30–4

Fifth Week of Ordinary Time (Weekday Cycle I)

✠ Monday

In the beginning God created the heavens and the earth. Now the earth was a formless void, there was darkness over the deep, and God's spirit hovered over the water. (Genesis 1:1)

George spent three-quarters of his life trying to get himself in order before presenting himself to you, his creator. Finally, frustrated by his failure, he gave up his inner chaos to you in despair, and then, at last, your Spirit could begin its transforming action.

✠ Tuesday

And so it was. God saw all he had made, and indeed it was very good. (Genesis 1:31)

You declared that everything you had made was good. What subtle pride, therefore, seduces me into thinking that I alone am no good?

✠ Wednesday

At the time when the Lord God made earth and heaven, there was as yet no wild bush on the earth nor had any wild plant yet sprung up, for the Lord God had not sent rain on the earth, nor was there any man to till the soil. However, a flood was rising from the earth and watering all the surface of the soil. (Genesis 2:5–6)

And before any of our life's shape is formed or our circumstances determined, before ever we can speak or think, your life wells up in us, the origin of all we shall become in you, and the first source of all that our lives shall become for others.

❦ Thursday

By the labour of your hands you shall eat.
You will be happy and prosper. (Psalm 128:2)

What we make with the gifts you give us brings us joy, and leads to life . . .

❦ Friday

The woman saw that the tree was good to eat and pleasing to the eye, and that it was desirable for the knowledge that it could give, so she took some of its fruit and ate it. (Genesis 3:6)

. . . but what we take of what you have not given or seize of what you have witheld, brings us shame, and leads to death.

❦ Saturday

You sweep men away like a dream,
like grass which springs up in the morning.
In the morning it springs up and flowers:
by evening it withers and fades. (Psalm 90:5–6)

Will the dream, that is my life, leave the waking world the richer or the poorer for its having been dreamed? Will the flower of my years leave fragrance in its wake or will it fade into forgetfulness?

The week's readings

Monday	Genesis 1:1–19; Psalm 104(103); Mark 6:53–6
Tuesday	Genesis 1:20 – 2:4; Psalm 8; Mark 7:1–13
Wednesday	Genesis 2:4–9, 15–17; Psalm 104(103); Mark 7:14–23
Thursday	Genesis 2:18–25; Psalm 128(127); Mark 7:24–30
Friday	Genesis 3:1–8; Psalm 32(31); Mark 7:31–7
Saturday	Genesis 3:9–24; Psalm 90(89); Mark 8:1–10

Fifth Week of Ordinary Time *(Weekday Cycle II)*

✠ Monday

There was nothing in the ark except the two stone tablets Moses had placed in it at Horeb, the tablets of the covenant which the Lord had made with the Israelites when they came out of the land of Egypt; they are still there today. (1 Kings 8:9)

When we enter our innermost depths we sometimes find nothing but bare emptiness and the cold heavy stones of our covenant promises to remain faithfully in the place where we have said we will be. Yet this same bare, painful and uncompromising place is the place of the ark, where your Spirit dwells, making us ready for freedom.

✠ Tuesday

Yet will God really live with men on the earth? Why, the heavens and their own heavens cannot contain you. How much less this house that I have built. (1 Kings 8:27–8)

It may take a lifetime to clear space in our hearts for God; and can such space contain him? Only if it is big enough to contain the smallest and most insignificant of his creatures.

✠ Wednesday

'Nothing that goes into a man from outside can make him unclean; it is the things that come out of a man that make him unclean.' (Mark 7:15–16)

I ate some contaminated food and it made me ill for a week.
I spoke a bitter word to a friend and it blighted our relationship for ever.

✠ Thursday

They even offered their own sons
and their daughters in sacrifice to demons,
till his anger blazed against his people:
he was filled with horror at his chosen ones. (Psalm 106:36–40)

David saw no connection between his worries about his teenage daughter's casual attitude towards her relationship with her boyfriend and the 'adult' magazines he carried in his own briefcase.

Friday

Their admiration was unbounded. 'He has done all things well,' they said, 'he makes the deaf hear and the dumb speak.' (Mark 7:37)

Greg had always been uncontroversial as a local councillor, going along easily with the majority view or the line of least resistance. Until his daughter was refused an operation because of financial cuts. He watched his child in pain that night, and love and pity cut a swathe through his heart. His ears were opened to the cry of injustice, and from that day forward he became a fearless and vocal campaigner for the needs of the sick and the helpless.

Saturday

'How many loaves have you.' 'Seven,' they said. Then he instructed the crowd to sit down on the ground, and he took the seven loaves, and after giving thanks he broke them and handed them to his disciples to distribute, and they distributed them among the crowd . . . Now there had been about four thousand people. (Mark 8:5–6, 9)

The logic of the Lord is simple. The little we have must be divided before it can be multiplied. The things we cling to must be taken away before the fullness of his love can be added to our own.

The week's readings

Monday	1 Kings 8:1–7, 9–13; Psalm 132(131); Mark 6:53–6
Tuesday	1 Kings 8:22–3, 27–30; Psalm 84(83); Mark 7:1–13
Wednesday	1 Kings 10:1–10; Psalm 37(36); Mark 7:14–23
Thursday	1 Kings 11:4–13; Psalm 106(105); Mark 7:24–30
Friday	1 Kings 11:29–32; 12:19; Psalm 81(80); Mark 7:31–7
Saturday	1 Kings 12:26–32; 13:33–4; Psalm 106(105); Mark 8:1–10

Sixth Week of Ordinary Time *(Weekday Cycle I)*

✠ Monday

Listen to the sound of your brother's blood, crying out to me from the ground . . . When you till the ground it shall no longer yield you any of its produce. (Genesis 4:10–12)

Which nation on earth is not soaked in the blood of your brothers and sisters, Lord? Their cries echo down the centuries, and only the flow of your blood can bring healing to our blighted hearts and homes.

✠ Tuesday

The Lord's voice resounding on the waters,
the Lord on the immensity of waters;
the voice of the Lord, full of power,
the voice of the Lord, full of splendour. (Psalm 29:3–4)

When the cares and concerns of our lives engulf us, Lord, and threaten to drown us in the tides of despair, help us to remember that your creating Spirit, hovering over our chaos, is continually bringing us to new birth and fresh growth.

✠ Wednesday

As long as earth lasts,
sowing and reaping,
cold and heat,
summer and winter,
day and night
shall cease no more. (Genesis 8:22)

Today may have felt like a disaster. This year may have seemed like a failure. But our days and years are held in a vast continuum of life, and you have promised that this life is leading all your children home to your eternal love.

Thursday

God said, 'Here is the sign of the Covenant I make between myself and you and every living creature with you for all generations: I set my bow in the clouds and it shall be a sign of the Covenant between me and the earth.' (Genesis 9:12–13)

Give us the grace to see beyond the stinging of our tears the radiance of your promise, eternally shining through the clouds.

Friday

'Come,' they said, 'let us build ourselves a town and a tower with its top reaching heaven. Let us make a name for ourselves . . . It was named Babel . . . It was from there that the Lord scattered them over the whole face of the earth. (Genesis 11:4, 9)

Jim had plenty of time to look back over his life as he lived out his declining years in the nursing home, unvisited and unloved. In his heyday he had built a business empire out of nothing. He had made a name for himself. He had reached for the stars. But in the process he had lost all connection with his family and friends. They had scattered far and wide beyond his reach, and now he was a nameless old man, laid low by loneliness and regret.

Saturday

Only faith can guarantee the blessings that we hope for, or prove the existence of the realities that at present remain unseen. (Hebrews 11:1)

Carol was so proud of her son who had persevered through chronic illness and disability to become the wise and cheerful adult he had grown into. 'I could only do it, Mum,' he said, 'because you believed in me.'

The week's readings

Monday	Genesis 4:1–15, 25; Psalm 50(49); Mark 8:11–13
Tuesday	Genesis 6:5–8; 7:1–5, 10; Psalm 29(28); Mark 8:14–21
Wednesday	Genesis 8:6–13, 20–2; Psalm 116(115); Mark 8:22–6
Thursday	Genesis 9:1–13; Psalm 102(101); Mark 8:27–33
Friday	Genesis 11:1–9; Psalm 33(32); Mark 8:34 – 9:1
Saturday	Hebrews 11:1–7; Psalm 145(144); Mark 9:2–13

Sixth Week of Ordinary Time (Weekday Cycle II)

❦ Monday

A person who has doubts is like the waves thrown up in the sea when the wind drives. (James 1:6–7)

Doubting means failing to trust you; allowing myself to forget the deep wellspring of peace and joy that is my central reality in you; allowing myself to believe rather in the surface turbulences of my days, as if they were the final statements.

❦ Tuesday

God does not tempt anybody. Everyone who is tempted is attracted and seduced by his own wrong desire. Then the desire conceives and gives birth to sin, and when sin is fully grown, it too has a child, and the child is death. (James 1:13–15)

When I blame someone else for my temptations I am not only sinning, but excusing my sin, and the sinful desires have undergone a whole new growth spurt towards their deadly destination.

❦ Wednesday

To listen to the word and not obey is like looking at your own features in a mirror and then, after a quick look, going off and immediately forgetting what you looked like. But the man who looks steadily at the perfect law of freedom and makes that his habit – not listening and then forgetting, but actively putting it into practice – will be happy in all that he does. (James 1:23–5)

Your word is our feast. If we sit at the table and look at it, admire it, tell others how wonderful it is, yet fail to take it into ourselves, we can neither grow nor be transformed. The law of your freedom must be incorporated into every cell of our being and our doing.

❦ Thursday

On the way Jesus put this question to his disciples, 'Who do people say I am?' And they told him 'John the Baptist,' they said, 'Others Elijah; others again, one of the prophets.' 'But you,' he asked, 'Who do you say I am?' Peter spoke up and said to him: 'You are the Christ.' (Mark 8:27–9)

Who do I think you are, Lord? Just a bigger, better, idealised version of 'me'? Or the One who transcends everything I am and calls me to transcend myself?

❦ Friday

> *A body dies when it is separated from the spirit, and in the same way faith is dead if it is separated from good deeds.* (James 2:26)

Nancy's houseplants died while she was in hospital. And inwardly she died, too, when there was no message or greeting from Julie, her daughter. The third death that day was Julie's, who could have watered Nancy's heart with a few drops of love, but didn't.

❦ Saturday

> *Once we put a bit into the horse's mouth, to make it do what we want, we have the whole animal under our control. Or think of ships, no matter how big they are, even if a gale is driving them, the man at the helm can steer them anywhere he likes by controlling a tiny rudder.* (James 3:3–5)

If I trust you for my rudder, the whole unwieldy bulk of my wayward heart can be guided by your gentlest touch. If I rely on my own steering I will spend all my life's energy and fail to change my course by even a fraction.

The week's readings

Monday	James 1:1–11; Psalm 119(118); Mark 8:11–13
Tuesday	James 1:12–18; Psalm 94(93); Mark 8:14–21
Wednesday	James 1:19–27; Psalm 15(14); Mark 8:22–6
Thursday	James 2:1–9; Psalm 34(33); Mark 8:27–33
Friday	James 2:14–24, 26; Psalm 112(111); Mark 8:34 – 9:1
Saturday	James 3:1–10; Psalm 12(11); Mark 9:2–13

Seventh Week of Ordinary Time (Weekday Cycle I)

Monday

The father of the boy [in convulsions] cried out: 'I do have faith. Help the little faith I have.' (Mark 9:25)

We may have beliefs enough to fill a catechism, but do we trust you, Lord? We may believe in everything we read on the seed packet, but will we plant the seed? And will we tend its growing?

Tuesday

'Anyone who welcomes one of these little children in my name, welcomes me, and anyone who welcomes me welcomes not me but the one who sent me.' (Mark 9:37)

The one who can see the bird inside the egg and the oak inside the acorn, can see the Lord of all creation in a little child.

Wednesday

'Anyone who is not against us is for us.' (Mark 9:40)

I would rather assume that everyone is friendly, and be fooled a few times but keep my heart open to everyone around me, than hold my image and my wallet safe, but die with a closed-up heart.

Thursday

Jesus said: 'If your hand should cause you to sin, cut it off; it is better for you to enter into life crippled, than to have two hands and go to hell.' (Mark 9:43)

Cutting free from anything that cuts us off from you may feel like bleeding to death, but, in your love, it will become an entry into a fuller depth of life.

Friday

A faithful friend is the elixir of life,
and those who fear the Lord will find one.
Whoever fears the Lord makes true friends,
for as a man is, so is his friend. (Ecclesiasticus 6:16–17)

Jamie's parents were concerned about his friendship with Gary. Gary was a trouble-maker at school, and yet Jamie was always there alongside him, not in the trouble-making, but in the pain and punishment that followed after. Only years later did they begin to realise how, gradually, Gary had started to model himself on his faithful friend and was slowly learning how to become a friend himself.

Saturday

The Lord fashioned man from the earth . . .
and gave them a heart to think with. (Ecclesiasticus 17:15)

In the frantic circles of living there is a still centre that only our hearts know how to find. Only in that still centre will our thinking become clear and true.

The week's readings

Monday	Ecclesiasticus 1:1–10; Psalm 93(92); Mark 9:14–29
Tuesday	Ecclesiasticus 2:1–11; Psalm 37(36); Mark 9:30–7
Wednesday	Ecclesiasticus 4:11–19; Psalm 119(118); Mark 9:38–40
Thursday	Ecclesiasticus 5:1–8; Psalm 1; Mark 9:41–50
Friday	Ecclesiasticus 6:5–17; Psalm 119(118); Mark 10:1–12
Saturday	Ecclesiasticus 17:1–15; Psalm 103(102); Mark 10:13–16

Seventh week of Ordinary Time (Weekday Cycle II)

✠ Monday

> *'If you can do anything,' said the child's father, 'have pity on us and help us.' 'If you can?' retorted Jesus. 'Everything is possible for anyone who has faith.' Immediately the father of the boy cried out: 'I do have faith. Help the little faith I have.'* (Mark 9:23–5)

Out of our darkness we cry, 'Help the little faith we have!' And that turns out to be the most potent prayer of all. It opens us up to your healing and makes all things possible.

✠ Tuesday

> *Where do these wars and battles between yourselves first start? Isn't it precisely in the desires fighting inside your own selves? You want something and you haven't got it; so you are prepared to kill. You have an ambition that you cannot satisfy; so you fight to get your way by force.* (James 4:1–2)

I switched on the television news and saw my own inner conflicts writ large. I saw the inner struggles of every member of the human family stamped onto a barren battlefield and scarred indelibly across the faces of the innocent. Then I switched off the television and knew that peace could only begin with me.

✠ Wednesday

> *You never know what will happen tomorrow: you are no more than a mist that is here for a little while and then disappears.* (James 4:14)

A mist can obscure the beauty of life, from ourselves and from others. Or it can soak into the earth and give life to new growth. Which shall our lives become: an obscuring cloud or a refreshing dewfall?

✠ Thursday

> *'Salt is a good thing, but if salt has become insipid, how can you season it again? Have salt in yourselves and be at peace with one another.'* (Mark 9:50)

May the salt of our faith be the salt that preserves and the salt that gives flavour, the salt that melts frozen hearts and the salt that tempts the seeker to taste and see. May the salt of our faith become the salt of the earth.

❦ Friday

If you mean 'Yes', you must say 'Yes'; if you mean 'No', say 'No.' (James 5:12)

The hallmark of truth is its simplicity. Complications and convolutions are the symptoms of concealment. Simplicity is of God. The complications are our own.

❦ Saturday

My brothers, if one of you strays away from the truth and another brings him back to it, he may be sure that anyone who can bring back a sinner from the wrong way that he has taken will be saving a soul from death and covering up a great number of sins. (James 5:20)

One return to the way of truth is worth a hundred reproaches for deviating from it.

The week's readings

Monday	James 3:13–18; Psalm 19(18); Mark 9:14–29
Tuesday	James 4:1–10; Psalm 55(54); Mark 9:30–7
Wednesday	James 4:13–17; Psalm 49(48); Mark 9:38–40
Thursday	James 5:1–6; Psalm 49(48); Mark 9:41–50
Friday	James 5:9–12; Psalm 103(102); Mark 10:1–12
Saturday	James 5:13–20; Psalm 141(140); Mark 10:13–16

Eighth Week of Ordinary Time (Weekday Cycle I)

❦ Monday

> *Jesus looked steadily at him and loved him, and he said: 'There is one thing you lack. Go and sell everything you own and give the money to the poor, and you will have treasure in heaven; then come, follow me.'* (Mark 10:21–2)

Arnold lay dying, surrounded by all his memories – everything that he had valued and loved in life. Day by day he loosened himself from everything, saying goodbye with gratitude, not with regret. And when he was free of everything that held him, he was light enough to follow you into eternal life.

❦ Tuesday

> *By showing gratitude, a man makes an offering of fine flour,*
> *by giving alms, he offers praise.* (Ecclesiasticus 35:2–4)

Marie received two gifts on Mother's Day. Her elder son sent her a bottle of expensive perfume, gift-wrapped and dispatched by courier from his company address in the city. Her younger son, who still hadn't found a job, came round to see her, gave her a hug and said, 'Thank you, Mum; I love you.'

❦ Wednesday

> *'Can you drink the cup that I must drink, or be baptised with the baptism with which I must be baptised?'* (Mark 10:38)

The waters of baptism that flow over us in infancy may become floods of grief in which adult care would drown us, and the cup of our first communion may become a bitter chalice of suffering; yet, wherever we are, there are *you*.

❦ Thursday

> *Throwing off his cloak, blind Bartimaeus jumped up and went to Jesus. Then Jesus spoke, 'What do you want me to do for you?'* (Mark 10:50–1)

If, in our blindness, we can penetrate to the roots of what our hearts most deeply desire, then we shall know what you desire for us; then we shall know your Will.

❦ Friday

'When you stand in prayer, forgive whatever you have against anybody, so that your Father in heaven may forgive your failings too.' (Mark 11:25)

Janice found no peace in her heart for prayer that evening. The words were there, but they rattled emptily away, without touching her heart. It was during the small hours of the night that she awoke, heavy-hearted with regrets and resentments from the quarrel with her friend. The tears flowed, and then she knew that her desire for reconciliation was so much greater than her wounded pride. As she slipped back, exhausted, into sleep, her evening prayer had been made whole again.

❦ Saturday

In my prayers I asked outright for wisdom . . .
Outside the sanctuary I would pray for her.
From her blossoming to the ripening of her grape
my heart has taken its delight in her. (Ecclesiasticus 51:13–15)

Those first insights that you give us as we seek your face, Lord, delight us as the blossoms of our springtime. But your wisdom will grow and ripen in us, like fruits on the vine, until, at the end, all we have left is a crushed grape, whose essence has been distilled for those who follow after.

The week's readings

Monday	Ecclesiasticus 17:24–9; Psalm 32(31); Mark 10:17–27
Tuesday	Ecclesiasticus 35:1–12; Psalm 50(49); Mark 10:28–31
Wednesday	Ecclesiasticus 36:1, 4–5, 10–17; Psalm 79(78); Mark 10:32–45
Thursday	Ecclesiasticus 42:15–25; Psalm 33(32); Mark 10:46–52
Friday	Ecclesiasticus 44:1, 9–13; Psalm 149; Mark 11:11–26
Saturday	Ecclesiasticus 51:12–20; Psalm 19(18); Mark 11:27–33

Eighth Week of Ordinary Time (Weekday Cycle II)

❦ Monday

Through your faith, God's power will guard you until the salvation which has been prepared is revealed at the end of time. This is a cause of great joy to you, even though you may for a short time have to bear being plagued by all sorts of trials; so that, when Jesus Christ is revealed, your faith will have been tested and proved like gold – only it is more precious than gold. (1 Peter 1:5–7)

In the crucible of your redeeming grace, it sometimes feels as though our faith, our hope and everything we think we are is consumed to ashes. Yet those ashes are Gethsemane ashes, from which alone the fullness of your resurrection will arise.

❦ Tuesday

'Many who are first will be last, and the last first.' (Mark 10:31)

The prayer group gathered as usual for their reflections and faith sharing. They had been praying together for several years and felt confident and experienced. Sally had never been before and hardly knew how to begin. But as soon as she shared with them, quietly and shyly, the joy of her meeting with you in prayer, they knew they were in the presence of one who knew you in her heart and carried that knowledge unconsciously to all around her.

❦ Wednesday

Remember, the ransom that was paid to free you from the useless way of life your ancestors handed down was not paid in anything corruptible, neither in silver nor gold, but in the precious blood of a lamb without spot or stain, namely Christ. (1 Peter 1:18–20)

The checkout girl took my £20 note and routinely examined it for signs of forgery before completing the transaction. I packed my shopping, reflecting that this basket of perishable food had been purchased with corruptible currency, yet remembering that what is indestructible in me has been purchased by your incorruptible and indestructible love.

❦ Thursday

Throwing off his cloak, Bartimaeus jumped up and went to Jesus. Then Jesus spoke, 'What do you want me to do for you?' 'Rabbuni,' the blind man said to him. 'Master, let me see again.' (Mark 10:50–1)

The heart of our own deepest desires and longings is the place where we shall meet your dream for us, and realise the certainty of its fulfilment.

❦ Friday

My dear people, you must not think it unaccountable that you should be tested by fire . . . If you can have some share in the sufferings of Christ, be glad, because you will enjoy a much greater gladness when his glory is revealed. (1 Peter 4:12–13)

When Hilary's terminal illness was diagnosed, she noticed two things: some of her friends drifted away, repelled by her pain and the imminence of death, until they became mere acquaintances; other friends drew closer, bringing real compassion alongside her suffering and fear, until they became intimate companions. You give us the same choice, Lord, when our hurting and aching meets yours.

❦ Saturday

Keep yourselves within the love of God and wait for the mercy of our Lord Jesus Christ to give you eternal life. (Jude, verse 21)

After the massacre by the crazed gunman, the dazed survivors of the shattered community crept helplessly into the church to huddle together in their grief, their need of each other, and their overwhelming need of you.

The week's readings

Monday	1 Peter 1:3–9; Psalm 111(110); Mark 10:17–27
Tuesday	1 Peter 1:10–16; Psalm 98(97); Mark 10:28–31
Wednesday	1 Peter 1:18–25; Psalm 147; Mark 10:32–45
Thursday	1 Peter 2:2–5, 9–12; Psalm 100(99); Mark 10:46–52
Friday	1 Peter 4:7–13; Psalm 96(95); Mark 11:11–26
Saturday	Jude 17:20–5; Psalm 63(62); Mark 11:27–33

Ninth Week of Ordinary Time (Weekday Cycle I)

❦ Monday

> *'The tenants of the master's vineyard said to each other: "This is the heir. Come on, let us kill him and the inheritance will be ours". So they seized him and killed him and threw him out of the vineyard.'* (Mark 12:7–8)

What we take by force we may hold for a season. What you give through grace is our inheritance for all eternity.

❦ Tuesday

> *They handed him a denarius and he said: 'Whose head is this? Whose name?' 'Caesar's' they told him. Jesus said to them, 'Give back to Caesar what belongs to Caesar – and to God what belongs to God.'* (Mark 12:15–17)

How shall I draw my life's energy? In the currency of Caesar, with its punitive interest rates? Or in the currency of God, that is given unearned?

❦ Wednesday

> *Lord, make me know your ways.*
> *Lord, teach me your paths.*
> *Make me walk in your truth, and teach me,*
> *for you are God, my saviour.* (Psalm 25:4–5)

The unique pathways that you walk with each of us are not on any map. Instead we must trust the compass you have planted in our hearts.

❦ Thursday

> *One of the scribes came up to Jesus and put a question to him: 'Which is the first of all the commandments?' Jesus replied: 'This is the first. Listen, Israel, the Lord your God is the one Lord, and you must love the Lord your God with all your heart, with all your soul, with all your mind and with all your strength. The second is this: you must love your neighbour as yourself. There is no commandment greater than these.'* (Mark 12:28–31)

All of me: not just the Sunday slot. All of me: not just my conscious thoughts. All of me: not just the span of years I call my life on earth. All of me: just space enough to hold a seed of God.

❧ Friday

It is the Lord who keeps faith for ever,
who is just to those who are oppressed.
It is he who gives bread to the hungry,
the Lord, who sets prisoners free. (Psalm 146:6–7)

When we look into the eyes of one who is caring for the oppressed, the hungry, the prisoners, we are looking into the heart of God, whether the one who is caring is aware of God or not.

❧ Saturday

He sat down opposite the treasury and watched the people putting money into the treasury, and many of the rich put in a great deal. A poor widow came and put in two small coins, the equivalent of a penny. Then he called his disciples and said to them: 'I tell you solemnly, this poor widow has put in more than all who have contributed to the treasury; for they have all put in money they had over, but she from the little she had has put in everything she possessed, all she had to live on.' (Mark 12:41–4)

My eyes were blinded by the tears that the ugly incident had caused. The richest gifts, the most lavish promises, would have left me unconsoled. Then my two-year-old came up to me, looked at me with mute, sad eyes, and placed her teddy in my lap. It was everything she had: it was everything I needed.

The week's readings

Monday	Tobit 1:1; 2:1–8; Psalm 112(111); Mark 12:1–12
Tuesday	Tobit 2:9–14; Psalm 112(111); Mark 12:13–17
Wednesday	Tobit 3:1–11, 16–17; Psalm 25(24); Mark 12:18–27
Thursday	Tobit 6:11; 7:1, 9–14; 8:4–8; Psalm 128(127); Mark 12:28–34
Friday	Tobit 11:5–15; Psalm 146(145); Mark 12:35–7
Saturday	Tobit 12:1, 5–15, 20; Tobit 13:2, 6–8; Mark 12:38–44

Ninth Week of Ordinary Time *(Weekday Cycle II)*

✠ Monday

By his divine power, he has given us all the things that we need for life and for true devotion, bringing us to know God himself, who has called us by his own glory and goodness. In making these gifts, he has given us the guarantee of something very great and wonderful to come. (2 Peter 1:3–4)

In every lived moment we discover your gifts, and every gift is a sacrament, at once both fulfilling the needs of the 'now' and pointing to, and bringing to fulfilment, the promise of the 'not yet'.

✠ Tuesday

Show forth your work to your servants;
let your glory shine on their children. (Psalm 90:16–17)

The brilliance of the full moon held me rooted to the spot in awe and wonder. Yet it was only a lump of rock spinning through space, and its glory came entirely from the light of the unseen sun, shining upon it in the darkness of my night. It shed upon me its promise that we too, your lumps of clay, might reflect the light of your unseen presence into the darkness we find around us.

✠ Wednesday

'He is God, not of the dead, but of the living.' (Mark 12:27)

When I dwell on the follies and the failures of the past, I find nothing but an empty tomb. But when I hear you call my name in the garden of my grief, I know that you are touching that which is alive in me, and calling it into resurrection.

❦ Thursday

If we disown him, then he will disown us.
We may be unfaithful, but he is always faithful,
for he cannot disown his own self. (2 Timothy 2:12–13)

We can only disown what is not part of us. When God has made his dwelling in our hearts then faithfulness must follow.

❦ Friday

Though my foes and oppressors are countless
I have not swerved from your will.
Your word is founded on truth:
your decrees are eternal. (Psalm 119:157, 160)

Every day we live seems to open up new quicksands and landslides that threaten to engulf us. But when, in the middle of the turmoil, we reach out to you in prayer, we discover just sufficient solid ground for one more step towards you.

❦ Saturday

As for me, my life is already being poured away as a libation, and the time has come for me to be gone. (2 Timothy 4:6)

The power of your Spirit in our hearts is only released when we take the risk of our own emptying and allow you to pour us out for others.

The week's readings

Monday	2 Peter 1:2–7; Psalm 91(90); Mark 12:1–12
Tuesday	2 Peter 3:11–15, 17–18; Psalm 90(89); Mark 12:13–17
Wednesday	2 Timothy 1:1–3, 6–12; Psalm 123(122); Mark 12:18–27
Thursday	2 Timothy 2:8–15; Psalm 25(24); Mark 12:28–34
Friday	2 Timothy 3:10–17; Psalm 119(118); Mark 12:35–7
Saturday	2 Timothy 4:1–8; Psalm 71(70); Mark 12:38–44

Tenth Week of Ordinary Time (Weekday Cycle I)

✠ Monday

> *'How happy are the poor in spirit; theirs is the kingdom of heaven.'* (Matthew 5:3)

The first thing she noticed out of the emptiness following her husband's death was a tiny wild rose shoot, pushing through the gap between the paving stones. A flower blooming in her desert space. A fullness that needed emptiness in which to grow. An emptied heart, full of space for the coming of a kingdom.

✠ Tuesday

> *Jesus said to his disciples: 'You are the salt of the earth. But if salt becomes tasteless, what can make it salty again? It is good for nothing, and can only be thrown out to be trampled underfoot by men.'* (Matthew 5:13)

We are called, not to add piquancy to our own private meal, but to let the flavour of God spread through the whole human stew, so that everyone's appetite is sharpened.

✠ Wednesday

> *Jesus said to his disciples: 'Do not imagine that I have come to abolish the Law or the Prophets. I have come not to abolish but to complete them.'* (Matthew 5:17)

Faithful obedience leads at last to the fullness of love, as surely as the laws received by the children of Israel led to the dawn of resurrection, as surely as the seed yields the perfection of the flower.

✠ Thursday

> *'So then, if you are bringing your offering to the altar and there remember that your brother has something against you, leave your offering there before the altar, go and be reconciled with your brother first, and then come back and present your offering.'* (Matthew 5:23–4)

You could almost see the wall of tension between them as they sat icily side by side through the first part of the Eucharist, each brooding bitterly over last night's row. But there was no escaping the moment of truth. Eyes lowered, they reached out reluctant hands. 'Peace be with you,' he muttered. 'And peace be with you,' she almost choked. Then their eyes met. Something snapped. Something changed. Tonight would be different. It was possible to try again. They went forward together, to receive communion.

☙ Friday

> *We are only the earthenware jars that hold this treasure, to make it clear that such an overwhelming power comes from God and not from us.* (2 Corinthians 4:7)

Even when we are shattered, the worst that can happen is that God's love and grace and power spill over into the waiting world.

☙ Saturday

> *And for anyone who is in Christ there is a new creation; the old creation has gone, and now the new one is here. It is all God's work. It was God who reconciled us to himself through Christ and gave us the work of handing on this reconciliation.* (2 Corinthians 5:17–19)

To see the world as you see it would be a daily miracle. But you call us to even more than this: you call us to become the means of sharing the vision, of multiplying the miracle.

The week's readings

Monday	2 Corinthians. 1:1–7; Psalm 34(33); Matthew 5:1–12
Tuesday	2 Corinthians 1:18–22; Psalm 119(118); Matthew 5:13–16
Wednesday	2 Corinthians 3:4–11; Psalm 99(98); Matthew 5:17–19
Thursday	2 Corinthians 3:15 – 4:1, 3–6; Psalm 85(84); Matthew 5:20–6
Friday	2 Corinthians 4:7–15; Psalm 116(115); Matthew 5:27–32
Saturday	2 Corinthians 5:14–21; Psalm 103(102); Matthew 5:33–7

Tenth Week of Ordinary Time *(Weekday Cycle II)*

❧ Monday

> *'Happy are you when people abuse you and persecute you and speak all kinds of calumny against you on my account. Rejoice and be glad, for your reward will be great in heaven.'* (Matthew 5:11–12)

Etty went to her death in a concentration camp with her eyes open: not condoning or co-operating with the evil, but knowing that the inner source of joy in her heart was more powerful still. Knowing you, and blessed in that knowledge that has its roots deeper than all destruction.

❧ Tuesday

> *You have put into my heart a greater joy than they have from abundance of corn and new wine.* (Psalm 4:7)

We rejoice briefly in the harvest suppers of our lives, but you give a joy that will sustain us all through our wintering.

❧ Wednesday

> *Answer me, Lord, answer me, so that this people may know that you, Lord, are God and are winning back their hearts.* (1 Kings 18:37)

When our own lives reveal the radiance of our joy in you, then we co-operate in your winning back of the hearts of all your creation.

❧ Thursday

> *And thus you provide for the earth;*
> *you drench its furrows,*
> *you level it, soften it with showers,*
> *you bless its growth.* (Psalm 65:10)

Sometimes our lives fill up with sorrow and the sharp blades of pain drive furrows through our hearts. Saturate us, then, with your grace, so that we might know that in just such times you are blessing and nourishing our growth.

Friday

> *'If your right hand should cause you to sin, cut it off and throw it away, for it will do you less harm to lose one part of you than to have your whole body go to hell.'* (Matthew 5:30)

When I look around the inner rooms of my heart I find gifts from you that I have allowed to become the centre of my life. Help me to give them back to you, Lord, and to build my life on the Giver and not the gifts.

Saturday

> *'All you need say is "Yes" if you mean yes, "No" if you mean no; anything more than this comes from the evil one.'* (Matthew 5:37)

Mary eventually put down the letter in irritation, annoyed by all its expressions of 'You really shouldn't have gone to all that trouble' and 'How can we ever repay you for your kindness?' They didn't quite ring true. It was so refreshing to read the simple response of her friend: 'Thank you for the evening. I loved it.'

The week's readings

Monday	1 Kings 17:1–6; Psalm 121(120); Matthew 5:1–12
Tuesday	1 Kings 17:7–16; Psalm 4; Matthew 5:13–16
Wednesday	1 Kings 18:20–39; Psalm 16(15); Matthew 5:17–19
Thursday	1 Kings 18:41–6; Psalm 65(64); Matthew 5:20–6
Friday	1 Kings 19:9, 11–16; Psalm 27(26); Matthew 5:27–32
Saturday	1 Kings 19:19–21; Psalm 16(15); Matthew 5:33–7

Eleventh Week of Ordinary Time (Weekday Cycle I)

☙ Monday

> *Jesus said: 'And if anyone orders you to go one mile, go two miles with him. Give to anyone who asks, and if anyone wants to borrow, do not turn away.'* (Matthew 5:42)

I simmer inwardly as I force myself to do the chores that life imposes on me. For the first mile I feel like a slave. Yet when the obligation is lifted I can do exactly the same tasks again, in a free spirit, and discover joy in doing them. I walk the second mile like a prince.

☙ Tuesday

> *'But I say this to you: love your enemies and pray for those who persecute you; in this way you will be sons of your Father in heaven, for he causes his sun to rise on bad men as well as good, and his rain to fall on honest and dishonest men alike.'* (Matthew 5:44–6)

I need all my energy for living towards your fullness. The energy I expend in anger and resentment is diverted and lost. The energy I use for loving and praying is multiplied. It helps to neutralise my enemy's destructive feelings and it protects me from my own.

☙ Wednesday

> *'When you pray, go to your private room and, when you have shut your door, pray to your Father who is in that secret place, and your Father who sees all that is done in secret will reward you.'* (Matthew 6:6)

The Israelites carried Yahweh with them on their journeying, in the tabernacle-tent. To pray is to discover our own tabernacle-tent in the deep silence of our heart and to enter its secret, sacred space to meet with the Lord of the journey.

☙ Thursday

> *Jesus said to his disciples: 'In your prayers do not babble as the pagans do, for they think that by using many words they will make themselves heard. Do not be like them; your Father knows what you need before you ask him.'* (Matthew 6:7–8)

In the excitement of first meeting, the friends hardly stopped talking. But as their friendship deepened, they discovered that their most profound feelings could only be communicated in a receptive silence.

✠ Friday

> *'The lamp of the body is the eye. It follows that if your eye is sound, your whole body will be filled with light. But if your eye is diseased, your whole body will be all darkness. If, then, the light inside you is darkness, what darkness will that be?'* (Matthew 6:22–3)

Our prayer is a window through which the sunlight of your love streams in to us, filling our whole being with your light. We can choose to keep it curtained or shuttered, or we can let it be clean and clear and open.

✠ Saturday

> *'That is why I am telling you not to worry about your life and what you are to eat, nor about your body and how you are to clothe it. Surely life means more than food, and the body more than clothing! . . . Set your hearts on his kingdom first, and on his righteousness, and all these other things will be given you as well. So do not worry about tomorrow: tomorrow will take care of itself.'* (Matthew 6:25, 33–4)

The day had been so hectic. She had spent hours in the kitchen devising something to tempt the baby's appetite. Then she had rushed round the shops, searching for toys for his birthday. She sighed, as she leaned over his cot that night and stroked his sleeping head, with its soft, downy hair. The day was over, and she had come close to missing it completely. It would never return. He was a day older, and she was a day wiser.

The week's readings

Monday	2 Corinthians 6:1–10; Psalm 98(97); Matthew 5:38–42
Tuesday	2 Corinthians 8:1–9; Psalm 146(145); Matthew 5:43–8
Wednesday	2 Corinthians 9:6–11; Psalm 112(111); Matthew 6:1–6, 16–18
Thursday	2 Corinthians 11:1–11; Psalm 111(110); Matthew 6:7–15
Friday	2 Corinthians 11:18, 21–30; Psalm 34(33); Matthew 6:19–23
Saturday	2 Corinthians 12:1–10; Psalm 34(33); Matthew 6:24–34

Eleventh Week of Ordinary Time *(Weekday Cycle II)*

✠ Monday

> *'Give to anyone who asks, and if anyone wants to borrow, do not turn away.'* (Matthew 5:42)

Peter was getting tired of opening the vicarage door to beggars and vagrants. Enough was enough. Then Charlie knocked. And Peter looked into his eyes. And Peter gave again. And a tear of gratitude trickled across Charlie's cheek. There will never be enough of giving until all is spent

✠ Tuesday

> *Have mercy on me, God, in your kindness.*
> *In your compassion blot out my offence.*
> *O wash me more and more from my guilt*
> *and cleanse me from my sin.* (Psalm 51:1–2)

The pick-axe of reproach may hack at our stony hearts, but only the ceaseless, gentle, cleansing flow of grace will soften them into flesh.

✠ Wednesday

> *'When you give alms, your left hand must not know what your right hand is doing; your almsgiving must be secret, and your Father who sees all that is done in secret will reward you.'* (Matthew 6:3–4)

Everyone in the neighbourhood knew of Eileen's legendary generosity. Everyone, that is, except Eileen herself, who never gave it a thought as she lived out her life in unselfconscious attentiveness to the needs of those around her.

❦ Thursday

The Lord is king, let earth rejoice,
the many coastlands be glad.
Cloud and darkness are his raiment;
his throne, justice and right. (Psalm 97:1–2)

Why, Lord, do you walk the earth in the shape of those who are clouded with despair and darkened by suffering? Is it to awaken in us the desire to bring them your justice and your healing love?

❦ Friday

'Where your treasure is, there will your heart be also.' (Matthew 6:21)

It began harmlessly for Jim. First a few overtime hours for an extra holiday, then a few more for a bigger house, and finally a compulsive, workaholic lifestyle leaving his heart stranded on the beach of his ebbing life.

❦ Saturday

I will punish their offences with the rod,
I will scourge them on account of their guilt.
But I will never take back my love:
my truth will never fail. (Psalm 89:32–3)

It had been a terrible day, and Susan's temper was in shreds. A fractious toddler, a disobedient child and a moody teenager had all taken their toll on their mother's nerves. Finally, in the silence of the night, she slipped into their rooms one last time. As she kissed them softly in their sleep, her heart tugged itself back into place, and she knew, again, just how much she loved them.

The week's readings

Monday	1 Kings 21:1–16; Psalm 5; Matthew 5:38–42
Tuesday	1 Kings 21:17–29; Psalm 51(50); Matthew 5:43–8
Wednesday	2 Kings 2:1, 6–14, Psalm 31(30); Matthew 6:1–6, 16–18
Thursday	Ecclesiasticus 48:1–14; Psalm 97(96); Matthew 6:7–15
Friday	2 Kings 11:1–4, 9–18, 20; Psalm 132(131); Matthew 6:19–23
Saturday	2 Chronicles 24:17–25; Psalm 89(88); Matthew 6:24–34

Twelfth Week of Ordinary Time *(Weekday Cycle I)*

✠ Monday

'Do not judge, and you will not be judged; because the judgements you give are the judgements you will get, and the amount you measure out is the amount you will be given. Why do you observe the splinter in your brother's eye and never notice the plank in your own?' (Matthew 7:1–3)

Every time I criticise my friends I alienate them from me a little more; we move further apart, away from the centre of warmth and trust that we might have shared. Every time I acknowledge my own shortcomings, instead of exposing theirs, we are drawn closer together into a new understanding and mutual compassion.

✠ Tuesday

Abram was a very rich man, with livestock, silver and gold. Lot, who was travelling with Abram, had flocks and cattle of his own and tents too. The land was not sufficient to accommodate them both at once, for they had too many possessions to be able to live together. (Genesis 13:2)

Archaeologists tell us that the first general evidence of murder is linked to the time when people ceased to be nomadic and started to settle in one place, accumulate possessions and envy each others' treasures. From then on they had too many possessions to be able to live together.

✠ Wednesday

'Beware of false prophets who come to you disguised as sheep but underneath are ravenous wolves. You will be able to tell them by their fruits. Can people pick grapes from thorns, or figs from thistles? In the same way, a sound tree produces good fruit but a rotten tree bad fruit.' (Matthew 7:15–18)

Words of reproach, spoken unjustly, yielding resentment. Words of reproach, spoken in love, yielding growth and healing. The fruit reveals the nature of the tree. The harvest identifies the seed.

❦ Thursday

'Therefore, everyone who listens to these words of mine and acts on them will be like a sensible man who built his house on rock. Rain came down, floods rose, gales blew and hurled themselves against that house, and it did not fall: it was founded on rock.' (Matthew 7:24–6)

It was when I was dashed against the rocks of experience that I discovered the only solid foundation for my life, in the maker of the rocks and the healer of the experience.

❦ Friday

After Jesus had come down from the mountain, large crowds followed him. A leper now came up and bowed low in front of him. 'Sir,' he said, 'if you want to, you can cure me.' Jesus stretched out his hand, touched him and said, 'Of course I want to! Be cured!' (Matthew 8:1–3)

The television films of the refugee camps showed scenes of total desolation. Parents' faces were frozen in anguish as they gazed helplessly at their dying children. The cameras traced the passage of their tears. Then I knew that *you* were there. I saw your longing etched on their faces – a parent's love and longing: 'Of course I want to cure you!'

❦ Saturday

A centurion came up and pleaded with Jesus. 'Sir', he said, 'my servant is lying at home paralysed and in great pain.' 'I will come myself and cure him,' said Jesus. The centurion replied, 'Sir, I am not worthy to have you under my roof; just give the word, and my servant will be cured.' (Matthew 8:5–8)

The Word that made us heals us, and lodges eternally under the roof of our own hearts.

The week's readings

Monday	Genesis 12:1–9; Psalm 33(32); Matthew 7:1–5
Tuesday	Genesis 13:2, 5–18; Psalm 15(14); Matthew 7:6, 12–14
Wednesday	Genesis 15:1–12, 17–18; Psalm 105(104); Matthew 7:15–20
Thursday	Genesis 16:1–12, 15–16; Psalm 106(105); Matthew 7:21–9
Friday	Genesis 17:1, 9–10, 15–22; Psalm 128(127); Matthew 8:1–4
Saturday	Genesis 18:1–15; Luke 1:46–50, 53–5; Matthew 8:5–17

Twelfth Week of Ordinary Time *(Weekday Cycle II)*

✠ Monday

You have made the earth quake, torn it open.
Repair what is shattered for it sways.
You have inflicted hardships on your people
and made us drink a wine that dazed us. (Psalm 60:2–3)

Drunk with our illusions, and high on the drug of our own self-sufficiency, we stagger through the tumbling structures of our world. Yet there is still just enough vision left to show us our plight and our need, and to give voice to our cry to you for rescue.

✠ Tuesday

A remnant shall go out from Jerusalem, and survivors from Mount Zion.
The love of the Lord shall accomplish this. (2 Kings 19:31)

The seamless garment of your kingdom is not made from the finest rolls of fabric, but from the scraps and remnants of faith that you have gathered from your people through the ages and made one in your love.

✠ Wednesday

'Beware of false prophets who come to you disguised as sheep but underneath are ravenous wolves. You will be able to tell them by their fruits. Can people pick grapes from thorns, or figs from thistles? In the same way, a sound tree produces good fruit but a rotten tree bad fruit.' (Matthew 7:15–18)

The creatures of the woodland know how to distinguish between the colourful, seductive toadstools and the humble, hidden mushrooms, because they have noticed their effects. Lord, please give us the same wisdom in our lives and in our world.

✠ Thursday

'Therefore, everyone who listens to these words of mine and acts on them will be like a sensible man who built his house on rock. Rain came down, floods rose, gales blew and hurled themselves against that house, and it did not fall: it was founded on rock.' (Matthew 7:24–6)

We place our trust in our homes and our jobs and our investments, yet the storms of recession or of war dissolve them in flash floods of destruction. And when all is gone, we find nothing but the hard rock, and the shocked realisation that only that Rock is able to hold us.

❦ Friday

By the rivers of Babylon
there we sat and wept, remembering Zion . . .
O how could we sing the song of the Lord
on alien soil? (Psalm 137:1, 4)

Yet when we find the heart to sing your song in a world that rejects you, then our little patch of alien soil becomes your home again, and a place where others might find you.

❦ Saturday

And going into Peter's house Jesus found Peter's mother-in-law in bed with fever. He touched her hand and the fever left her, and she got up and began to wait on him. (Matthew 8:14–15)

You touch us with your love and the fever of our lives subsides. Our hearts become whole again, able to respond to you in joyful service.

The week's readings

Monday	2 Kings 17:5–8, 13–15, 18; Psalm 60(59); Matthew 7:1–5
Tuesday	2 Kings 19:9–11, 14–21, 31–6; Psalm 48(47); Matthew 7:6, 12–14
Wednesday	2 Kings 22:8–13; 23:1–3; Psalm 119(118); Matthew 7:15–20
Thursday	2 Kings 24:8–17; Psalm 79(78); Matthew 7:21–9
Friday	2 Kings 25:1–12; Psalm 137(136); Matthew 8:1–4
Saturday	Lamentations 2:2, 10–14, 18–19; Psalm 74(73); Matthew 8:5–17

Thirteenth Week of Ordinary Time *(Weekday Cycle I)*

✠ Monday

One of the scribes then came up and said to him, 'Master, I will follow you wherever you go.' Jesus replied, 'Foxes have holes and the birds of the air have nests, but the Son of Man has nowhere to lay his head.' (Matthew 8:19–20)

There are moments of desolation when there is no one, nowhere to turn to, and every direction seems to lead to despair. And there, at the still centre of the storm, the homeless One is waiting.

✠ Tuesday

When dawn broke the angel urged Lot: 'Come, take your wife and these two daughters of yours, or you will be overwhelmed in the punishment of the town [Sodom and Gomorrah] . . . As they were leading him out he said: 'Run for your life. Neither look behind you nor stop anywhere on the plain. Make for the hills if you would not be overwhelmed.' . . . But the wife of Lot looked back and was turned to salt. (Genesis 19:15–18, 26)

I stop in my tracks and look back to the plain below me. There, spread out, I see the memories of all that has hurt me and all those I have hurt. Then I turn forwards to the hills ahead of me. There I see an open sky, full of unknown possibilities. Which view will I choose? Which view will lead to life?

✠ Wednesday

When Jesus reached the country of the Gadarenes on the other side, two demoniacs came towards him out of the tombs – creatures so fierce that no one could pass that way. They stood there shouting: 'What do you want with us, Son of God? Have you come here to torture us before the time?' (Matthew 8:28–30)

I don't know what made me say it. My dark mood took control of me. My darkness couldn't handle the meeting with your light and hurled all its strength against you, and it all came out in a torrent of angry words against my friend. But your light was even stronger, and my darkness knew your power and acknowledged its sovereignty.

❦ Thursday

> *When they arrived at the place God had pointed out to him, Abraham built an altar there, and arranged the wood. Then he bound his son Isaac and put him on the altar on top of the wood. Abraham stretched out his hand and seized the knife to kill his son. But the angel of the Lord called to him from heaven . . . 'Do not raise your hand against the boy,' the angel said: 'Do not harm him, for now I know you fear God. You have not refused me your son, your own son.'* (Genesis 22:9–12)

Love beyond the limits of all that is reasonable or logical. Calvary-love, taking faith through the eye of the needle into the possibility of resurrection.

❦ Friday

> *The Pharisees said to the disciples: 'Why does your master eat with tax collectors and sinners?' When he heard this he replied, 'It is not the healthy who need the doctor, but the sick.'* (Matthew 9:11–13)

The sick at heart lie in the streets, because they don't recognise the hospital and can't see your healing hands revealed in ours. Strip us, Lord, of our disguises.

❦ Saturday

> *'No one puts new wine into old wineskins; if they do, the skins burst, the wine runs out, and the skins are lost. No, they put new wine into fresh skins and both are preserved.'* (Matthew 9:17)

The first moments of life are the most hazardous, as old and safe containers are left behind to make space for all that is new. The risk of letting go is the price of life and growth.

The week's readings

Monday	Genesis 18:16–33; Psalm 103(102); Matthew 8:18–22
Tuesday	Genesis 19:15–29; Psalm 26(25); Matthew 8:23–7
Wednesday	Genesis 21:5, 8–20; Psalm 34(33); Matthew 8:28–34
Thursday	Genesis 22:1–19; Psalm 115(114); Matthew 9:1–8
Friday	Genesis 23:1–4, 19; 24:1–8, 62–7; Psalm 106(105); Matthew 9:9–13
Saturday	Genesis 27:1–5, 15–29; Psalm 135(134); Matthew 9:14–17

Thirteenth Week of Ordinary Time *(Weekday Cycle II)*

❦ Monday

One of the scribes then came up and said to him, 'Master, I will follow you wherever you go.' Jesus replied, 'Foxes have holes and the birds of the air have nests, but the Son of Man has nowhere to lay his head.' (Matthew 8:19–20)

Everyone said that Mark had really 'arrived'. He seemed to have achieved all his dreams and his lifestyle reflected his success. Then he met you, and became one of your people of the Way, for whom there is no arrival, except in you and your homeless journeying.

❦ Tuesday

Without warning a storm broke over the lake, so violent that the waves were breaking right over the boat. But Jesus was asleep. So they went to him and woke him saying, 'Save us, Lord, we are going down.' (Matthew 8:23–5)

Jennie came crying to her mother in the middle of the night, to be comforted from the nightmare. A more independent child – or one less loved – might have struggled on alone, suppressing the terror, and never known the calming reassurance of the loving presence of one who was always there for her.

❦ Wednesday

Let me have no more of the din of your chanting,
no more of your strumming on harps.
But let justice flow like water,
and integrity like an unfailing stream. (Amos 5:23–4)

Not the justice that merely shouts from the soapbox, but that which flows quietly through all our daily dealings. Not the exhortations to be sinless, but the opportunities to be kind. Your grace, Lord, not our efforts.

❦ Thursday

Then some people appeared, bringing him a paralytic stretched out on a bed. Seeing their faith, Jesus said to the paralytic 'Courage, my child, your sins are forgiven.' (Matthew 9:1–2)

When we are paralysed by the knowledge of our own failures and fears, you free us by giving us the courage to acknowledge our need and let you gently lift the crippling burdens of the past from our hearts.

❧ Friday

See what days are coming – it is the Lord who speaks – days when I will bring a famine on the country, a famine not of bread, a drought not of water, but of hearing the word of the Lord. They will stagger from sea to sea, wander from north to east, seeking the word of the Lord and failing to find it. (Amos 8:11–12)

Lord, we are one with your staggering, wandering people, but we carry your living water in our hearts to quench their parching need, because we are also one with you.

❧ Saturday

'No one puts a piece of unshrunken cloth onto an old cloak, because the patch pulls away from the cloak and the tear gets worse. No one puts new wine into old wineskins; if they do, the skins burst, the wine runs out, and the skins are lost. No, they put new wine into fresh skins and both are preserved.' (Matthew 9:16–17)

You do not call us into minor adjustments and repairs of our accustomed lives in the world, but to the radical transformation of a life lived in you.

The week's readings

Monday	Amos 2:6–10, 13–16; Psalm 50(49); Matthew 8:18–22
Tuesday	Amos 3:1–8; 4:11–12; Psalm 5; Matthew 8:23–7
Wednesday	Amos 5:14–15, 21–4; Psalm 50(49); Matthew 8:28–34
Thursday	Amos 7:10–17; Psalm 19(18); Matthew 9:1–8
Friday	Amos 8:4–6, 9–12; Psalm 119(118); Matthew 9:9–13
Saturday	Amos 9:11–15; Psalm 85(84); Matthew 9:14–17

Fourteenth Week of Ordinary Time *(Weekday Cycle I)*

✠ Monday

When he had reached a certain place, Jacob passed the night there, since the sun had set. Taking one of the stones to be found at that place, he made it his pillow and lay down where he was. He had a dream: a ladder was there, standing on the ground with its top reaching to heaven, and there were angels of God going up it and coming down. And the Lord was there, standing over him . . . Jacob awoke from his sleep and said: 'Truly, the Lord is in this place and I never knew it.' (Genesis 28:10–17)

Between the stones of our despair we catch a glimpse of the diamonds of your presence and your love, in the place where we never thought to find you.

✠ Tuesday

Hide me in the shadow of your wings. (Psalm 17:8)

The hidden camera filmed the nest of the newly hatched owl chicks. Soon there would be flight and the struggle for survival, but tonight there was only a warm mound of tawny feathers, breathing as one. Four chicks completely enfolded under their mother's wings: source of love today, and power for tomorrow's flight.

✠ Wednesday

'Go to the lost sheep of the House of Israel. And as you go, proclaim that the kingdom of heaven is close at hand.' (Matthew 10:7)

It was an arduous climb and the summit seemed to get further away with every step. Then a fellow walker greeted us: 'Not far to go now,' he smiled. Immediately our steps were lightened, our hearts rejoiced and our tired trudging became hope-filled again.

✠ Thursday

Jesus instructed the Twelve as follows: 'As you go, proclaim that the kingdom of heaven is close at hand. Cure the sick, raise the dead, cleanse the lepers, cast out devils. You received without charge, give without charge.' (Matthew 10:7–9)

She was old and lonely and lived on her memories. The years of her youth had been given unstintingly to her children and grandchildren. Her love for them was its own reward. Yet how nice it would be if they would find a few minutes to visit her now and again. It would cost so little and mean so much.

❦ Friday

'Do not worry about how to speak or what to say; what you are to say will be given to you when the time comes; because it is not you who will be speaking; the Spirit of your Father will be speaking in you.' (Matthew 10:19–20)

He was renowned for his talks and lectures, and the hall was packed with people who had come a long way to hear him. A cold shudder ran through him as he realised that he had left his notes at home. He panicked for a moment, but then steadied himself in a few moments of prayerful calm, before walking into the auditorium. Afterwards they said that it was the best talk he had ever given.

❦ Saturday

'What I say to you in the dark, tell in the daylight; what you hear in whispers, proclaim from the housetops.' (Matthew 10:27)

What is given in the dark silence of prayer is for carrying out into the bright lights and clamour of everyday, for the transforming of our lived experience.

The week's readings

Monday	Genesis 28:10–22; Psalm 91(90); Matthew 9:18–26
Tuesday	Genesis 32:23–33; Psalm 17(16); Matthew 9:32–8
Wednesday	Genesis 41:55–7; 42:5–7, 17–24; Psalm 33(32); Matthew 10:1–7
Thursday	Genesis 44:18–21, 23–9; 45:1–5; Psalm 105(104); Matthew 10:7–15
Friday	Genesis 46:1–7, 28–30; Psalm 37(36), Matthew 10:16–23
Saturday	Genesis 49:29–33; 50:15–25; Psalm 105(104); Matthew 10:24–33

Fourteenth Week of Ordinary Time *(Weekday Cycle II)*

✠ Monday

It is the Lord who speaks:
I am going to lure her
and lead her into the wilderness
and speak to her heart. (Hosea 2:14)

When we are walking through the desert spaces in our lives and the searing sun is burning away all our masks and our defences – there, where nothing comes between us, we meet you face to face and you speak to our hearts.

✠ Tuesday

And when Jesus saw the crowds he felt sorry for them because they were harassed and dejected, like sheep without a shepherd. Then he said to his disciples, 'The harvest is rich but the labourers are few, so ask the Lord of the harvest to send labourers to this harvest.' (Matthew 9:36–8)

The fields of my life are rich with the harvest of gifts you have planted uniquely in my heart. Yet if I fail to gather in their fruits and share them with a hungry world, you will have planted them in vain.

✠ Wednesday

Sow integrity for yourselves,
reap a harvest of kindness,
break up your fallow ground:
it is time to go seeking the Lord
until he comes to rain salvation on you. (Hosea 10:12)

Katy had lived a good and law-abiding life, yet when she looked back there seemed little to show for it. Then came the ground-breaking years, when unseen stirrings shook her life's soil apart. The waiting time was yielding to the coming of the harvest, and she knew that it was time to seek the Lord in the hidden roots of her being.

Thursday

'You received without charge, give without charge.' (Matthew 10:8)

As long as we attach price tags and conditions to our loving, we shall not be fully free. And until we are free we can never fully love.

Friday

I will heal their disloyalty,
I will love them with all my heart,
for my anger has turned from them.
I will fall like dew on Israel.
He shall bloom like the lily
and thrust out roots like the poplar,
his shoots will spread far. (Hosea 14:5–7)

When the waves of anger and resentment recede, then I shall see the firm sands and solid rock of love. And there I learn that what I resent, I hold captive, and am myself enslaved by it. What I learn to love I set free for growth and fruitfulness and am myself made fruitful by it.

Saturday

Then I heard the voice of the Lord saying:
'Whom shall I send? Who will be our messenger?'
I answered, 'Here I am, send me.' (Isaiah 6:8)

Barbara was terrified of driving, but when her neighbour had an accident she forgot her fear and drove him through the rush-hour traffic to the hospital. There had been no time to spare for asking 'Who will drive?' There had only been time to make the instant response of love.

The week's readings

Monday	Hosea 2:16–18, 21–2; Psalm 145(144); Matthew 9:18–26
Tuesday	Hosea 8:4–7, 11–13; Psalm 115(113b); Matthew 9:32–8
Wednesday	Hosea 10:1–3, 7–8, 12; Psalm 105(104); Matthew 10:1–7
Thursday	Hosea 11:1, 3–4, 8–9; Psalm 80(79); Matthew 10:7–15
Friday	Hosea 14:2–10; Psalm 51(50); Matthew 10:16–23
Saturday	Isaiah 6:1–8; Psalm 93(92); Matthew 10:24–33

Fifteenth Week of Ordinary Time *(Weekday Cycle I)*

❦ Monday

Our life, like a bird, has escaped from the snare of the fowler. Indeed the snare has been broken and we have escaped. (Psalm 124:7–8)

The pet rabbit gnawed away at his hutch until one day he broke loose. The driver found him sitting in the middle of the road, hypnotised by the glare of the lights. Gaining his freedom had been easy. Living out its consequences and its potential was altogether harder.

❦ Tuesday

I have sunk into the mud of the deep and there is no foothold.
I have entered the waters of the deep and the waves overwhelm me.
This is my prayer to you, my prayer for your favour.
In your great love, answer me, O God, with your help that never fails. (Psalm 69:2–4)

At the bottom of the deepest layer of mud there will be the solid rock that will hold me and let me fall no further. I know it from my experience. Why do I always forget it while I am sinking?

❦ Wednesday

Jesus exclaimed, 'I bless you, Father, Lord of heaven and of earth, for hiding these things from the learned and the clever and revealing them to mere children.' (Matthew 11:25)

We still had three miles to walk and we had promised to be home for lunch. Our toddler suddenly sat down in the meadow, gazing in rapture at the ambling journey of a shiny black beetle. She was seeing the very first beetle with the very first eyes – seeing it as you see it. For a moment we forgot our haste and then we saw it too.

❦ Thursday

'Come to me, all you who labour and are over-burdened, and I will give you rest. Shoulder my yoke and learn from me, for I am gentle and humble in heart, and you will find rest for your souls. Yes, my yoke is easy and my burden light.' (Matthew 11:28–30)

The Palestinian woman lifted the huge weight of the filled water jug onto her head.

An impossible burden, I thought. Impossible for me, but she was walking in perfect balance, and that made her burden light.

❦ Friday

You shall eat the Passover like this: with a girdle round your waist, sandals on your feet, a staff in your hand. You shall eat it hastily; it is a passover in honour of the Lord. (Exodus 11:11)

The journey is unfinished, and you call us, your Passover people, to be always ready for the onward road, every communion with you a preparation for moving on.

❦ Saturday

'Here is my servant whom I have chosen, my beloved, the favourite of my soul. I will endow him with my spirit, and he will proclaim the true faith to the nations. He will not brawl or shout, nor will anyone hear his voice in the streets.' (Matthew 12:18–19)

Your voice speaks to us in the silence, and in your silent presence within us we proclaim that presence to everyone we meet.

The week's readings

Monday	Exodus 1:8–14, 22; Psalm 124(123); Matthew 10:34 – 11:1
Tuesday	Exodus 2:1–15; Psalm 69(68); Matthew 11:20–4
Wednesday	Exodus 3:1–6, 9–12; Psalm 103(102); Matthew 11:25–7
Thursday	Exodus 3:13–20; Psalm 105(104); Matthew 11:28–30
Friday	Exodus 11:10 – 12:14; Psalm 116(115); Matthew 12:1–8
Saturday	Exodus 12:37–42; Psalm (136)135; Matthew 12:14–21

Fifteenth Week of Ordinary Time *(Weekday Cycle II)*

✠ Monday

'Do not suppose that I have come to bring peace to the earth: it is not peace I have come to bring, but a sword.' (Matthew 10:34)

We do not reach your peace by staying out of trouble, but by setting our course painfully through all the struggles on our way, and slicing through the obstructions that keep us from our truest destination.

✠ Tuesday

'Pay attention, keep calm, have no fear,
do not let your heart sink.' (Isaiah 7:4)

When my heart sinks, it sinks into the quicksands of my own fears and preoccupations, where it can see nothing except itself. When I lift it up to you, it rises into freedom where it can see your world and your suffering children.

✠ Wednesday

Jesus exclaimed, 'I bless you, Father, Lord of heaven and of earth, for hiding these things from the learned and the clever and revealing them to mere children.' (Matthew 11:25)

Underneath all the layers of our learning and our skills lies a heart that once knew how to marvel at the simple miracle of life – a heart that once received life without needing to conquer or control it, and a heart that can still recapture that first dawn of wonder.

✠ Thursday

As a woman with child near her time
writhes and cries out in her prayer,
so are we, O Lord, in your presence.
We have conceived, we writhe
as if we were giving birth. (Isaiah 26:17–18)

Once your love has been conceived in our hearts we have no choice but to bring it to birth in our world. We consented to the conception, Lord, and we consent to the pains of labour, for the sake of the coming of your kingdom.

❧ Friday

For you, Lord, my heart will live,
you gave me back my spirit;
you cured me, kept me alive,
changed my sickness into health. (Isaiah 38:16–17)

More than anything, it was Jim's attentive, unobtrusive care that kept Mike going through the long months of depression and despair. He nurtured him, like a sickening plant in need of food and water and light. Once recovered, Mike knew that he owed everything to the friend who had kept his heart alive and given him back his spirit.

❧ Saturday

Woe to those who plot evil,
who lie in bed planning mischief!
No sooner is it dawn than they do it. (Micah 2:1)

When we lie and brood in our own inner darkness, our worst fears take us over and our worst intentions can become reality. But when we surrender ourselves to you in the dark silence of prayer, your joy can become incarnate and your dream can come to fulfilment.

The week's readings

Monday	Isaiah 1:11–17; Psalm 50(49); Matthew 10:34 – 11:1
Tuesday	Isaiah 7:1–9; Psalm 48(47); Matthew 11:20–4
Wednesday	Isaiah 10:5–7, 13–16; Psalm 94(93); Matthew 11:25–7
Thursday	Isaiah 26:7–9, 12, 16–19; Psalm 102(101); Matthew 11:28–30
Friday	Isaiah 38:1–6, 21–2, 7–8; Isaiah 38:10–12, 16; Matthew 12:1–8
Saturday	Micah 2:1–5; Psalm 10(9b); Matthew 12:14–21

Sixteenth Week of Ordinary Time *(Weekday Cycle I)*

✠ Monday

Moses answered the people, 'Have no fear! Stand firm, and you will see what the Lord will do to save you today. The Lord will do the fighting for you: you have only to keep still.' (Exodus 14:13–14)

The lifeguard could do nothing until the victim stopped struggling and fell into unconsciousness. From then on it was easy to draw him gently but firmly to the shore. Give us the grace, Lord, to trust in your strength more than in our own efforts, and to stop getting in the way of your saving power.

✠ Tuesday

You will lead them and plant them on your mountain,
the place, O Lord, where you have made your home,
the sanctuary, Lord, which your hands have made. (Exodus 15:17)

Jason watched over the seedlings in his greenhouse with loving devotion. One by one, when the time was right, he planted them in their permanent place in his garden – in a special place that he had chosen and prepared for each one of them – a place where they would be for ever a part of his home.

✠ Wednesday

'The kingdom of heaven is like treasure hidden in a field which someone has found; he hides it again, goes off happy, sells everything he owns and buys the field.' (Matthew 13:44)

The life-saving operation would cost them their life's savings. They gave it gladly, because they loved their little daughter beyond all measure.

✠ Thursday

At every stage of their journey, whenever the cloud rose from the tabernacle the sons of Israel would resume their march. If the cloud did not rise, they waited and would not march until it did. For the cloud of the Lord rested on the tabernacle by day, and a fire shone within the cloud by night, for all the House of Israel to see. And so it was for every stage of their journey. (Exodus 40:34–8)

The clouds are down so often, and I seem to spend much more of my life in waiting than in marching. But I know from experience that they *will* lift eventually and I *will* move on, because that has been so for every stage of my journey, and I trust it for the remainder.

✠ Friday

Coming to his home town, Jesus taught the people in their synagogue in such a way that they were astonished and said: 'Where did the man get this wisdom and these miraculous powers? This is the carpenter's son, surely?' (Matthew 13:54–5)

She was a non-entity in the village. She was John's wife and Sally's mother, the doctor's daughter and the school's secretary. Then she met a friend who called her by her name and knew her for herself, and who released all her unique potential. And the villagers were amazed.

✠ Saturday

During the celebrations for Herod's birthday, the daughter of Herodias danced before the company and so delighted Herod that he promised on oath to give her anything she asked. Prompted by her mother she said, 'Give me John the Baptist's head, here, on a dish.' The king was distressed, but, thinking of the oaths he had sworn and of his guests, he ordered it to be given her, and sent and had John beheaded in the prison. (Matthew 14:6–10)

He had had too much to drink and was in no mood to be coaxed home by his embarrassed wife. Instead he told a crude story against her. His pride was saved, but something irreplaceable was lost that evening.

The week's readings

Monday	Exodus 14:5–18; Exodus 15:1–6; Matthew 12:38–42
Tuesday	Exodus 14:21 – 5:1; Exodus 15:8–10, 12, 17; Matthew 12:46–50
Wednesday	Exodus 16:1–5, 9–15; Psalm 78(77); Matthew 13:1–9
Thursday	Exodus 19:1–2, 9–11, 16–20; Daniel 3:52–6; Matthew 13:10–17
Friday	Exodus 20:1–17; Psalm 19(18); Matthew 13:18–23
Saturday	Exodus 24:3–8; Psalm 50(49); Matthew 13:24–30

Sixteenth Week of Ordinary Time (Weekday Cycle II)

❧ Monday

This is what the Lord asks of you:
only this, to act justly,
to love tenderly
and to walk humbly with your God. (Micah 6:8)

When we walk humbly with you, we cannot fail to be touched by your tenderness, and when your tender love has touched us, truth and justice are our only options.

❧ Tuesday

Jesus replied: 'Who is my mother? Who are my brothers?' And stretching out his hand towards his disciples he said: 'Here are my mother and my brothers. Anyone who does the will of my Father in heaven, he is my brother and sister and mother.' (Matthew 12:48–50)

It is you, Lord, who are refused asylum by a 'friendly' government. It is you who are reduced to poverty in an affluent society. You, Lord – our brother and our sister.

❧ Wednesday

'Before I formed you in the womb I knew you;
before you came to birth, I consecrated you.' (Jeremiah 1:5)

Bernard grew prize gladioli. Each year he lovingly planted the bulbs, and for every bulb he planted he had a vision in his heart of the perfect flower it would become, nurtured by him until it should reveal the fullness of its still-hidden mystery.

❧ Thursday

'My people have abandoned me,
the fountain of living water,
only to dig cisterns for themselves,
leaky cisterns, that hold no water.' (Jeremiah 2:13)

For years I used all my energy in trying to dig my own wells of wisdom. When I returned to you, defeated and exhausted. I found once more the spring of living water, undiminished and unpolluted, freely given and effortlessly received.

Friday

'The one who received the seed in rich soil is the person who hears the word and understands it; he is the one who yields a harvest.' (Matthew 13:23)

The yield of the harvest lies not in the labour of our hands but in the receptiveness of our hearts.

Saturday

'The kingdom of heaven may be compared to a man who sowed good seed in his field. While everyone was asleep his enemy came, sowed darnel all among the wheat, and made off. When the new wheat sprouted and ripened, the darnel appeared as well. The owner's servants went to him and said: "Sir, was it not good seed that you sowed in your field? If so, where does the darnel come from?" "Some enemy has done this," he answered.' (Matthew 13:24–8)

Like weeds, my persistent fears grow fast and furious, taking over my mind and my heart. Yet it is the sure and steady growth of joy that will have the final word; the good seed of joy that is the original inhabitant and rightful heir of my life's soil, and will be its eternal harvest.

The week's readings

Monday	Micah 6:1–4, 6–8; Psalm 50(49); Matthew 12:38–42
Tuesday	Micah 7:14–15, 18–20; Psalm 85(84); Matthew 12:46–50
Wednesday	Jeremiah 1:1, 5–10; Psalm 71(70); Matthew 13:1–9
Thursday	Jeremiah 2:1–3, 7–8, 12–13; Psalm 36(35); Matthew 13:10–17
Friday	Jeremiah 3:14–17; Jeremiah 31:10–13; Matthew 13:18–23
Saturday	Jeremiah 7:1–11; Psalm 84(83); Matthew 13:24–30

Seventeenth Week of Ordinary Time (Weekday Cycle I)

❧ Monday

They fashioned a calf at Horeb
and worshipped an image of metal,
exchanging the God who was their glory
for the image of a bull that eats grass. (Psalm 106:19–20)

James was a self-made man. He had a successful career, a well-organised family and a tidy, prosperous lifestyle. Self-made, from head to toe, but unable to face the empty space where God had intended his heart to be.

❧ Tuesday

And Moses bowed down to the ground at once, and worshipped. 'If I have indeed won your favour, Lord,' he said, 'let my Lord come with us, I beg. True, they are a headstrong people, but forgive us our faults and our sins, and adopt us as your heritage.' (Exodus 34:8–9)

You have walked with me down every cul-de-sac into which my wilfulness has led me, waiting for your headstrong child to find her destination in the One who walks beside her.

❧ Wednesday

Whenever he went into the Lord's presence to speak with him, Moses would remove the veil until he came out again. And when he came out, he would tell the sons of Israel what he had been ordered to pass on to them, and the sons of Israel would see the face of Moses radiant. (Exodus 34:34–5)

Martin was a person of prayer. Though he never said so, you could see it in his eyes and hear it in the quiet authority with which he shared what he had heard in the darkness.

❧ Thursday

Jesus said to them: 'Well then, everyone who becomes a disciple of the kingdom of heaven is like a householder who brings out from his storeroom things both old and new.' (Matthew 13:52)

The freshness of my life's stream flows boldly through every day's new landscape, but it flows out of old, almost forgotten sources.

❦ Friday

> *When you enter the land that I give you, and gather in the harvest there, you must bring the first sheaf of your harvest to the priest, and he is to present it to the Lord.* (Leviticus 23:10–11)

You give me all the gifts of my life, and to you I return them, for you know far better than I how they might best be used.

❦ Saturday

> *O God, be gracious and bless us,*
> *and let your face shed its light upon us.* (Psalm 67:1)

The ward sister was exhausted after the long, demanding night shift. She stopped by Jane's bedside and noticed that she had, at last, sunk into peaceful sleep. And then the first shaft of dawn came slanting down through the window, as if to add your blessing to the long night's ending.

The week's readings

Monday	Exodus 32:15–24, 30–4; Psalm 106(105); Matthew 13:31–5
Tuesday	Exodus 33:7–11; 34:5–9, 28; Psalm 103(102); Matthew 13:36–43
Wednesday	Exodus 34:29–35; Psalm 99(98); Matthew 13:44–6
Thursday	Exodus 40:16–21, 34–8; Psalm 84(83); Matthew 13:47–53
Friday	Leviticus 23:1, 4–11, 15–16, 27, 34–7; Psalm 81(80); Matthew 13:54–8
Saturday	Leviticus 25:1, 8–17; Psalm 67(66); Matthew 14:1–12

Seventeenth Week of Ordinary Time *(Weekday Cycle II)*

✠ Monday

> *'The kingdom of heaven is like the yeast a woman took and mixed in with three measures of flour till it was leavened all through.'* (Matthew 13:33)

A teaspoon of the yeast of *your* kingdom can leaven a whole lifetime of the dough of mine.

✠ Tuesday

> *If I go into the countryside,*
> *there lie men killed by the sword;*
> *if I go into the city,*
> *I see people sick with hunger . . .*
> *O God, you are our hope.* (Jeremiah 14:18, 22)

Our pangs of hunger make us seek out the food we need; our pains cause us to look for healing; our anger makes us work for justice and our encounters with evil set us journeying in search of our redeeming.

✠ Wednesday

> *'The kingdom of heaven is like a merchant looking for fine pearls; when he finds one of great value he goes and sells everything he owns and buys it.'* (Matthew 13:45–6)

The deepest desire of my heart is the one that I will follow, letting go of all the lesser ones. Will it lead me to the fullness of your kingdom, or to the bankruptcy of my own?

✠ Thursday

> *So I went down to the potter's house; and there he was, working at the wheel. And whenever the vessel he was making came out wrong, he would start afresh and work it into another vessel, as potters do . . . As the clay is in the potter's hand, so you are in mine.* (Jeremiah 18:3–5, 7)

We are held in hands that assure us that every false start is a new beginning and every failure an opportunity for a new creation.

✠ Friday

> *'Where did the man get this wisdom and these miraculous powers? This is the carpenter's son, surely.'* (Matthew 13:54–5)

We strain our eyes to see miracles on our life's horizon, and fail to see them lying on the doorstep of our own experience.

✠ Saturday

> *The Lord listens to the needy*
> *and does not spurn his servants in their chains.* (Psalm 69:33)

Our circumstances hold us captive, as a fence surrounds a field. Yet we have the choice, to focus our gaze on the fence that encloses us or on the view that our field affords, on the clamour of our needs or on the Lord who listens.

The week's readings

Monday	Jeremiah 13:1–11, Deuteronomy 32:18–21; Matthew 13:31–5
Tuesday	Jeremiah 14:17–22; Psalm 79(78); Matthew 13:36–43
Wednesday	Jeremiah 15:10, 16–21; Psalm 59(58); Matthew 13:44–6
Thursday	Jeremiah 18:1–6; Psalm 146(145); Matthew 13:47–53
Friday	Jeremiah 26:1–9; Psalm 69(68); Matthew 13:54–8
Saturday	Jeremiah 26:11–16, 24; Psalm 69(68); Matthew 14:1–12

Eighteenth Week of Ordinary Time *(Weekday Cycle I)*

✠ Monday

The sons of Israel [freed from slavery in Egypt and now journeying through the desert towards the Promised Land] began to wail, 'Who will give us meat to eat?' they said. 'Think of the fish we used to eat free in Egypt, the cucumbers, melons, leeks, onions and garlic! Here we are wasting away, stripped of everything; there is nothing but manna for us to look at!' (Numbers 11:4–6)

For a while the newly liberated citizens of Eastern Europe relished their freedom to live their lives in their own way and to make their own decisions and their own mistakes. Then the memory of full employment and fixed prices and guaranteed pensions began to return. The smell of onions, leeks and garlic made them wonder whether freedom was worth its cost. For me, too, the smell of all I crave can seduce me away from the larger vision towards which you are calling me.

✠ Tuesday

Jesus went towards them, walking on the water . . . He called out to them saying 'Courage! It is I. Do not be afraid.' It was Peter who answered, 'Lord,' he said, 'if it is you, tell me to come to you across the water.' 'Come', said Jesus. Then Peter got out of the boat and started walking towards Jesus across the water, but as soon as he felt the force of the wind he took fright and began to sink. (Matthew 14:25–30)

Philip was well in the lead and seemed certain to win the race. All his energy was focused on that one supreme goal. Then there was a disturbance among the spectators. He glanced sideways at the crowd, suddenly conscious of his surroundings and their dangers. From that moment his focus was lost, and so was the race.

✠ Wednesday

At the end of forty days they came back from the reconnaissance of the land . . . They told them this story, 'We went into the land to which you sent us. It does indeed flow with milk and honey; this is its produce. At the same time its inhabitants are a powerful people.' (Numbers 13:25–8)

Just when I begin to taste the joy of the milk and the honey, I come face to face with one of the powerful giants of fear, or doubt, or pride, who populate my inner kingdom. The honey of your promise is not drawn from a bed of roses.

☙ Thursday

The Lord spoke to Moses and said: 'Take the branch and call the community together, you and your brother Aaron. Then, in full view of them, order this rock to give water. You will make water flow for them out of the rock, and provide drink for the community and their cattle.' (Numbers 20:8)

The hard immovable rocks of our lives sometimes prove to be the hidden, unsuspected sources of your greatest gifts to us, if we only have the courage and the trust to face them in faith.

☙ Friday

Jesus said to his disciples, 'If anyone wants to be a follower of mine, let him renounce himself and take up his cross and follow me. For anyone who wants to save his life will lose it; but anyone who loses his life for my sake will find it.' (Matthew 16:24–5)

The less there is of me, the more space there is for you. And the more I let you fill me, the more completely I become who I really am.

☙ Saturday

Moses said to the people: 'Listen, Israel: the Lord our God is the one Lord. You shall love the Lord your God with all your heart, with all your soul, with all your strength. Let these words I urge on you today be written on your heart. You shall fasten them on your hand and on your forehead; you shall write them on the doorposts of your house.' (Deuteronomy 6:4–9)

Sue and David's home is always open. All sorts of people seek them out and find a welcome there. If you could see into the deep recesses of their being, you would find these words inscribed on the doorposts of their hearts: 'God lives here.'

The week's readings

Monday	Numbers 11:4–15; Psalm 81(80); Matthew 14:13–21
Tuesday	Numbers 12:1–13; Psalm 51(50); Matthew 14:22–36
Wednesday	Numbers 13:1–2, 25 – 14:1, 26–9, 34–5; Psalm 106(105); Matthew 15:21–8
Thursday	Numbers 20:1–13; Psalm 95(94); Matthew 16:13–23
Friday	Deuteronomy 4:32–40; Psalm 77(76); Matthew 16:24–8
Saturday	Deuteronomy 6:4–13; Psalm 18(17); Matthew 17:14–20

Eighteenth Week of Ordinary Time (Weekday Cycle II)

✠ Monday

When Jesus received the news of John the Baptist's death he withdrew by boat to a lonely place where they could be by themselves. But the people heard of this and, leaving the towns, went after him on foot. So as he stepped ashore he saw a large crowd; and he took pity on them and healed their sick. (Matthew 14:13–14)

In the grieving times of our lives we want to be alone with our hurting. But the cries of those who are hurting more than we are draws us back to them, carrying your compassion.

✠ Tuesday

The Lord leaned down from his sanctuary on high.
He looked down from heaven to the earth
that he might hear the groans of the prisoners
and free those condemned to die. (Psalm 102:19–20)

You do not hear our groanings from somewhere high above us, Lord, or even from alongside us, but from right inside us, inside the locked cells of our hearts and holding the key to our freedom.

✠ Wednesday

They have found pardon in the wilderness,
those who have survived the sword. (Jeremiah 31:2)

The quarrel with his former friend left Richard devastated and inwardly bleeding. For months he existed in an inner desert. Only two things grew in that desert. One was the choking tangle of his remorse and his regrets. The other was the soft, determined flower of your forgiveness and your peace.

✠ Thursday

'You are Peter and on this rock I will build my Church.' (Matthew 16:18)

The rocks that bruise and batter us are the same rocks on which you are building us up into the People of God.

❦ Friday

> *'What, then, will a man gain if he wins the whole world and ruins his life? Or what has a man to offer in exchange for his life?'* (Matthew 16:25–6)

Let our energies be spent for living, and not for building up mere monuments to life.

❦ Saturday

> *'If your faith were the size of a mustard seed you could say to this mountain, "Move from here to there, and it would move; nothing would be impossible for you." '* (Matthew 17:20)

Your faith in us transforms us from frightened by-standers into partners in your kingdom-building. And you call us to make more and more room for the impossible, by believing more and more in each other.

The week's readings

Monday	Jeremiah 28:1–17; Psalm 119(118); Matthew 14:13–21
Tuesday	Jeremiah 30:1–2, 12–15, 18–22; Psalm 102(101); Matthew 14:22–36
Wednesday	Jeremiah 31:1–7; Jeremiah 31:10–13; Matthew 15:21–8
Thursday	Jeremiah 31:31–4; Psalm 51(50); Matthew 16:13–23
Friday	Nahum 2:1, 3; 3:1–3, 6–7; Deuteronomy 32:35–6, 39, 41; Matthew 16:24–8
Saturday	Habakkuk 1:12 – 2:4; Psalm 9; Matthew 17:14–20

Nineteenth Week of Ordinary Time (Weekday Cycle I)

✠ Monday

Moses said to the people: 'Love the stranger then, for you were strangers in the land of Egypt.' (Deuteronomy 10:19)

The children stood round in a huddle and stared at the newcomer, as he trailed shyly, fearfully, across the playground. It was Martin who broke the wall of tension with a friendly word for the frightened stranger. Martin had been new here himself last term.

✠ Tuesday

Jesus called a little child to him and set the child in front of him. Then he said: 'I tell you solemnly, unless you change and become like little children you will never enter the kingdom of heaven. And so, the one who makes himself as little as this little child is the greatest in the kingdom of heaven.' (Matthew 18:2–4)

The Reception Class is well named. It is not only the place for those who are to be received, but also for those who, of all people, are the ones most receptive to the wonders that lie around them, waiting for discovery.

✠ Wednesday

Jesus said: 'I tell you solemnly, whatever you bind on earth shall be considered bound in heaven; whatever you loose on earth shall be considered loosed in heaven.' (Matthew 18:18)

For years I nursed the memory of the harm she had done to me. When I finally reached the point when I could freely let it go, I discovered, to my joy, that not only was I freed of its burden myself, but she too was freed from the burden I had been forcing her to carry.

✠ Thursday

Joshua said to the Israelites: 'Come closer and hear the words of the Lord your God. By this you shall know that a living God is with you.' (Joshua 3:10)

Jane's correspondence with her pen-friend had been, necessarily, a little forced and stilted. But when they finally met and stayed in each other's homes, their paper connection changed into a living relationship that was a source of richness and joy to them both. Help us to change our long-distance acquaintance with you into the close and living encounter you long for it to be.

❦ Friday

'I gave you a land where you never toiled, you live in towns you never built, you eat now from vineyards and olive groves you never planted.' (Joshua 24:13)

Maureen used her parents' home like a hotel, and frequently filled it with her teenage friends. She seemed to have no appreciation of all that they had put into creating a home for her. Then one night she flung her arms round her parents' necks and hugged them. Nothing was said, but at that moment they realised that the seeds they had sown had taken root in her heart, and would yield their own fruits in a home that she herself would one day create, for children yet unborn.

❦ Saturday

People brought little children to Jesus, for him to lay his hands on them and say a prayer. The disciples turned them away, but Jesus said, 'Let the little children alone and do not stop them coming to me; for it is to such as these that the kingdom of heaven belongs.' (Matthew 19:13–14)

Carol's kitchen was always full of children. No one was ever sent away. Among them were those who found no such welcome in their own cold homes, and flocked to Carol for their warming. Probably she never realised how perfectly she was carrying out your command.

The week's readings

Monday	Deuteronomy 10:12–22; Psalm 147; Matthew 17:22–7
Tuesday	Deuteronomy 31:1–8; Deuteronomy 32:3–4, 7–9, 12; Matthew 18:1–5, 10, 12–14
Wednesday	Deuteronomy 34:1–12; Psalm 66(65); Matthew 18:15–20
Thursday	Joshua 3:7–11, 13–17; Psalm 114(113a); Matthew 18:21 – 19:1
Friday	Joshua 24:1–13; Psalm 136(135); Matthew 19:3–12
Saturday	Joshua 24:14–29; Psalm 16(15); Matthew 19:13–15

Nineteenth Week of Ordinary Time (Weekday Cycle II)

✠ Monday

> *I saw something that looked like the glory of the Lord. I looked, and prostrated myself.* (Ezekiel 1:28)

If I look back over each day's living, I will find a speck of gold among the sand-grains, a moment in which I have recognised your *I AM* in mine.

✠ Tuesday

> *The Lord said, 'Son of Man, eat what is given to you; eat this scroll, then go and speak to the House of Israel.' I opened my mouth; he gave me the scroll to eat and said, 'Son of Man, feed and be satisfied by the scroll I am giving you.' I ate it, and it tasted sweet as honey.* (Ezekiel 3:1–3)

Your Word is not for filing in the Reference sections of our heads, but for taking into ourselves and digesting, and for *becoming* the truth with which it feeds us.

✠ Wednesday

> *'If your brother does something wrong . . . and if he refuses to listen to the community, treat him like a pagan or a tax collector.'* (Matthew 18:17)

. . . yet remembering, Lord, that you also treated the pagans and the tax collectors with love.

✠ Thursday

> *'I cancelled all that debt of yours when you appealed to me. Were you not bound, then, to have pity on your fellow servant just as I had pity on you?'* (Matthew 18:33)

Chris was amazed when his boss let him off so lightly after he had messed up such an important contract through his carelessness. The tension of the day was still driving him when he arrived home and lashed out at his son for not doing his homework conscientiously. It was only when he lay in bed that night that he remembered the grace of the day, and its shame.

❦ Friday

With joy you will draw water from the wells of salvation. (Isaiah 12:3)

The springs of grace that flow in the privacy of our hearts are deeper than drought and pure beyond pollution. Private wells, but flowing with a love for universal sharing.

❦ Saturday

The upright man is law-abiding and honest: he does not seduce his neighbour's wife; he oppresses no one, returns pledges, never steals, gives his own bread to the hungry, his clothes to the naked. He never charges usury on loans, takes no interest, abstains from evil, gives honest judgement between man and man, keeps my laws and sincerely respects my observances. (Ezekiel 18:5–9)

You walked along the High Street, looking for an upright man. You stopped at the newsagents and noticed the magazines on the top shelf. You stopped by the homeless man crouched on a doorstep, and noticed us hurrying by. You stopped outside the bank and noticed the posters advertising bank loans and credit cards. You stopped outside the police station and noticed the peace demonstrators being herded inside. Then you stopped by the school, and watched the lollipop lady stop the cars and lead a little child to safety through the hazards of the city traffic, and I knew that you had found what you were looking for.

The week's readings

Monday	Ezekiel 1:2–5, 24–8; Psalm 148; Matthew 17:22–7
Tuesday	Ezekiel 2:8 – 3:4; Psalm 119(118); Matthew 18:1–5, 10, 12–14
Wednesday	Ezekiel 9:1–7; 10:18–22; Psalm 113(112); Matthew 18:15–20
Thursday	Ezekiel 12:1–12; Psalm 78(77); Matthew 18:21 – 19:1
Friday	Ezekiel 16:1–15, 60, 63; Isaiah 12:2–6; Matthew 19:3–12
Saturday	Ezekiel 18:1–10, 13, 30–2; Psalm 51(50); Matthew 19:13–15

Twentieth Week of Ordinary Time *(Weekday Cycle I)*

✠ Monday

> *The young man said to Jesus: 'I have kept all the commandments. What more do I need to do, to possess eternal life?' Jesus said: 'If you wish to be perfect, go and sell what you own and give the money to the poor, and you will have treasure in heaven; then come, follow me.'* (Matthew 19:20–1)

You are a tenant of my heart, sharing its space with so many lesser lodgers. Become its owner and its whole possessor, Lord, for only where there is no room for any other, then there will be infinity for all.

✠ Tuesday

> *Jesus said to his disciples, 'I tell you solemnly, it will be hard for a rich man to enter the kingdom of heaven. Yes, I tell you again, it is easier for a camel to pass through the eye of a needle than for a rich man to enter the kingdom of heaven.'* (Matthew 19:23–4)

When I let go of my need to possess, and surrender to the emptiness of the needle's eye, I stand on the threshold of an unimaginable fullness.

✠ Wednesday

> *'Thus the last will be first, and the first, last.'* (Matthew 20:16)

In your human life, Lord, you were usually at the back of the world's queues, among the rejects and outcasts of society. Why, then, am I so anxious to be at the front of life's queues, among the achievers and succeeders? Please give me the grace to let you love me in my failures.

✠ Thursday

> *You do not ask for sacrifice and offerings, but an open ear.*
> *You do not ask for holocaust and victim.*
> *Instead, here am I.* (Psalm 40:6–7)

Emily was the envy of her classmates. She had everything a teenager could wish for. Her parents worked from morning till night to buy her all she could desire. Jenny had nothing – except a Mum and Dad who were there for her and listened to her dreams.

✠ Friday

Ruth said to Naomi: 'Do not press me to leave you and to turn back from your company, for wherever you go, I will go, wherever you live, I will live. Your people shall be my people, and your God, my God.' (Ruth 1:3–6)

If we wear a disciple's sandals, they may lead us where we would rather not walk, alongside people we would rather not know. If your Father is our Father, too, then your ways shall be ours.

✠ Saturday

'The greatest among you must be your servant. Anyone who exalts himself will be humbled, and anyone who humbles himself will be exalted.' (Matthew 23:11–12)

After the accident the headmistress summoned the school together and gave them an impressive lecture on the dangers of running in the corridors and the importance of dignified behaviour. Meanwhile one of the dinner ladies was quietly wiping David's tears away and gently bathing his cut knee.

The week's readings

Monday	Judges 2:11–19; Psalm 106(105); Matthew 19:16–22
Tuesday	Judges 6:11–24; Psalm 85(84); Matthew 19:23–30
Wednesday	Judges 9:6–15; Psalm 21(20); Matthew 20:1–16
Thursday	Judges 11:29–39; Psalm 40(39); Matthew 22:1–14
Friday	Ruth 1:1, 3–6, 14–16, 22; Psalm 146(145); Matthew 22:34–40
Saturday	Ruth 2:1–3, 8–11; 4:13–17; Psalm 128(127); Matthew 23:1–12

Twentieth Week of Ordinary Time *(Weekday cycle II)*

✠ Monday

I am about to deprive you suddenly of the delight of your eyes. But you are not to lament, not to weep, not to let your tears run down . . . do not go into mourning for the dead. (Ezekiel 24:16–17)

Let me light a candle in my heart for everything I have loved and lost. Let the silent tears flow like softened wax. But let the light of the flame of hope be the final word, and my companion forward into life.

✠ Tuesday

Jesus said to his disciples, 'I tell you solemnly, it will be hard for a rich man to enter the kingdom of heaven. Yes, I tell you again, it is easier for a camel to pass through the eye of a needle than for a rich man to enter the kingdom of heaven.' (Matthew 19:23–4)

The climbers had to leave their rucksacks behind, before attempting the summit. The most beautiful and mysterious places of the mountain were only accessible through the slimmest of openings between the rocks, where there was no room for any baggage.

✠ Wednesday

Shepherds ought to feed their flock, yet you have fed on milk, you have dressed yourselves in wool, you have sacrificed the fattest sheep, but failed to feed the flock. You have failed to make weak sheep strong, or to care for the sick ones, or bandage the wounded ones. (Ezekiel 34:3–4)

Forgive us, Lord, for we have shorn you of your wool, and not even bound the wounds of that shearing. We have drained you of your milk, yet failed to nourish you for its replenishing. We have done this to our brothers and sisters, Lord. We have done it to you.

✠ Thursday

I shall give you a new heart, and put a new spirit in you; I shall remove the heart of stone from your bodies and give you a heart of flesh instead. (Ezekiel 36:26–7)

We seek to by-pass our hearts with all the defences and delusions we can muster. Give us the courage to surrender ourselves instead to your transplant operation.

❧ Friday

> *The Spirit of the Lord set me down in the middle of a valley, a valley full of bones . . . He said, 'Dry bones, hear the word of the Lord. The Lord says this to these bones: I am now going to make the breath enter you, and you will live. I shall put sinews on you, I shall make flesh grow on you. I shall cover you with skin and give you breath, and you will live; and you will learn that I am the Lord.'* (Ezekiel 37:1–7)

Hannah was numbed with grief after her life companion died. She sat, day after day, gazing at faded photographs of their childhood and their youth, immobilised by sadness and regret. Until one day the neighbour's little girl knocked on her door, with a message from her parents. It was the start of a new friendship. The old lady and the child would sit and chat together, until Hannah's faded photographs became a new and living love.

❧ Saturday

> *Mercy and faithfulness have met;*
> *justice and peace have embraced.* (Psalm 85:10)

Greg's son was blinded in the terrorist attack. His outraged sense of justice demanded retaliation, but his son's new vision saw things differently. 'They are blinder than I am, Dad,' he said quietly. 'Don't let them blind you, too.'

The week's readings

Monday	Ezekiel 24:15–24; Deuteronomy 32:18–21; Matthew 19:16–22
Tuesday	Ezekiel 28:1–10; Deuteronomy 32:26–8, 30, 35–6; Matthew 19:23–30
Wednesday	Ezekiel 34:1–11; Psalm 23(22); Matthew 20:1–16
Thursday	Ezekiel 36:23–8; Psalm 51(50); Matthew 22:1–4
Friday	Ezekiel 37:1–14; Psalm 107(106); Matthew 22:34–40
Saturday	Ezekiel 43:1–7; Psalm 85(84); Matthew 23:1–12

Twenty-first Week of Ordinary Time *(Weekday Cycle I)*

✠ Monday

When we brought the Good News to you, it came to you not only as words, but as power and as the Holy Spirit and as utter conviction. (1 Thessalonians 1:4–5)

The Word that inspires us is the Word who created us and the Word who empowers us to become ourselves a word for others.

✠ Tuesday

Oh Lord, you search me and you know me,
you know my resting and my rising,
you discern my purpose from afar. (Psalm 139:1–2)

Like a shy and secret bird, I try to conceal myself from your knowledge of me. Yet hear my muted prayer-song, Lord. It is my call to you, to know me in spite of my concealment.

✠ Wednesday

If I say: 'Let the darkness hide me
and let the light around me be night,'
even darkness is not dark for you
and the night is as clear as the day. (Psalm 139:11–12)

Christine wraps herself in the thick blanket of depression, refusing to open the door or answer the telephone. No one can reach her. She needs the One who walked through his own Gethsemane darkness.

✠ Thursday

Jesus said to his disciples: 'Stay awake, because you do not know the day when your master is coming . . . Stand ready because the Son of Man is coming at an hour you do not expect.' (Matthew 24:42, 44)

It was a bleak January day up on the high fells, and the snow-laden clouds seemed uniformly grey. Then, just for a moment, the sun broke through the cloud cover and the hills were transfigured with light. The vision was over in a few seconds, but it was enough to sustain us through a long, cold, winter walk.

❦ Friday

'The kingdom of heaven will be like this: Ten bridesmaids took their lamps and went to meet the bridegroom. Five of them were foolish and five were wise . . . The foolish bridesmaids had gone off to buy oil when the bridegroom arrived. Those who were ready went in with him to the wedding hall and the door was closed. The other bridesmaids arrived later. "Lord, Lord," they said, "Open the door for us." But he replied "I tell you solemnly, I do not know you." So stay awake, because you do not know either the day or the hour.' (Matthew 25:1–2, 10–13)

Your surprises catch us up in their joy. Yet how easily we miss them among the clouds of our distractions and pre-occupations, and never even realise the value of what we have lost.

❦ Saturday

'A man on his way abroad summoned his servants and entrusted his property to them. To one he gave five talents, to another two, to a third, one; each in proportion to his ability. Then he set out. The man who had received the five talents promptly went and traded with them and made five more. The man who had received two made two more in the same way. But the man who had received one went off and dug a hole in the ground and hid his master's money.' (Matthew 25:14–18)

Alice had been looking forward so much to seeing her grandsons again. She noticed straight away that they were wearing the sweaters she had knitted for them last year. John's was getting thin and worn. It had been through many a playground scuffle and received its share of life's batterings and hugs. Her heart rejoiced. But Jim's looked as smart as on the day she had given it to him. Barely worn, she thought. And her heart sank.

The week's readings

Monday	1 Thessalonians 1:2–5, 8–10; Psalm 149; Matthew 23:13–22
Tuesday	1 Thessalonians 2:1–8; Psalm 139(138); Matthew 23:23–6
Wednesday	1 Thessalonians 2:9–13; Psalm 139(138); Matthew 23:27–32
Thursday	1 Thessalonians 3:7–13; Psalm 90(89); Matthew 24:42–51
Friday	1 Thessalonians 4:1–8; Psalm 97(96); Matthew 25:1–13
Saturday	1 Thessalonians 4:9–12; Psalm 98(97); Matthew 25:14–30

Twenty-first Week of Ordinary Time *(Weekday Cycle II)*

❦ Monday

> *'You blind men! For which is of greater worth, the offering, or the altar that makes the offering sacred?'* (Matthew 23:19)

I unwrapped the gift carefully. The beautiful wrapping made it special, but the real specialness was in the love with which you gave it to me.

❦ Tuesday

> *'You blind guides! Straining out gnats and swallowing camels! You who clean the outside of cup and dish and leave the inside full of extortion and intemperance. Blind Pharisee! Clean the inside of cup and dish first so that the outside may become clean as well.'* (Matthew 23:25–6)

In your presence, Lord, we are turned inside out. Perhaps that is why we are so hesitant to enter it.

❦ Wednesday

> *From me, Paul, these greetings in my own handwriting, which is the mark of genuineness in every letter; this is my own writing.* (2 Thessalonians 3:17–18)

So you, too, Lord, write your name, by your own hand, in each believer's heart, marking us with the sign of your authenticity, and drawing us towards the same genuineness as yours, whose name we bear.

❦ Thursday

> *'Stay awake, because you do not know the day when your master is coming.'* (Matthew 24:42)

Not with the anxious wakefulness of night we await you, but with the eager wakefulness of dawning.

❦ Friday

> *While the Jews demand miracles and the Greeks look for wisdom, here are we preaching a crucified Christ; to the Jews an obstacle that they cannot get over, to the pagans madness,*

but to those who have been called, whether they are Jews or Greeks, a Christ who is the power and the wisdom of God. (1 Corinthians 1:23–5)

Katy admired David's ability to engage the attention of their friends in what he said and did, and she had great respect for the understanding he revealed in their conversations, but it wasn't until she saw him, weak and broken, in a hospital bed, that she knew how much she *loved* him.

Saturday

'To everyone who has will be given more, and he will have more than enough; but from the man who has not, even what he has will be taken away.' (Matthew 25:29)

The nudge of inspiration comes quietly, urging us to exercise a hidden talent and let it bear fruit. If we respond, it will grow, strengthening our confidence and ability. If we ignore it, it will fade and be lost, and we may never know what gifts we have left buried in the unexplored depths of our lives.

The week's readings

Monday	2 Thessalonians 1:1–5, 11–12; Psalm 96(95); Matthew 23:13–22
Tuesday	2 Thessalonians 2:1–3, 14–17; Psalm 96(95); Matthew 23:23–6
Wednesday	2 Thessalonians 3:6–10, 16–18; Psalm 128(127); Matthew 23:27–32
Thursday	1 Corinthians 1:1–9; Psalm 145(144); Matthew 24:42–51
Friday	1 Corinthians 1:17–25; Psalm 33(32); Matthew 25:1–13
Saturday	1 Corinthians 1:26–31; Psalm 33(32); Matthew 25:14–30

Twenty-second Week of Ordinary Time (Weekday Cycle I)

❧ Monday

Unrolling the scroll he found the place where it is written:
The Spirit of the Lord has been given to me, for he has anointed me.
He has sent me to bring the good news to the poor,
to proclaim liberty to captives and to the blind new sight,
to set the downtrodden free, to proclaim the Lord's year of favour.

He then rolled up the scroll, gave it back to the assistant and sat down. And all eyes in the synagogue were fixed on him. Then he began to speak to them, 'This text is being fulfilled today even as you listen.' (Luke 4:16–22)

The words rang hollow as I walked through the up-market estate and wondered about its inhabitants. Yet the words wouldn't leave me, for all that. Words that spoke of the poor, encased in wealth yet starved of love, and of captives who have purchased every luxury and had to fence themselves in to defend it. These, too, are your poor and your blind and your oppressed, and claimants on your love.

❧ Tuesday

I am sure I shall see the Lord's goodness in the land of the living.
Hope in him, hold firm and take heart. Hope in the Lord! (Psalm 27:13–14)

There was nothing meaningful she could do to reach him in his despair. All she could offer was a hand on his shoulder, with the words: 'Let me carry the hope for you, until you are strong enough to pick it up again for yourself.'

❧ Wednesday

I am like a growing olive tree in the house of God.
I trust in the goodness of God for ever and ever. (Psalm 52:8)

Like seeds we are called to growth, trusting in the unseen goodness of the soil that holds us; called to yield fruits for the nourishing of many.

❦ Thursday

Jesus caught sight of two boats close to the bank. The fishermen had gone out of them and were washing their nets . . . And Jesus said to Simon, 'Do not be afraid; from now on it is people you will catch.' (Luke 5:1–2, 10)

The love of God is caught, not taught, and we are called to be the source of the contagion.

❦ Friday

Christ Jesus is the image of the unseen God
and the first-born of all creation,
for in him were created
all things in heaven and in earth. (Colossians 1:15–16)

Everywhere I look, in every part of your creation, I see your face in what you have created, each image reflecting that special aspect of your nature which it alone – uniquely – can reflect.

❦ Saturday

One sabbath Jesus happened to be taking a walk through the cornfields, and his disciples were picking ears of corn, rubbing them in their hands and eating them. Some of the Pharisees said: 'Why are you doing something that is forbidden on the sabbath day?' And he said to them, 'The Son of Man is master of the sabbath.' (Luke 6:1–3, 5)

For years Mary stayed away from church, for fear of revealing her ignorance of its customs and practices. But one day her need overcame her fear, and she discovered that your love is so much greater than the rules in which we try to wrap it up.

The week's readings

Monday	1 Thessalonians 4:13–18; Psalm 96(95); Luke 4:16–30
Tuesday	1 Thessalonians 5:1–6, 9–11; Psalm 27(26); Luke 4:31–7
Wednesday	Colossians 1:1–8; Psalm 52(51); Luke 4:38–44
Thursday	Colossians 1:9–14; Psalm 98(97); Luke 5:1–11
Friday	Colossians 1:15–20; Psalm 100(99); Luke 5:33–9
Saturday	Colossians 1:21–3; Psalm 54(53); Luke 6:1–5

Twenty-second Week of Ordinary Time *(Weekday Cycle II)*

❧ Monday

'The Spirit of the Lord has been given to me, for he has anointed me.
He has sent me to bring the good news to the poor,
to proclaim liberty to captives and to the blind new sight,
to set the downtrodden free, to proclaim the Lord's year of favour.' (Luke 4:18–19)

When we share a word of love with the lonely; when we take a trembling hand into our own; when we help a child to solve a problem or intervene to curb a playground fight, we are sharing your anointing, Lord, and letting your kingdom show.

❧ Tuesday

The Spirit reaches the depths of everything, even the depths of God. After all, the depths of a man can only be known by his own spirit, not by any other man, and in the same way the depths of God can only be known by the Spirit of God. (1 Corinthians 2:10)

When I seek the depths of my own spirit in prayer, I discover your Spirit, waiting to receive me, where deep calls to deep.

❧ Wednesday

I did the planting, Apollos did the watering, but God makes things grow. Neither the planter nor the waterer matters; only God, who makes things grow. (1 Corinthians 3:6–7)

Without your seed, all our planting would be futile. Without your power of growth, all our cultivation would be in vain. Let our work be in the service of your life, and our lives be lived in the presence of the One who makes us grow.

❧ Thursday

Paul, Appollos, Cephas, the world, life and death, the present and the future, are all your servants, but you belong to Christ and Christ belongs to God. (1 Corinthians 3:22–3)

Time, and all that it brings to us and takes away again, is just a stream in which we flow home to fullness.

❧ Friday

When the Lord comes he will light up all that is hidden in the dark and reveal the secret intentions of men's hearts. (1 Corinthians 4:5)

If we could see each others' hearts as God sees us, we might be surprised to see what selfish motives sometimes prompt our generosity, and what love is often buried underneath our worst mistakes.

❧ Saturday

One sabbath Jesus happened to be taking a walk through the cornfields, and his disciples were picking ears of corn, rubbing them in their hands and eating them. Some of the Pharisees said: 'Why are you doing something that is forbidden on the sabbath day?' And he said to them, 'The Son of Man is master of the sabbath.' (Luke 6:1–3, 5)

Forgive us, Lord, when the complications we impose upon ourselves and on each other prevent us from simply living.

The week's readings

Monday	1 Corinthians 2:1–5; Psalm 119(118); Luke 4:16–30
Tuesday	1 Corinthians 2:10–16; Psalm 145(144); Luke 4:31–7
Wednesday	1 Corinthians 3:1–9; Psalm 33(32); Luke 4:38–44
Thursday	1 Corinthians 3:18–23; Psalm 24(23); Luke 5:1–11
Friday	1 Corinthians 4:1–5; Psalm 37(36); Luke 5:33–9
Saturday	1 Corinthians 4:6–15; Psalm 145(144); Luke 6:1–5

Twenty-third Week of Ordinary Time *(Weekday Cycle I)*

❦ Monday

It makes me happy to suffer for you, as I am suffering now, and in my own body to do what I can to make up all that has still to be undergone by Christ for the sake of his body, the Church. (Colossians 1:24)

Judith endures chronic pain and immobility. It could have hardened her heart into bitterness. Instead she consciously joins it to the pain of Gethsemane and Calvary, living out in her own time and place the struggle and the power of the cross. It has softened her heart into a tenderness that flows over into every other heart that it encounters.

❦ Tuesday

He then came down with them and stopped at a piece of level ground where there was a large gathering of his disciples with a great crowd of people . . . and everyone in the crowd was trying to touch him because power came out of him that cured them all. (Luke 6:17–19)

You do not call us to climb mountains in your name or to stand on the pinnacles of achievement. Instead you invite us to come down, humbly, to the level ground, where your people wait and hope and trust. You invite us only to be there, carrying you in our hearts, trusting in your healing power, for us, and for all.

❦ Wednesday

And now the life you have is hidden with Christ in God. But when Christ is revealed – and he is your life – you too will be revealed in all your glory with him. (Colossians 3:3–4)

Our daffodil bulbs can have no idea of what they will become next April. But we, who have planted them in the darkness, we know what glory lies hidden in their hearts and we rejoice in the joy and trust of anticipation.

❦ Thursday

'I say this to you, who are listening: Love your enemies, do good to those who hate you, bless those who curse you, pray for those who treat you badly.' (Luke 6:27)

When I disarm my enemy with a smile, I achieve far more than when I arm myself with sarcasm and disdain. Something negative is prevented and reversed, and one little arrow of pain is rendered harmless.

Friday

I will bless the Lord who gives me counsel,
who even at night directs my heart. (Psalm 16:7)

I thought I was trying to steer the boat of my life all alone, while you, Lord, lay sleeping in the bows. Then I awoke, to find that it is I who have been asleep while you captained my craft, lonely and patient, through the dark nights of my faithlessness.

Saturday

'Everyone who comes to me and listens to my words and acts on them is like the man who, when he built his house, dug and dug deep, and laid the foundations on rock; when the river was in flood it bore down on that house but could not shake it, it was so well built.' (Luke 6:47–9)

The builders' estimate arrived. It seemed incredible that the foundations of the house should cost such a high proportion of the total price. A bit of concrete and steel that would never be seen again. And my own foundations, Lord? That part of me that no one sees except you? Will they hold firm when my life-floods rise? Are they built on the rock of you, or on the sand of me?

The week's readings

Monday	Colossians 1:24 – 2:3; Psalm 62(61); Luke 6:6–11
Tuesday	Colossians 2:6–15; Psalm 145(144); Luke 6:12–19
Wednesday	Colossians 3:1–11; Psalm 145(144); Luke 6:20–6
Thursday	Colossians 3:12–17; Psalm 150; Luke 6:27–38
Friday	1 Timothy 1:1–2, 12–14; Psalm 16(15); Luke 6:39–42
Saturday	1 Timothy 1:15–17; Psalm 113(112); Luke 6:43–9

Twenty-third Week of Ordinary Time *(Weekday Cycle II)*

✠ Monday

On the sabbath Jesus went into the synagogue and began to teach, and a man was there whose right hand was withered . . . and Jesus said to the man 'Stretch out your hand.' He did so, and his hand was better. (Luke 6:6, 10–11)

The broken one who reaches out to you for healing is already halfway to wholeness.

✠ Tuesday

Jesus went out into the hills to pray; and he spent the whole night in prayer to God. When day came he summoned his disciples and picked out twelve of them; he called them 'apostles'. (Luke 6:12–13)

If every moment of decision were preceded by a night of prayer, how differently our lives might run – if every daylight choice were shaped by your presence in our darkness.

✠ Wednesday

'Happy you who are hungry now: you shall be satisfied.' (Luke 6:20)

Jack had never known hunger. Long years of business lunches had dulled his appetite and taken a terrible toll on his heart. Now, just out of intensive care, he took the glass of water from the nurse's hand, and nothing in the world had ever tasted so good.

✠ Thursday

'Be compassionate as your Father is compassionate. Do not judge, and you will not be judged yourselves; do not condemn, and you will not be condemned; grant pardon, and you will be pardoned.' (Luke 6:36–7)

Marion used to criticise every other driver on the road, until one day her small son said, 'But *you* do that too, Mum.' It was a moment of truth and the remarkable thing was that when she stopped criticising others she had more energy to concentrate on being a better driver herself.

❦ Friday

> *'Can one blind man guide another? Surely both will fall into a pit.'* (Luke 6:39)

The pits open up in front of us when we try to *lead* each other. The way is much safer if we remain humbly *alongside* each other, equally in need and dependent on you.

❦ Saturday

> *The blessing-cup that we bless is a communion with the blood of Christ, and the bread that we break is a communion with the body of Christ. The fact that there is only one loaf means that, though there are many of us, we form a single body because we all have a share in this one loaf.'* (1 Corinthians 10:15–17)

Our bread is consecrated only when we share it with our neighbour. Our cup is blessed only when we pass it on.

The week's readings

Monday	1 Corinthians 5:1–8; Psalm 5; Luke 6:6–11
Tuesday	1 Corinthians 6:1–11; Psalm 149; Luke 6:12–19
Wednesday	1 Corinthians 7:25–31; Psalm 45(44); Luke 6:20–6
Thursday	1 Corinthians 8:1–7, 11–13; Psalm 139(138), Luke 6:27–38
Friday	1 Corinthians 9:16–19, 22–7; Psalm 84(83); Luke 6:39–42
Saturday	1 Corinthians 10:14–22; Psalm 116(115); Luke 6:43–9

Twenty-fourth Week of Ordinary Time (Weekday Cycle I)

❧ Monday

The Lord is my strength and my shield;
in him my heart trusts. (Psalm 28:7)

How strong is my trust in you, Lord? Weaker than the power of my greatest fear! But you are asking me to trust that your power is greater than the combined force of all my fears, all the world's fears. And such trust is possible, because you have pinned it on the cross for all to see and share.

❧ Tuesday

When he was near the gate of the town of Nain, it happened that a dead man was being carried out for burial, the only son of his mother, and she was a widow. When the Lord saw her he felt sorry for her. 'Do not cry,' he said. Then he went up and put his hand on the bier and the bearers stood still and he said 'Young man, I tell you to get up.' And the dead man sat up and began to talk, and Jesus gave him to his mother. (Luke 7:11–16)

The miracle of healing begins with compassion and leads to the giving back of life. Give us compassion for each other, Lord, that we too may restore each other to the fullness of life.

❧ Wednesday

Without any doubt, the mystery of our religion is very deep indeed. (1 Timothy 3:16)

Your nature is a mystery infinitely beyond our understanding, yet, like life itself, it is revealed in everyone we meet, in everything we experience, in every stirring of our deepest hearts.

❧ Thursday

Do not let people disregard you because you are young, but be an example to all the believers in the way you speak and behave, and in your love, your faith and your purity. (1 Timothy 4:12)

Nothing would persuade Christopher to go to church with his parents. He just couldn't see the point. But while they were out he rang his schoolfriend, Mark, who was in trouble with the police. There wasn't much he could say; but he could listen, and understand, and offer the solid rock of his own integrity for Mark to lean on for a while.

❧ Friday

> *Jesus made his way through towns and villages preaching, and proclaiming the Good News of the kingdom of God. With him went the Twelve, as well as certain women who had been cured of evil spirits and ailments.* (Luke 8:1–2)

Five minutes in the presence of someone who has been cured of what is ailing me is more precious to me than an hour of expert consultancy.

❧ Saturday

> *'A sower went out to sow his seed. As he sowed some fell on the edge of the path and was trampled on; and the birds of the air ate it up. Some seed fell on rock, and when it came up it withered away, having no moisture. Some seed fell amongst thorns and the thorns grew with it and choked it. And some seed fell into rich soil and grew and produced its crop a hundredfold.'* (Luke 8:5–8)

Sometimes the seed of your truth falls onto my soil, my friend. But I feel threatened by it and trample it to death. Or I receive it with a stony silence, and deprive it of life-giving encouragement. Or I crowd it out with my own concerns and ideas and choke it. Forgive me, my friend. Give me the grace to give your seed the space for growth and fruitfulness.

The week's readings

Monday	1 Timothy 2:1–8; Psalm 28(27); Luke 7:1–10
Tuesday	1 Timothy 3:1–13; Psalm 101(100); Luke 7:11–17
Wednesday	1 Timothy 3:14–16; Psalm 111(110); Luke 7:31–5
Thursday	1 Timothy 4:12–16; Psalm 111(110); Luke 7:36–50
Friday	1 Timothy 6:2–12; Psalm 49(48); Luke 8:1–3
Saturday	1 Timothy 6:13–16; Psalm 100(99); Luke 8:4–15

Twenty-fourth Week of Ordinary Time (Weekday Cycle II)

✠ Monday

You do not ask for sacrifice and offerings, but an open ear.
You do not ask for holocaust and victim; instead, here I am. (Psalm 40:6–7)

As long as I bring you my own sacrifices, my own offerings, I keep my relationship with you under *my* control. When I bring you myself, and my unconditional attentiveness, I hand over that control to *you.*

✠ Tuesday

Then Jesus went up and put his hand on the bier and the bearers stood still and he said 'Young man, I tell you to get up.' And the dead man sat up and began to talk, and Jesus gave him to his mother. (Luke 7:14–16)

When you touch our frozen hearts and draw us back to the fullness of life in you, you do it not just for our own sakes, but in order to give us back to the world, charged with your living spirit.

✠ Wednesday

Now we are seeing a dim reflection in a mirror; but then we shall be seeing face to face. The knowledge that I have now is imperfect; but then I shall know as fully as I am known. (1 Corinthians 13:12)

When I stop looking at my own mirror image, and turn instead to look into your face, then, at last, in your clear, love-filled gaze, I shall see your promise of who I really am.

✠ Thursday

'Simon', Jesus said, 'you see this woman? . . . I tell you that her sins, her many sins, must have been forgiven her, or she would not have shown such great love. It is the man who is forgiven little who shows little love.' (Luke 7:47)

If we are tempted to feel that we love you more than others do, help us to remember, Lord, that the measure of our love for you is the measure of the forgiveness you have poured out upon us, and the measure of that forgiveness is the measure of our need of it.

❧ Friday

Hide me in the shadow of your wings. (Psalm 17:8)

When I feel weak, I run to you for shelter, like a chick to the mother hen. When I feel strong, let me not forget that it is your eagles' wings that are carrying me above the storm.

❧ Saturday

Whatever you sow in the ground has to die before it is given new life and the thing that you sow is not what is going to come . . . the thing that is sown is perishable but what is raised is imperishable. (1 Corinthians 15:36–7, 42)

Jane rolled the wrinkled little rowan berry around in her hand. In another few weeks it would have rotted away into the ground. Yet it held within itself the entire reality of a new and living tree that would rise out of its falling.

The week's readings

Monday	1 Corinthians 11:17–26, 33; Psalm 40(39); Luke 7:1–10
Tuesday	1 Corinthians 12:12–14, 27–31; Psalm 100(99); Luke 7:11–17
Wednesday	1 Corinthians 12:31 – 3:13; Psalm 33(32); Luke 7:31–5
Thursday	1 Corinthians 15:1–11; Psalm 118(117); Luke 7:36–50
Friday	1 Corinthians 15:12–20; Psalm 17(16); Luke 8:1–3
Saturday	1 Corinthians 15:35–7, 42–9; Psalm 56(55); Luke 8:4–15

Twenty-fifth Week of Ordinary Time (Weekday Cycle I)

✠ Monday

Those who are sowing in tears
will sing when they reap.
They go out, they go out, full of tears,
carrying seed for the sowing:
they come back, they come back, full of song,
carrying their sheaves. (Psalm 126:5–6)

The grey wintry sky depressed Jake as he seeded the crop, his skin gradually soaking up the cold seeping drizzle. Somewhere in his memory was the dream of a harvest supper, but it seemed a long way off. At home his wife was struggling to persuade their baby to eat his meal. Her frustration all but smothered her hopes for the full-grown son he would become. Then evening came, and they sat beside the fire, and silently warmed their dreams together.

✠ Tuesday

I rejoiced when I heard them say:
'Let us go to God's house.'
And now our feet are standing
within your gates, O Jerusalem. (Psalm 122:1–2)

Stefan grew up in an oppressive atheistic regime. But on Christmas Eve some power far greater than that of the oppressor drew him, like a magnet, to the carol concert in the city's church. For an hour he stood at the gates of the Holy City, and when his feet had to leave, he left his heart there in the manger.

✠ Wednesday

Jesus called the Twelve together and gave them power and authority over all devils and to cure diseases, and he sent them out to proclaim the kingdom of God and to heal. He said to them, 'Take nothing for the journey: neither staff, nor haversack, nor bread, nor money.' (Luke 9:1–3)

Why can we not heal and save our brothers and sisters as you commissioned us to do? Is it because the hands we need for the task are so full with the many things we are trying to take with us on the journey?

✠ Thursday

So now the Lord of hosts says this: Reflect carefully how things have gone for you. You have sown much and harvested little; you eat but never have enough, drink but never have your fill, put on clothes but do not feel warm. The wage earner gets his wages only to put them in a purse riddled with holes. (Haggai 1:5–8)

When I bank my wages, Lord, help me to remember that I am dealing with a dangerously addictive substance that, without your grace, will leave me for ever longing for more.

✠ Friday

One day when Jesus was praying alone in the presence of his disciples he put this question to them, 'Who do the crowds say I am?' And they answered, 'John the Baptist; others Elijah; and others say one of the ancient prophets come back to life.' 'But you,' he said, 'who do you say I am?' (Luke 9:18–20)

The 5-year-olds were coming out of school at the end of their first day. 'Which one's your Mum?' David asked Jim. 'I know her, she's the lady at the check-out in the supermarket,' broke in Simon. 'No, she's our Sunday School teacher,' David corrected him. Only Jim knew the full truth. He ran up to her and gave her a big hug, because only he knew who she *really* was.

✠ Saturday

At a time when everyone was full of admiration for all he did, Jesus said to his disciples, 'For your part, you must have these words constantly in mind: the Son of Man is going to be handed over into the power of men.' (Luke 9:43–4)

The crowds follow you eagerly, Lord, all wanting to be with you, to be part of who you are. We see ourselves among them. But the road leads to Jerusalem, to betrayal, to suffering and to death. Can we hear your warning words? And will we follow you anyway?

The week's readings

Monday	Ezra 1:1–6; Psalm 126(125); Luke 8:16–18
Tuesday	Ezra 6:7–8, 12, 14–20; Psalm 122(121); Luke 8:19–21
Wednesday	Ezra 9:5–9; Tobias 13:2, 4, 6–8; Luke 9:1–6
Thursday	Haggai 1:1–8; Psalm 149; Luke 9:7–9
Friday	Haggai 1:15 – 2:9; Psalm 43(42); Luke 9:18–22
Saturday	Zechariah 2:5–9, 14–15; Jeremiah 31:10–13; Luke 9:43–5

Twenty-fifth Week of Ordinary Time *(Weekday Cycle II)*

Monday

Do not say to your neighbour: 'Go away! Come another time. I will give it you tomorrow,' if you can do it now. (Proverbs 3:28)

Mary had to pass old Hannah's door every day when she came home from work. During the cold snap she even wondered whether Hannah was keeping warm enough, and whether perhaps she should go round and check. Then one evening she saw the police car and ambulance parked outside. The finality of death had frozen her good intentions into inescapable reproach.

Tuesday

A man's conduct may strike him as upright; the Lord, however, weighs the heart. (Proverbs 21:2)

The leadenness of sorrow and of pain can add weight and substance to our hearts that the feathers of mere pleasure can never bring.

Wednesday

'As for those who do not welcome you, when you leave their town shake the dust from your feet as a sign to them.' (Luke 9:5)

The dust of old hurts and resentments accumulates and clings to my feet like a solid layer of mud, until it finally prevents me from moving on at all. To shake it off is to set myself free, as well as those who caused the hurting.

Thursday

You sweep men away like a dream,
like grass which springs up in the morning.
In the morning it springs up and flowers:
by evening it withers and fades. (Psalm 90:5–6)

When we acknowledge the transience of our lives and are content to let ourselves become a space through which life flows, we begin to grasp the meaning of eternity.

❦ Friday

There is a season for everything, a time for every occupation under heaven:
A time for giving birth; a time for dying;
A time for planting; a time for uprooting what has been planted . . .
A time for throwing stones away; a time for gathering them up . . .
A time for searching; a time for losing;
A time for keeping; a time for throwing away. (Ecclesiastes 3:1–3, 6)

Bill and Emma had grown old together, he the dominant decision-maker, she the meek peace-maker. Now he was helpless and dependent in his infirmity and she marvelled at his new-found calm, while she had found in herself a new strength of leadership in the life of the community. Times and seasons for growth and change and for discovering new depths and breadths of personality in the opposite of who they thought they were.

❦ Saturday

Yet the almond tree is in flower,
the grasshopper is heavy with food
and the caper bush bears its fruit,
while man goes to his everlasting home. (Ecclesiastes 11:9 – 12:8)

The village cemetery was alive with cherry blossom and daffodils. Burgeoning life in the midst of the monuments of death. It was a place where it was impossible to believe that death could have the final word.

The week's readings

Monday	Proverbs 3:27–34; Psalm 15(14); Luke 8:16–18
Tuesday	Proverbs 21:1–6, 10–13; Psalm 119(118); Luke 8:19–21
Wednesday	Proverbs 30:5–9; Psalm 119(118); Luke 9:1–6
Thursday	Ecclesiastes 1:2–11; Psalm 90(89):3–6, 12–14, 17, Luke 9:7–9
Friday	Ecclesiastes 3:1–11; Psalm 144(143); Luke 9:18–22
Saturday	Ecclesiastes 11:9 – 12:8; Psalm 90(89); Luke 9:43–5

Twenty-sixth Week of Ordinary Time *(Weekday Cycle I)*

❦ Monday

> *Jesus took a little child and set him by his side and then said to them, 'Anyone who welcomes this little child in my name welcomes me; and anyone who welcomes me welcomes the one who sent me. For the least among you all, that is the one who is great.'* (Luke 9:47–8)

In all the huge world I have built around myself, is there still room for the little child I once was, who was small enough to capture all the wonder of the present moment? Help me welcome her for your sake, and in welcoming her, let me welcome you.

❦ Tuesday

> *As the time drew near for him to be taken up to heaven, Jesus resolutely took the road for Jerusalem.* (Luke 9:51)

There are days when we can see the shadow of a cross looming darkly on our personal horizons. How easy then to sink into our fears and griefs. How hard to walk resolutely along the road you have walked ahead of us, risking the pain in order to remain close to you.

❦ Wednesday

> *O how could we sing the song of the Lord*
> *on alien soil?*
> *If I forget you, Jerusalem,*
> *let my right hand wither.* (Psalm 137:4–5)

Janice was often depressed and lonely in the old people's home. It was hard to raise a smile for the nurses. She had only her memories to nourish her spirit, but in those memories were the pearls of experience that had made her life precious, and nothing could wrest them from her.

❦ Thursday

> *He then said, 'Go, eat the fat, drink the sweet wine, and send a portion to the man who has nothing prepared ready. For this day is sacred to our Lord. Do not be sad: the joy of the Lord is your stronghold.'* (Nehemiah 8:10–11)

You ask only this of those who come to your table: that we enjoy your feast, and that we share it.

❦ Friday

How long, O Lord? Will you be angry for ever,
how long will your anger burn like fire? . . .
Do not hold the guilt of our fathers against us.
Let your compassion hasten to meet us
for we are in the depths of distress. (Psalm 79:5, 8)

The hurt child becomes the hurting parent, in a chain of pain that only your grace can break. How long, O Lord, before we allow your healing compassion to meet us in the hurting?

❦ Saturday

It was then that, filled with joy by the Holy Spirit, he said, 'I bless you, Father, Lord of heaven and of earth, for hiding these things from the learned and the clever and revealing them to mere children.' (Luke 10:21)

As we build the mountains of knowledge in our children's minds, help us to tread carefully, lest we bury the treasure of wisdom that you have planted in their hearts.

The week's readings

Monday	Zechariah 8:1–8; Psalm 102(101); Luke 9:46–50
Tuesday	Zechariah 8:20–3; Psalm 87(86); Luke 9:51–6
Wednesday	Nehemiah 2:1–8; Psalm 137(136); Luke 9:57–62
Thursday	Nehemiah 8:1–12; Psalm 19(18); Luke 10:1–12
Friday	Baruch 1:15–22; Psalm 79(78); Luke 10:13–16
Saturday	Baruch 4:5–12, 27–9; Psalm 69(68); Luke 10:17–24

Twenty-sixth Week of Ordinary Time *(Weekday Cycle II)*

☙ Monday

Naked I came from my mother's womb,
naked I shall return.
The Lord gave, the Lord has taken back.
Blessed be the name of the Lord! (Job 1:21)

When gain and loss become as simple as breathing in and breathing out, then we shall begin to see how close you have been to us when we thought we were most grievously alone.

☙ Tuesday

Lord my God, I call for help by day;
I cry at night before you.
Let my prayer come into your presence.
O turn your ear to my cry. (Psalm 88:1–2)

I beg you to receive my prayer into your presence, and you respond by opening my heart to your presence in my prayer.

☙ Wednesday

As Jesus and his disciples travelled along they met a man on the road who said to him: 'I will follow you wherever you go.' (Luke 9:57)

To follow wherever *you* go is to court humiliation and contempt, disgrace and destruction. Our following of you may take us to the depths of hell, but it will never lead where you have not walked yourself.

☙ Thursday

'The harvest is rich but the labourers are few, so ask the Lord of the harvest to send labourers to his harvest.' (Luke 10:2)

When we pray to you to call more people to your service, give us the grace to hear the ways in which you are calling *us*.

❦ Friday

O Lord, you search me and you know me,
you know my resting and my rising,
you discern my purpose from afar.
You mark when I walk or lie down,
all my ways lie open to you. (Psalm 139:1–3)

Once it filled me with apprehension, that nothing I could do or say or think could be concealed from you. Now it fills me with hope and trust, knowing that whichever paths I take, everything has the potential to lead me to you.

❦ Saturday

Job died, an old man and full of days. (Job 42:16)

To die an old man is one thing; but to have lived a life in which every day was really *lived*, that is quite another.

The week's readings

Monday	Job 1:6–22; Psalm 17(16); Luke 9:46–50
Tuesday	Job 3:1–3, 11–17, 20–3; Psalm 88(87); Luke 9:51–6
Wednesday	Job 9:1–12, 14–16; Psalm 88(87); Luke 9:57–62
Thursday	Job 19:21–7; Psalm 27(26); Luke 10:1–12
Friday	Job 38:1, 12–21; 40:3–5; Psalm 139(138); Luke 10:13–16
Saturday:	Job 42:1–3, 5–6, 12–17; Psalm 119(118); Luke 10:17–24

Twenty-seventh Week of Ordinary Time (Weekday Cycle I)

❧ Monday

The word of the Lord was addressed to Jonah son of Amittai: 'Up!' he said 'Go to Nineveh, the great city, and inform them that their wickedness has become known to me.' Jonah decided to run away from the Lord, and to go to Tarshish. He went down to Joppa and found a ship bound for Tarshish; he paid his fare and went aboard, to go with them to Tarshish, to get away from the Lord. But the Lord unleashed a violent wind on the sea, and there was such a great storm at sea that the ship threatened to break up. (Jonah 1:1–5)

I *know* when I am trying to avoid your stirrings in my life, and to run away from your guiding. I know it because the turmoil inside me rises to storm force and my life starts to come apart at the seams.

❧ Tuesday

Martha, who was distracted with all the serving said, 'Lord, do you not care that my sister is leaving me to do the serving all by myself? Please tell her to help me.' But the Lord answered: 'Martha, Martha,' he said, 'you worry and fret about so many things, and yet few are needed, indeed only one. It is Mary who has chosen the better part; it is not to be taken from her.' (Luke 10:40–2)

By the evening Christine felt exhausted and fragmented. She felt as if she had been all things to all people: wife, mother, colleague, friend, secretary, teacher and nurse. She lay awake in bed, too tired to sleep, and watched the sky. One single star shone out above her. It steadied her heart, until she could hear your voice inside her: 'For me, you are one; you are whole; you are Christine.'

❧ Wednesday

Once Jesus was in a certain place praying, and when he had finished, one of his disciples said, 'Lord, teach us to pray.' (Luke 11:1)

We learn to pray by being in the presence of the One who is always in his Father's presence.

❦ Thursday

'What father among you would hand his son a stone when he asked for bread? Or hand him a scorpion if he asked for an egg? If you, then, who are evil, know how to give your children what is good, how much more will the heavenly Father give the Holy Spirit to those who ask him?' (Luke 11:11–13)

One of the best parts of Christmas is choosing those little gifts that the recipient hasn't even thought to ask for. When I choose gifts like that, I remember the surprises of your Spirit that you choose for us and place along our path, for the sheer joy of giving.

❦ Friday

The nations have fallen in the pit which they made, their feet caught in the snare they laid. (Psalm 9:15)

There is a causal connection between the greed and pride of empire and the barbarity and squalor of war. There is a causal connection between our every selfish gesture and the deep discontent that reigns in and around us.

❦ Saturday

When that day comes,
the mountains will run with new wine
and the hills flow with milk,
and all the river beds of Judah
will run with water. (Joel 4:18)

When God breaks out inside us, something overflows: nourishing, intoxicating, unceasingly replenished. Then God is in flood, and there will be an abundant harvest.

The week's readings

Monday	Jonah 1:1 – 2:1, 11; Jonah 2:3–5, 8; Luke 10:25–37
Tuesday	Jonah 3:1–10; Psalm 130(129); Luke 10:38–42
Wednesday	Jonah 4:1–11; Psalm 86(85); Luke 11:1–4
Thursday	Malachi 3:13–20; Psalm 1; Luke 11:5–13
Friday	Joel 1:13–15; 2:1–2; Psalm 9; Luke 11:15–26
Saturday	Joel 4:12–21; Psalm 97(96); Luke 11:27–8

Twenty-seventh Week of Ordinary Time (Weekday Cycle II)

☙ Monday

'A Samaritan traveller who came upon him was moved with compassion when he saw him. He went up and bandaged his wounds, pouring oil and wine on them. He then lifted him onto his own mount, carried him to the inn and looked after him.' (Luke 10:33–4)

A crowd of bystanders gathered round the scene of the accident. They watched the paramedics carrying the old lady to the ambulance, and they were relieved that none of their own family had been involved. In the emergency ward the nurses did all they could to ease her pain and bind her wounds, but there was neither the time nor the funding for any more. It was when she was sent home that the unemployed immigrant family from next door came round. They turned their compassion into an unobtrusive, undemanding, day-by-day caring for their wounded neighbour.

☙ Tuesday

The Lord said: 'Martha, Martha, you worry and fret about so many things, and yet few are needed, indeed only one.' (Luke 10:41)

We fret for so much that is out of reach, when all we really need is waiting to be claimed in the treasure of the present moment.

☙ Wednesday

'Lord, teach us to pray.' (Luke 11:1)

When we teach our children about our world, we give them something of our knowledge. When you teach us how to pray, you give us something of yourself.

☙ Thursday

'Ask, and it will be given to you; search, and you will find; knock, and the door will be opened to you.' (Luke 11:9)

Lord, give us the courage to ask you for what we most desire, so that we may hear ourselves acknowledge our deepest needs and most fervent hopes in your presence, and so that, in acknowledging them, we may open ourselves up to your fulfilling of them.

❦ Friday

I will thank the Lord with all my heart
in the meeting of the just and their assembly.
Great are the works of the Lord;
to be pondered by all who love them. (Psalm 111:1–2)

To hear the parish gossips talking, you might think that everything was wrong with the church. Their criticism ranged from the vicar to the altar flowers, from the liturgy to the summer fete. Maeve stayed behind, to be alone in prayer with her confusion. Yet surely it was in this place, among these people, that she had found her way home to God! As she prayed, the parish critics shrank into perspective, and her heart expanded with the love that bound them all to each other, in spite of themselves.

❦ Saturday

You are, all of you, sons of God through faith in Christ Jesus. All baptised in Christ, you have clothed yourselves in Christ. (Galatians 3:26–7)

When I am dressed for the ball, I don't go wading through the mud. Lord, may the ways of my heart and the pattern of my living become consistent with the words in which I clothe my faith.

The week's readings

Monday	Galatians 1:6–12; Psalm 111(110); Luke 10:25–37
Tuesday	Galatians 1:13–24; Psalm 139(138); Luke 10:38–42
Wednesday	Galatians 2:1–2, 7–14; Psalm 117(116); Luke 11:1–4
Thursday	Galatians 3:1–5; Luke 1:69–75; Luke 11:5–13
Friday	Galatians 3:7–14; Psalm 111(110); Luke 11:15–26
Saturday	Galatians 3:22–9; Psalm 105(104); Luke 11:27–8

Twenty-eighth Week of Ordinary Time *(Weekday Cycle I)*

❧ Monday

Sing a new song to the Lord,
for he has worked wonders. (Psalm 98:1)

The world has turned through thousands of years since life began, yet still the song of every life is uniquely new and fresh and brings joy to you, our creator.

❧ Tuesday

The Pharisee was surprised that Jesus had not first washed before the meal. But the Lord said to him 'Oh, you Pharisees! You clean the outside of cup and plate, while inside yourselves you are filled with extortion and wickedness.' (Luke 11:38–9)

Aunt Agatha kept an immaculate household, and insisted on orderly behaviour in her home. She cringed as her small nephew came bursting in from the garden with muddy feet and sticky hands. But her protests were stifled by his exuberant hug, and the stiffness in her heart was softened by the warmth of his dirty face.

❧ Wednesday

In God alone is my soul at rest;
my help comes from him.
He alone is my rock, my stronghold,
my fortress: I stand firm. (Psalm 62:1–2)

Beneath the most turbulent waves of my life lie the still and silent ocean depths of prayer. And beneath the depths, holding them in the palms of your hands, I find you, my sea bed, my rock and my place of rest.

❧ Thursday

Out of the depths I cry to you, O Lord,
Lord hear my voice!
O let your ears be attentive
to the voice of my pleading. (Psalm 130:1–2)

At the depths of our greatest griefs and needs we will also find the seeds of our deepest trust and faith, hidden in our darkness.

✠ Friday

And Jesus began to speak, first of all to his disciples: 'Be on your guard against the yeast of the Pharisees – that is, their hypocrisy. Everything that is now hidden will be made clear. For this reason, whatever you have said in the dark will be heard in the daylight, and what you have whispered in hidden places will be proclaimed on the housetops.' (Luke 12:1–3)

One worm can make the apple bad. One grain of yeast can make the loaf rise. Our lies can multiply into a torrent of evil, but our truth can swell the ocean of redeeming love.

✠ Saturday

Jesus said to his disciples, 'I tell you, if anyone openly declares himself for me in the presence of men, the Son of Man will declare himself for him in the presence of God's angels. But the man who disowns me in the presence of men will be disowned in the presence of God's angels.' (Luke 12:8–9)

Max was always kind to the young prisoners-of-war who had been forcibly drafted into his place of work. He risked his own life to make their burden lighter, and he did it quietly and without fuss. When the war ended and the conquering armies stormed the city there was little mercy for the former oppressors. But those ex-prisoners remembered Max. They spoke up for him, their humanity acknowledging his. A life for a life.

The week's readings

Monday	Romans 1:1–7; Psalm 98(97); Luke 11:29–32
Tuesday	Romans 1:16–25; Psalm 19(18); Luke 11:37–41
Wednesday	Romans 2:1–11; Psalm 62(61); Luke 11:42–6
Thursday	Romans 3:21–30; Psalm 130(129); Luke 11:47–54
Friday	Romans 4:1–8; Psalm 32(31); Luke 12:1–7
Saturday	Romans 4:13, 16–18; Psalm 105(104); Luke 12:8–12

Twenty-eighth Week of Ordinary Time (Weekday Cycle II)

☙ Monday

When Christ freed us, he meant us to remain free. Stand firm, therefore, and do not submit again to the yoke of slavery. (Galatians 5:1)

Barbara caught the cat firmly and gently took the terrified little bird from its jaws. As she carried it to a safe distance and let it fly free, she knew that it would need strength, courage and constant vigilance to stay free and to live.

☙ Tuesday

If you look to the Law to make you justified, then you have separated yourselves from Christ, and have fallen from grace . . . what matters is faith that makes its power felt through love. (Galatians 5:4, 6)

Every time I think I have managed, by my own efforts, to act in accordance with your will, I move a little bit further from that helpless acknowledgement of my utter need of you, which alone can break me open to your love.

☙ Wednesday

What the Spirit brings is very different: love, joy, peace, patience, kindness, goodness, trustfulness, gentleness and self-control. (Galatians 5:22)

Paul and Monica sent out their wedding list in good time and the toasters, towels and tablecloths duly arrived from friends and relatives. But the gifts that came silently and unseen, through the sacrament of their vows, were altogether different, and much more necessary.

☙ Thursday

'Alas for you who build the tombs of the prophets, the men your ancestors killed! In this way you both witness what your ancestors did and approve it; they did the killing, you do the building.' (Luke 11:47–8)

Reg never talked about the war. He tried never even to think about it. Sometimes his walks would bring him face to face with the war memorial, with its fine marble and the names of his friends who had been pitched along with him into wholesale slaughter. Then he would flinch inwardly, swallow his anger and his grief, and walk resolutely in the opposite direction.

❧ Friday

> *'Everything that is now covered will be uncovered, and everything now hidden will be made clear. Whatever you have said in the dark will be heard in the daylight, and what you have whispered in hidden places will be proclaimed on the housetops.'* (Luke 12:2–3)

The paradox of your grace turns us inside-out, until our trembling, sin-stained hearts are fully exposed to the light of your healing, all-revealing love.

❧ Saturday

> *May he enlighten the eyes of your mind so that you can see what hope his call holds for you.* (Ephesians 1:18)

The light of your hope, like the light of the stars, shines most clearly through the deepest darkness. It may seem so distant, yet it is the truest beacon and companion of our night.

The week's readings

Monday	Galatians 4:22–4, 26–7, 31 – 5:1; Psalm 113(112); Luke 11:29–32
Tuesday	Galatians 5:1–6; Psalm 119(118); Luke 11:37–41
Wednesday	Galatians 5:18–25; Psalm 1; Luke 11:42–6
Thursday	Ephesians 1:1, 3–10; Psalm 98(97); Luke 11:47–54
Friday	Ephesians 1:11–14; Psalm 33(32); Luke 12:1–7
Saturday	Ephesians 1:15–23; Psalm 8; Luke 12:8–12

Twenty-ninth Week of Ordinary Time (Weekday Cycle I)

✠ Monday

Then he told them a parable: 'There was once a rich man who, having a good harvest from his land, thought to himself "What am I to do? I have not enough room to store my crops." Then he said: "This is what I will do: I will pull down my barns and build bigger ones, and store all my grain and my goods in them" . . . But God said to him "Fool! This very night the demand will be made for your soul; and this hoard of yours, whose will it be then?" ' (Luke 12:16–19, 20–1)

Jane worked tirelessly for charity, raising funds and stirring people into action. She committed more and more of her time and energy to this all-consuming passion. By the time she got to bed each night she was too exhausted to hear the sobbing of her little son, lying alone with his fears in the next room.

✠ Tuesday

'However great the number of sins committed, grace was even greater.' (Romans 5:20)

We try to carry your grace up the mountains of our lives like a litre of water in a plastic bottle, and we pass by the streams of your living spirit unnoticed and untasted.

✠ Wednesday

Our life, like a bird, has escaped from the snare of the fowler. Indeed the snare has been broken and we have escaped. (Psalm 124:7–8)

When I receive your gift of freedom, Lord, do I let its power carry me on eagle's wings, or do I tremble at the cage door like a stranded budgerigar, unable to risk a life beyond captivity?

✠ Thursday

The wage paid by sin is death; the gift given by God is eternal life in Christ Jesus our Lord. (Romans 6:23)

Will I settle for the predictable wage of fleeting satisfaction, paid by my slave-master sin, or will I risk the unimaginable, unpredictable, once-and-for-ever gift of your grace?

❦ Friday

Jesus said to the crowds: 'When you see a cloud looming up in the west you say at once that rain is coming, and so it does . . . You know how to interpret the face of the earth and the sky. How is it you do not know how to interpret these times?' (Luke 12:54, 56)

The early Polynesian explorers navigated the Pacific Ocean by reading the stars, watching the clouds and feeling the swell of the tides beneath their boats. How much more surely shall the constellations of our own circumstances, the moods and movements of our hearts and the swell of our deepest faith be our God-given guides today on our journey of discovery towards him?

❦ Saturday

Jesus told this parable: 'A man had a fig tree planted in his vineyard, and he came looking for fruit on it but found none. He said to the man who looked after the vineyard, "Look here, for three years now I have been coming to look for fruit on this fig tree and finding none. Cut it down: why should it be taking up the ground?" "Sir," the man replied, "leave it one more year and give me time to dig around it and manure it: it may bear fruit next year; if not, then you can cut it down." ' (Luke 13:6–9)

John's daughter was dyslexic. Already in her early years she had been dismissed as an under-achiever and that might have been the end of the road for her. John thought back over the long evenings spent at home encouraging her to read and to express herself. And his heart warmed with a father's love and care as he watched her graduation ceremony.

The week's readings

Monday	Romans 4:20–5; Luke 1:69–75; Luke 12:13–21
Tuesday	Romans 5:12, 15, 17–21; Psalm 40(39); Luke 12:35–8
Wednesday	Romans 6:12–18; Psalm 124(123); Luke 12:39–48
Thursday	Romans 6:19–23; Psalm 1; Luke 12:49–53
Friday	Romans 7:18–25; Psalm 119(118); Luke 12:54–9
Saturday	Romans 8:1–11; Psalm 24(23); Luke 13:1–9

Twenty-ninth Week of Ordinary Time (Weekday Cycle II)

✠ Monday

We are God's work of art, created in Christ Jesus to love the good life as from the beginning he had meant us to live it. (Ephesians 2:10)

The old painting had been buried in the vaults for long forgotten years, yet in the hands of the restorers it was cleansed and re-created until the full glory of the artist's first intention shone from the canvas. It was a unique expression of his mind and heart, and the world had been incomplete without it.

✠ Tuesday

He is the peace between us . . . In his own person he killed the hostility. (Ephesians 2:14)

May we kill nothing except that which kills the wholeness of each other. May we destroy nothing except the barriers that divide us.

✠ Wednesday

'When a man has had a great deal given him, a great deal will be demanded of him.' (Luke 12:48)

Diane knew that the brightest and most gifted children in her class of 8-year-olds could be prone to boredom, so she sometimes asked them to help the slower ones with their reading and writing. They passed their own skills on to their classmates, and in return they learned patience and responsibility. It was a sharing of gifts that helped to change the class into a real community.

✠ Thursday

May he give you the power through his Spirit for your hidden self to grow strong, so that Christ may live in your hearts through faith, and then, planted in love and built on love, you will grasp the breadth and the length, the height and the depth. (Ephesians 3:16–18)

The soil of our circumstances, that sometimes seems so hostile to our growth, is the very place – and the *only* place – where our hidden roots find the hold and the nutrients that keep them in being and lead in time to the full height and breadth of our life's flowering and fruiting.

❧ Friday

'You know how to interpret the face of the earth and the sky. How is it you do not know how to interpret these times?' (Luke 12:56)

We are so immersed in the laboratory of human knowledge that we sometimes forget to look out of the window and see what is actually happening to us. Lord, take our knowledge, and transform it into wisdom.

❧ Saturday

If we live by the truth and in love,
we shall grow in all ways into Christ. (Ephesians 4:16)

When we live out the dream you have planted in our hearts, discerning it gradually in the light of your truth and your love, then we shall become who you are calling us to be, as surely as the acorn becomes an oak.

The week's readings

Monday	Ephesians 2:1–10; Psalm 100(99); Luke 12:13–21
Tuesday	Ephesians 2:12–22; Psalm 85(84); Luke 12:35–8
Wednesday	Ephesians 3:2–12; Isaiah 12:2–6; Luke 12:39–48
Thursday	Ephesians 3:14–21; Psalm 33(32); Luke 12:49–53
Friday	Ephesians 4:1–6; Psalm 24(23); Luke 12:54–9
Saturday	Ephesians 4:7–16; Psalm 122(121); Luke 13:1–9

Thirtieth Week of Ordinary Time *(Weekday Cycle I)*

✠ Monday

> *God gives the lonely a home to live in;*
> *he leads the prisoners forth into freedom.* (Psalm 68:6)

We need to know the ache of loneliness before we can receive the full depth of your companionship. We need to know how it feels to be trapped, before we can savour the taste of your freedom. Our pain is the passport to a greater joy.

✠ Tuesday

> *'The kingdom of God is like the yeast a woman took and mixed in with three measures of flour till it was leavened all through.'* (Luke 13:20–1)

The packet of yeast stood beside the bag of flour on the kitchen table. It thought to itself: 'I'm so glad I'm yeast, with my special gifts to transform flour into bread.' Then the baker took it in his hands and crumbled it into tiny fragments, dissolved it in warm water and mixed it into the flour, until it was totally broken down and lost. Give us the grace to allow the yeast in us to be crumbled, mingled and lost in the flour of our lived lives, and still to trust the promised transformation.

✠ Wednesday

> *We know that by turning everything to their good, God cooperates with all those who love him.* (Romans 8:28)

The falling leaves, the rotting berries, the crushed acorns, seem to hold all our regrets and disappointments in their autumn dying. But they also hold our dreams and hopes and faith within their seeding.

✠ Thursday

> *With God on our side who can be against us? . . . Could anyone accuse those that God has chosen? When God acquits, could anyone condemn?* (Romans 8:31, 34)

Since God has forgiven me, why do I so stubbornly refuse to forgive myself? Why do I seek to subvert God's perfect justice by continuing to condemn those things in myself of which he has acquitted me? Why do I water the weeds in my field, instead of nurturing the crop?

❦ Friday

> *Jesus addressed the lawyers and Pharisees, 'Is it against the law,' he asked, 'to cure a man on the sabbath, or not?' But they remained silent, so he took the man and cured him and sent him away. Then he said to them, 'Which of you here, if his son falls into a well, or his ox, will not pull him out on a sabbath day without hesitation?' And to this they could find no answer.* (Luke 14:3–6)

The demands of love always take precedence over the demands of law. They are the demands of our hearts and of God's, to which there can be no other answer.

❦ Saturday

> *'Everyone who exalts himself will be humbled, and the man who humbles himself will be exalted.'* (Luke 14:11)

Queues of tourists wait in line to visit the palace. Tomorrow their day will be just a memory. Once it was the other way round, and kings lined up to visit a stable. We are still talking about their visit two thousand years later.

The week's readings

Monday	Romans 8:12–17; Psalm 68(67); Luke 13:10–17
Tuesday	Romans 8:18–25; Psalm 126(125); Luke 13:18–21
Wednesday	Romans 8:26–30; Psalm 13(12); Luke 13:20–30
Thursday	Romans 8:31–9; Psalm 109(108); Luke 13:31–5
Friday	Romans 9:1–5; Psalm 147; Luke 14:1–6
Saturday	Romans 11:1–2, 11–12, 25–9; Psalm 94(93); Luke 14:1, 7–11

Thirtieth Week of Ordinary Time (Weekday Cycle II)

⁂ Monday

> *Jesus was teaching in one of the synagogues, and a woman was there who for eighteen years had been possessed by a spirit that left her enfeebled; she was bent double and quite unable to stand upright. When Jesus saw her, he called her over . . . and he laid his hands on her. And at once she straightened up, and she glorified God.* (Luke 13:10–13)

Mark would never have claimed to have a gift of healing; but he knew when one of the children in his care was crushed by a burden of self-doubt and inadequacy, and he knew how to nurture the crippled little sapling into a tall, straight tree.

⁂ Tuesday

> *A man never hates his own body, but he feeds it and looks after it; and that is the way Christ treats the Church, because it is his body, and we are its living parts.* (Ephesians 5:29–30)

With gentle, careful hand, I dressed the wound on my foot. Why am I, a living cell of your body, not just as gentle and careful when attending to the needs and wounds of your other living cells?

⁂ Wednesday

> *Work hard and willingly, but do it for the sake of the Lord and not for the sake of men.* (Ephesians 6:7)

Little Tricia dragged her feet and dawdled, and pulled with all her weight against her mother's urging. She had no desire to go shopping. It was different in the afternoon. She skipped lightly and buoyantly all the way to the park. It was the difference between duty and delight.

⁂ Thursday

> *'Jerusalem, Jerusalem . . . How often I have longed to gather your children, as a hen gathers her brood under her wings, and you refused.'* (Luke 13:34)

The mallard mother quickly tried to gather her six ducklings together in safety when she sensed the vibrations of the approaching motor boat. One of them refused. And then there were five.

☙ Friday

I am quite certain that the One who began this good work in you will see that it is finished when the Day of Christ Jesus comes. (Philippians 1:6)

The One who caused all creation to grow from a single spark of life will surely grow his seed in us to the fullness of its blossom and its fruitfulness.

☙ Saturday

'Everyone who exalts himself will be humbled, and the man who humbles himself will be exalted.' (Luke 14:11)

The two parliamentary candidates appeared on television. Bill used his slot to assassinate his opponent's character and policies. Stewart used the time to admit frankly to past mistakes and asked for a chance to put things right. Stewart won the seat.

The week's readings

Monday	Ephesians 4:32 – 5:8; Psalm 1; Luke 13:10–17
Tuesday	Ephesians 5:21–33; Psalm 128(127); Luke 13:18–21
Wednesday	Ephesians 6:1–9; Psalm 145(144); Luke 13:20–30
Thursday	Ephesians 6:10–20; Psalm 144(143); Luke 13:31–5
Friday	Philippians 1:1–11; Psalm 111(110); Luke 14:1–6
Saturday	Philippians 1:18–26; Psalm 42(41); Luke 14:1, 7–11

Thirty-first Week of Ordinary Time *(Weekday Cycle I)*

✠ Monday

How rich are the depths of God – how deep his wisdom and knowledge – and how impossible to penetrate his motives or understand his methods! Who could ever know the mind of the Lord? Who could ever be his counsellor? (Romans 11:33–5)

Your wisdom rises beyond us as the stars above the highest mountain peak. Yet still, Lord, we try to advise you on how to arrange your world and the details of our little lives. Still we try to capture the vastness of your purpose within the cramped cages of our minds.

✠ Tuesday

All of us, in union with Christ, form one body, and as parts of it we belong to each other. (Romans 12:5–6)

We stand together, each one a link in the circle of life, each needing our neighbours, each holding our neighbours, and all held in God.

✠ Wednesday

You must love your neighbour as yourself. Love is the one thing that cannot hurt your neighbour; that is why it is the answer to every one of the commandments. (Romans 13:9–10)

Love hurts. Love brings us up against our most painful choices. Love strips away our masks and exposes our deepest truth. And precisely because of that, love heals.

✠ Thursday

'What man among you with a hundred sheep, losing one would not leave the ninety-nine in the wilderness and go after the missing one till he found it? . . . I tell you, there will be more rejoicing in heaven over one repentant sinner than over ninety-nine virtuous men who have no need of repentance.' (Luke 15:4, 7)

Ted had all he needed, but still he spent most of his time in his old rocking-chair. It was polished with age and wear now, but he would never forget that, years ago, he had found it, mildewed, splintered and abandoned, at the tip. It had taken him years to restore it and now it meant everything to him. He had invested his heart in it, and made it live again.

Friday

'The children of this world are more astute in dealing with their own kind than are the children of light.' (Luke 16:8)

Gary regularly submitted fraudulent benefit claims while he went on moonlighting. Andrew did it once, out of desperation. Gary knew how to cover his tracks. It was Andrew who was caught. Gary never gave it a second thought. Andrew was shattered by remorse.

Saturday

'The man who can be trusted in little things can be trusted in great; the man who is dishonest in little things will be dishonest in great.' (Luke 16:10–11)

If I can trust you with the burdens of my heart, I do not need to wonder whether I can trust you with the contents of my purse.

The week's readings

Monday	Romans 11:29–36; Psalm 69(68); Luke 14:12–14
Tuesday	Romans 12:5–16; Psalm 131(130); Luke 14:15–24
Wednesday	Romans 13:8–10; Psalm 112(111); Luke 14:25–33
Thursday	Romans 14:7–12; Psalm 27(26); Luke 15:1–10
Friday	Romans 15:14–21; Psalm 98(97); Luke 16:1–8
Saturday	Romans 16:3–9, 22–7; Psalm 145(144); Luke 16:9–15

Thirty-first Week of Ordinary Time *(Weekday Cycle II)*

☙ Monday

Be united in your convictions and united in your love, with a common purpose and a common mind. (Philippians 2:2)

Your love is the apex of our lives and our desiring, that draws us all together into unity, however far apart our starting-points.

☙ Tuesday

'When the time for the banquet came, he sent his servant to say to those who had been invited, "Come along: everything is ready now." But all alike started to make excuses.' (Luke 14:17–18)

It always amazes me, with what ingenuity I try to avoid that which would make me whole, and with what tenacity I resist my own redemption.

☙ Wednesday

You will shine in the world like bright stars because you are offering it the word of life. (Philippians 2:15)

When we offer our friends our passing favours, we may win brief popularity, but when we share with them our friendship with you, your love will flood their lives with light.

☙ Thursday

'I tell you there will be more rejoicing in heaven over one repentant sinner than over ninety-nine virtuous men who have no need of repentance.' (Luke 15:7)

Jim's eyes filled up and spilled over into tears as he embraced his brother at the airport. Twenty-five years of sulky resentment melted away, as if their quarrel had never happened. The joy in this homecoming outshone the steady glow of more trouble-free relationships, yet even as it outshone them, it completed and fulfilled them.

❦ Friday

I rejoiced when I heard them say
'Let us go to God's house.'
And now our feet are standing
within your gates, O Jerusalem. (Psalm 122:1–2)

Prayer begins with the first quiver of desire to spend time in your presence, and before I know what has happened I am a guest in your heart and a pilgrim in your kingdom.

❦ Saturday

It was good of you to share with me in my hardships . . . It is not your gift that I value; what is valuable to me is the interest that is mounting up in your account. (Philippians 4:14,17)

You invest the capital of your love in our hearts, Lord, and the more we draw upon it, the more interest you pay us.

The week's readings

Monday	Philippians 2:1–4; Psalm 131(130); Luke 14:12–14
Tuesday	Philippians 2:5–11; Psalm 22(21); Luke 14:15–24
Wednesday	Philippians 2:12–18; Psalm 27(26); Luke 14:25–33
Thursday	Philippians 3:3–8; Psalm 105(104); Luke 15:1–10
Friday	Philippians 3:17 – 4:1; Psalm 122(121); Luke 16:1–8
Saturday	Philippians 4:10–19; Psalm 112(111); Luke 16:9–15

Thirty-second Week of Ordinary Time (Weekday Cycle I)

❦ Monday

Before ever a word is on my tongue
you know it, O Lord, through and through. (Psalm 139:4)

When I express my needs and hopes and fears in the words of my prayer, I know that you hear my call. But when I lay before you the nakedness of what I cannot express, then you enfold me in the deepest knowledge of your heart.

❦ Tuesday

The Lord turns his face against the wicked
to destroy their remembrance from the earth.
The Lord turns his eyes to the just
and his ears to their appeal. (Psalm 34:15–16)

It had been a bad day. As she climbed into bed, Jean nearly sank under the depressing weight of a series of mistakes, misjudgements and harsh, unnecessary words. But there had been that moment of kindness from a passing stranger that had made her feel more kindly to her fellow human beings, and there had been that new shoot on the camelia bush that had made her feel more kindly to herself. She switched off the light, let the destructive things fade, and turned her eyes instead to those moments of light.

❦ Wednesday

As Jesus entered one of the villages, ten lepers came to meet him. They stood some way off and called to him, 'Jesus! Master! Take pity on us.' When he saw them he said, 'Go and show yourselves to the priests.' Now as they were going away they were cleansed. Finding himself cured, one of them turned back praising God at the top of his voice and threw himself at the feet of Jesus and thanked him. The man was a Samaritan. This made Jesus say, 'Were not all ten made clean? The other nine, where are they? It seems that no one has come back to give praise to God except this stranger.' (Luke 17:12–19)

The sermon had been a great blessing. Everyone was talking about it as they made their way home for their Sunday lunch. Philip hung back. It was the first time he had been inside a church for years and the sermon had knocked him sideways. Slowly, tentatively, thankfully, he slipped back into the now silent church, knelt down and let his joy flow out in tears.

❦ Thursday

> *Jesus said: 'The coming of the kingdom of God does not admit of observation and there will be no one to say, "Look here! Look there!" For, you must know, the kingdom of God is among you.'* (Luke 17:20–2)

Hour by hour your kingdom comes, silently, powerfully as springtime, with all the fragile determination of the butterfly emerging from the caterpillar. We are called, not to watch anxiously for its coming, but joyfully to recognise its ever-present reality.

❦ Friday

> *'Remember Lot's wife. Anyone who tries to preserve his life will lose it; and anyone who loses it will keep it safe.'* (Luke 17:33–4)

I tried to protect myself behind a mask of cynicism, but became corroded by its salt sting. I tried to hide my hurting in a pool of vinegary sarcasm, but I drowned in its acid depths. Only when I let go my anxious grip on my own fears and frenzies did I discover the joy of flying free.

❦ Saturday

> *Overshadowing the camp there was a cloud,*
> *where water had been, dry land was seen to rise,*
> *the Red Sea became an unimpeded way,*
> *the tempestuous flood a green plain;*
> *sheltered by your hand, the whole nation passed across,*
> *gazing at those amazing miracles.* (Wisdom 19:7–8)

The clouds of mess and muddle seem to block our way impassably. But like the mists of morning they give way to a breathtaking sunrise and, in the distance we begin to glimpse the promise of dry land beyond our wildest storms.

The week's readings

Monday	Wisdom 1:1–7; Psalm 139(138); Luke 17:1–6
Tuesday	Wisdom 2:23 – 3:9; Psalm 34(33); Luke 17:7–10
Wednesday	Wisdom 6:1–11; Psalm 82(81); Luke 17:11–19
Thursday	Wisdom 7:22 – 8:1; Psalm 119(118); Luke 17:20–5
Friday	Wisdom 13:1–9; Psalm 19(18); Luke 17:26–37
Saturday	Wisdom 18:14–16; 19:6–9; Psalm 105(104); Luke 18:1–8

Thirty-second Week of Ordinary Time (Weekday Cycle II)

❧ Monday

The apostles said to the Lord, 'Increase our faith.' The Lord replied, 'Were your faith the size of a mustard seed you could say to this mulberry tree, "Be uprooted and planted in the sea," and it would obey you.' (Luke 17:5–6)

The faith that we hold as our own is your seed sown in our hearts. You are its source and the giver of its growth. We can only watch in wonder as its fullness unfolds in our lives.

❧ Tuesday

God's grace has been revealed . . . and taught us that what we have to do is to give up everything that does not lead to God. (Titus 2:11–12)

When our desire for you is so strong that we can allow nothing to distract us from you, then we shall find again all that we thought we had lost and surrendered made perfect in your love.

❧ Wednesday

As Jesus entered one of the villages, ten lepers came to meet him. They stood some way off and called to him, 'Jesus! Master! Take pity on us.' When he saw them he said, 'Go and show yourselves to the priests.' Now as they were going away they were cleansed. (Luke 17:12–15)

We call to you for help from afar off, hardly daring to approach you. And our healing begins when we hear your response, do as you bid us, and then walk on into the future, in the courage of trusting that our prayer has been answered.

❧ Thursday

'As the lightning flashing from one part of heaven lights up the other, so will be the Son of Man, when his day comes.' (Luke 17:24–5)

It was impossible to pinpoint the source of the flash at the centre of the storm, but its invisible power lit up the fields and forests all around, revealing their every detail. And so the unseen flashpoint of your love lights up our darkest corners and kindles fire in our hearts, that glows and flares far beyond the limits of our own lives and our own imagination.

❧ Friday

> *'Anyone who tries to preserve his life will lose it; and anyone who loses it will keep it safe.'* (Luke 17:33)

Lydia refused to get into the lifeboat without her bag of valuables. Her fellow passengers, shivering and bereft, were rowed to safety. Lydia still lies, with her treasure, in the wreckage on the ocean bed.

❧ Saturday

> *Happy the man who fears the Lord . . .*
> *He is a light in the darkness.* (Psalm 112:1, 4)

The first flickering light of our faith seems to reveal the intensity of the darkness all the more starkly. Remind us then, Lord, that as soon as even the most fragile of lights is kindled, the grip of the darkness has already been broken.

The week's readings

Monday	Titus 1:1–9; Psalm 24(23); Luke 17:1–6
Tuesday	Titus 2:1–8, 11–14; Psalm 37(36); Luke 17:7–10
Wednesday	Titus 3:1–7; Psalm 23(22); Luke 17:11–19
Thursday	Philemon 7–20; Psalm 146(145); Luke 17:20–5
Friday	2 John 4–9; Psalm 119(118); Luke 17:26–37
Saturday	3 John 5–8; Psalm 112(111); Luke 18:1–8

Thirty-third Week of Ordinary Time (Weekday Cycle I)

✠ Monday

Yet there were many in Israel who stood firm and found the courage to refuse unclean food. They chose death rather than contamination by such fare or profanation of the holy covenant, and they were executed. It was a dreadful wrath that visited Israel. (1 Maccabees 1:62–4)

There was a good degree and a bright future on offer for those who were willing to spy on their friends and denounce them to the totalitarian authorities. Yet at the start of the next term, only half of them returned to college. The rest had gone: some to freedom; some to death.

✠ Tuesday

Zacchaeus was anxious to see what kind of man Jesus was, but he was too short and could not see him for the crowd; so he ran ahead and climbed a sycamore tree to catch a glimpse of Jesus who was to pass that way. When Jesus reached the spot he looked up and spoke to him: 'Zacchaeus, come down. Hurry, because I must stay at your house today.' (Luke 19:3–6)

My only thought was to get a little closer to you, to get a better view. Yet that unspoken desire was all you needed to bring you to the very spot where I was so precariously perched. 'I'm looking for companions,' you said, 'not onlookers. Are you coming down?'

✠ Wednesday

Jesus said: 'I tell you, to everyone who has will be given more; but from the man who has not, even what he has will be taken away!' (Luke 19:26)

Moira was barely strong enough to get out of her hospital bed. But with what energy she could muster she went round to her fellow patients with words of encouragement. One by one they responded, with a smile, the clasp of a hand, a shared word, a tear, a glance of understanding. As she climbed back into bed, everyone on the ward had been enriched by her love, and a quite new energy was flowing with a power that defied their weakness.

❦ Thursday

> *As Jesus drew near Jerusalem and came in sight of the city he shed tears over it and said: 'If you in your turn had only understood on this day the message of peace! But, alas, it is hidden from your eyes! . . . and all because you did not recognise your opportunity when God offered it!'* (Luke 19:41–2, 44)

The phone call came a few moments too late. The car wouldn't start. There was a hold-up on the motorway. By the time he rushed into the intensive care unit his brother had just died. The word of forgiveness would never be spoken. Never again. His heart cracked . . . if only!

❦ Friday

> *Jesus went into the Temple and began driving out those who were selling. 'According to scripture,' he said, 'my house will be a house of prayer. But you have turned it into a robbers' den.'* (Luke 19:45)

There were whispered mutterings about the stranger at the back of the church. She had a 'past'. She wasn't entirely nice to know. What was she doing in church anyway, they wondered? She sensed the hostility and slipped quietly off into the shadows. Something of great value had been stolen from her – and that on consecrated ground!

❦ Saturday

> *When the king heard this news [of his defeat] he was amazed and profoundly shaken; he threw himself on his bed and fell into a lethargy from acute disappointment, because things had not turned out for him as he had planned.* (1 Maccabees 6:8–9)

How it amazes us, Lord, when our plans don't coincide with yours, and how it shakes us when life fails to conform to our requirements. How it must have surprised our ancestors, too, when they discovered that the earth revolves round the sun and not the sun around the earth.

The week's readings

Monday	1 Maccabees 1:10–15, 41–3, 54–7, 62–4; Psalm 119(118); Luke 18:35–43
Tuesday	2 Maccabees 6:18–31; Psalm 3; Luke 19:1–10
Wednesday	2 Maccabees 7:1, 20–31; Psalm 17(16); Luke 19:11–28
Thursday	1 Maccabees 2:15–29; Psalm 50(49); Luke 19:41–4
Friday	1 Maccabees 4:36–7, 52–9; 1 Chronicles 29:10–12; Luke 19:45–8
Saturday	1 Maccabees 6:1–13; Psalm 9; Luke 20:27–40

Thirty-third Week of Ordinary Time (Weekday Cycle II)

✠ Monday

I know all about you: how hard you work and how much you put up with . . . Nevertheless I have this complaint to make; you have less love now than you used to. Think where you were before you fell; repent and do as you used to at first. (Revelation 2:2, 4–5)

The home they had once built as a love-nest had become a chore, and the garden had become a backache. The children had become a worry and God himself had become a Sunday observance. So much work; so much to put up with – and underneath all that, there was *everything* waiting for rediscovery.

✠ Tuesday

'Look, I am standing at the door, knocking. If one of you hears me calling and opens the door, I will come in to share his meal, side by side with him.' (Revelation 3:20)

Only a door divides us, Lord. Only a door between my loneliness and your love. Only a door, and the handle is on my side.

✠ Wednesday

Let everything that lives and breathes
give praise to the Lord. Alleluia! (Psalm 150:6)

Remind us, Lord, that when we walk through our gardens and along our streets, we are moving through a hallowed cathedral where there is always a service in progress.

✠ Thursday

As Jesus drew near Jerusalem and came in sight of the city he shed tears over it and said: 'If you in your turn had only understood on this day the message of peace! But, alas, it is hidden from your eyes. Yes, a time is coming when your enemies will raise fortifications all around you, when they will encircle you and hem you in on every side; they will dash you and the children inside your walls to the ground; they will leave not one stone standing on another within you – and all because you did not recognise your opportunity when God offered it!' (Luke 19:41–4)

The uneasy ceasefire seemed to have ended, and the people of the war-torn city lived in fear again. At the crucial moment in the peace talks, the demons of revenge had broken loose, and the opportunity had been lost, perhaps for ever. And your tears flow, mingling with ours.

Friday

The chief priests and the scribes, with the support of the leading citizens, tried to do away with Jesus, but they did not see how they could carry this out because the people as a whole hung on his words. (Luke 19:47–8)

We are your people, Lord, and while we hold on to your Word, implanted in our hearts, no power on earth can do away with your Truth, incarnate in our lives.

Saturday

'He is God, not of the dead, but of the living;
for to him all men are in fact alive.' (Luke 20:38)

The sun and the rain nourish the garden alike in all seasons, as if they know, with a wisdom more profound than ours that the apparent death of winter is only the cradle of the spring.

The week's readings

Monday	Revelation 1:1–4; 2:1–5; Psalm 1; Luke 18:35–43
Tuesday	Revelation 3:1–6, 14–22; Psalm 15(14); Luke 19:1–10
Wednesday	Revelation 4:1–11; Psalm 150; Luke 19:11–28
Thursday	Revelation 5:1–10; Psalm 149; Luke 19:41–4
Friday	Revelation 10:8–11; Psalm 119(118); Luke 19:45–8
Saturday	Revelation 11:4–12; Psalm 144(143); Luke 20:27–40

Christ the King *(Weekday Cycle I) (Last week of the year)*

✠ Monday

> *Jesus happened to notice a poverty-stricken widow putting in two small coins [to the treasury] and he said, 'I tell you truly this poor widow has put in more than any of them; for these have all contributed money they had over, but she from the little she had has put in all she had to live on.'* (Luke 21:1–4)

Joan sat down thankfully for half an hour with a book and a cup of coffee, an oasis of peace and space for herself before the children came home from school. As always, the day had gone by in a whirlwind of jobs, one crowding out the other, and the evening would be the same. But this was her time and her space, the only bit she had. Then the phone rang. Maureen was in tears at the other end of the line. She needed a friend. Joan set her book aside, and gave her space to one who needed it even more than she did.

✠ Tuesday

> *'Take care not to be deceived,' he said, 'because many will come using my name and saying "I am he" and "The time is near at hand." Refuse to join them.'* (Luke 21:8)

Some of the imposters live in my own mind, Lord. They tell me I ought to do this or that, be someone different, convert the world to my own way of thinking, and they say it all in your name. Sometimes they clamour so loudly that I can barely hear the still small voice of your real self, deep in my heart.

✠ Wednesday

> *'Men will seize you and persecute you . . . and bring you before kings and governors because of my name – and that will be your opportunity to bear witness. Keep this carefully in mind: you are not to prepare your defence, because I myself shall give you an eloquence and a wisdom that none of your opponents will be able to resist or contradict.'* (Luke 21:12–15)

In our human *speaking* we are so often merely ourselves. But when we allow our human *being* to speak through our gestures and our silences, we are making space for the wisdom of your Word to shine through.

❦ Thursday

He is the living God, he endures for ever,
his sovereignty will never be destroyed
and his kingship never end.
He saves, sets free and works signs and wonders
in the heavens and on earth. (Daniel 6:26–7)

National sovereignty: fighting our corner against the others?
Personal sovereignty: surrendering our corner to your kingdom!

❦ Friday

Jesus told his disciples a parable. 'Think of the fig tree and indeed of every tree. As soon as you see them bud, you know that summer is now near. So when you see these things happening; know that the kingdom of God is near.' (Luke 21:29–31)

'I can't pray properly' I said. 'My spiritual life seems dead.'

'I want to be able to pray' is what *you* heard me say, and you rejoiced to see the first buds on the springtime tree.

❦ Saturday

'Stay awake, praying at all times for the strength to survive all that is going to happen, and to stand with confidence before the Son of Man.' (Luke 21:36)

I guard myself against drought not by filling up my spare bottles with water, but by remaining close to the spring.

The week's readings

Monday	Daniel 1:1–6, 8–20; Daniel 3:52–6; Luke 21:1–4
Tuesday	Daniel 2:31–45; Daniel 3:57–61; Luke 21:5–11
Wednesday	Daniel 5:1–6, 13–14, 16–17, 23–8; Daniel 3:62–7; Luke 21:12–19
Thursday	Daniel 6:12–28; Daniel 3:68–74; Luke 21:20–8
Friday	Daniel 7:2–14; Daniel 3:75–81; Luke 21:29–33
Saturday	Daniel 7:15–27; Daniel 3:82–7; Luke 21:34–6

Christ the King *(Weekday Cycle II) (Last Week of the Year)*

✠ Monday

As Jesus looked up he saw rich people putting their offerings into the treasury; then he happened to notice a poverty-stricken widow putting in two small coins and he said 'I tell you truly this poor widow has put in more than any of them; for these have all contributed money they had over, but she from the little she had has put in all she had to live on.' (Luke 21:1–4)

It cost Eric nearly a tenth of his salary to keep his invalid mother in the nursing home. It cost Gerry his health and strength, his freedom and his life, to keep his invalid mother at home.

✠ Tuesday

Jesus said, 'All these things you are staring at now – the time will come when not a single stone will be left on another: everything will be destroyed.' (Luke 21:6)

When I look around me at all the things, and places, and people that I cherish, and then imagine the empty space that would remain, were I to lose them all, then I begin to grasp the extent of my need and the depth of your love, that alone can fill it.

✠ Wednesday

'Men will seize you and persecute you; they will hand you over to the synagogues and to imprisonment, and bring you before kings and governors because of my name – and that will be your opportunity to bear witness.' (Luke 21:12)

When they make fun of us, Lord, because of our faith, we have a choice: we can feel sorry for ourselves, or we can feel proud of you.

✠ Thursday

'There will be signs in the sun and moon and stars; on earth nations in agony, bewildered by the clamour of the ocean and its waves; men dying of fear as they await what menaces the world, for the powers of heaven will be shaken . . . When these things begin to take place, stand erect, hold your heads high, because your liberation is near at hand.' (Luke 21:25–8)

The same earthquake that shatters our homes also breaks open our prisons. The same turmoil that rocks our certainties also shakes free the chains around our hearts.

❦ Friday

My soul is longing and yearning,
is yearning for the courts of the Lord. (Psalm 84:2)

My desires are the proof that my heart knows there is something beyond myself. My longings dislodge my heart from *me* and draw it towards the possibility of *you*.

❦ Saturday

The servants of the Lamb will worship him, they will see him face to face, and his name will be written on their foreheads. It will never be night again and they will not need lamplight or sunlight, because the Lord God will be shining on them. (Revelation 22:3–5)

It is the grace and gift of humility that we can never see your name upon our own foreheads, but we can see it clearly on each other's foreheads if we only take the time to look at each other with the eyes of love.

The week's readings

Monday	Revelation 14:1–5; Psalm 24(23); Luke 21:1–4
Tuesday	Revelation 14:14–19; Psalm 96(95); Luke 21:5–11
Wednesday	Revelation 15:1–4; Psalm 98(97); Luke 21:12–19
Thursday	Revelation 18:1–2, 21–3; 19:1–3, 9; Psalm 100(99), Luke 21:20–8
Friday	Revelation 20:1–4, 11 – 21:2; Psalm 84(83); Luke 21:29–33
Saturday	Revelation 22:1–7; Psalm 95(94); Luke 21:34–6

PART 4: ON THE SEVENTH DAY . . .

❦

Readings and reflections for the Sundays of the year

First Sunday of Advent

✠ Year A

He will wield authority over the nations
and adjudicate between many peoples;
these will hammer their swords into ploughshares,
their spears into sickles.
Nation will not lift sword against nation,
there will be no more training for war. (Isaiah 2:4–5)

Liz smiled wryly as she recalled her student days. She had been radical, even violent, in her demonstrations against the injustice of the system. There had been a time for wielding the sword of protest, she reflected, as she opened up the homeless shelter for the night, but now was the season for binding wounds, not for inflicting them.

✠ Year B

We have all withered like leaves
and our sins blew us away like the wind. (Isaiah 64:6)

Out in the garden the fallen leaves settle like a blanket over the withered grass. It looks as desolate as my own storm-swept heart so often feels, yet I know that this blanket of fallenness is covering and sheltering the unborn seeds of spring time.

✠ Year C

Jesus said to his disciples: 'There will be signs in the sun and moon and stars; on earth nations in agony, bewildered by the clamour of the ocean and its waves; men dying of fear as they await what menaces the world, for the powers of heaven will be shaken. And then they will see the Son of Man coming in a cloud with power and great glory.' (Luke 21:25–8)

In the beginning your Spirit hovered over the wild chaos of the unformed elements and brought forth all creation. So, now, your Spirit hovers over all our agony, our confusion, our bewilderment, our fear, bringing forth your new creation, until all is completed in your Son.

Readings

A Isaiah 2:1–5; Psalm 122(121); Romans 13:11–14; Matthew 24:37–44
B Isaiah 63:16–17; 64:1, 3–8; Psalm 80(79); 1 Corinthians 1:3–9; Mark 13:33–7
C Jeremiah 33:14–16; Psalm 25(24); 1 Thessalonians 3:12 – 4:2; Luke 21:25–8, 34–6

Second Sunday of Advent

Year A

The wolf lives with the lamb, the panther lies down with the kid,
calf and lion cub feed together with a little child to lead them . . .
They do no hurt, no harm, on all my holy mountain,
for the country is filled with the knowledge of the Lord
as the waters swell the sea. (Isaiah 11:6, 8–9)

For two minutes the whole nation was silent and still, honouring the memory of their recently assassinated leader. At the graveside of this man who had lived and died for peace, his former enemies stood alongside his most loyal supporters, while his grandchild spoke her simple words of love.

Year B

A voice cries in the wilderness:
Prepare a way for the Lord,
make his paths straight. (Mark 1:3)

In the good times, when my life's music is playing at top volume, I hear no voice except my own. But when I am lost and bewildered, a new voice breaks through into the wilderness of my heart, calling me to take just one next step along the path that leads me home.

Year C

'Every valley will be filled in,
every mountain and hill be laid low,
winding ways will be straightened
and rough roads made smooth.
And all mankind shall see the salvation of God.' (Luke 3:5–6)

When we come home to you, you will not look back and remind us of the years we have trudged up and down the hills and valleys of our griefs and joys. Nor will you reproach us for the detours we have followed, the signposts we have missed, the cul-de-sacs we have been trapped in. You will simply rejoice in our arrival and never let us be lost again.

Readings

A Isaiah 11:1–10; Psalm 72(71); Romans 15:4–9; Matthew 3:1–12
B Isaiah 40:1–5, 9–11; Psalm 85(84); 2 Peter 3:8–14; Mark 1:1–8
C Baruch 5:1–9; Psalm 126(125); Philippians 1:3–6, 8–11; Luke 3:1–6

Third Sunday of Advent

✠ Year A

John in his prison had heard what Christ was doing and he sent his disciples to ask him, 'Are you the one who is to come, or have we got to wait for someone else?' Jesus answered, 'Go back and tell John what you hear and see; the blind see again, and the lame walk, lepers are cleansed and the deaf hear, and the dead are raised to life and the Good News is proclaimed to the poor.' (Matthew 11:2–6)

When we see the life-giving power of your healing in our lives, we do not need to ask who you are.

✠ Year B

A man came, sent by God.
His name was John.
He came as a witness,
as a witness to speak for that Light
so that everyone might believe through him.
He was not the Light, only a witness to speak for the Light. (John 1:6–8)

We are not called to be lights ourselves, but to be the clear-glass panes through which your light might shine on others.

✠ Year C

'If anyone has two tunics he must share with the man who has none, and the one with something to eat must do the same.' (Luke 3:11)

The voice of the world says: multiply what you have;
the voice of the Lord says: divide what you have and share it with those who have not.
The voice of the world says: satisfy your hunger;
the voice of the Lord says: satisfy your neighbour's hunger.

Readings

A Isaiah 35:1–6, 10; Psalm 146(145); James 5:7–10; Matthew 11:2–11
B Isaiah 61:1–2, 10–11; Luke 1:46–50, 53–4; 1 Thessalonians 5:16–24; John 1:6–8, 19–28
C Zephaniah 3:14–18; Isaiah 12:2–6; Philippians 4:4–7; Luke 3:10–18

Fourth Sunday of Advent

❦ Year A

> *The maiden is with child and will soon give birth to a son whom she will call Immanuel, a name which means 'God-is-with-us'.* (Isaiah 7:14)

Nothing would ever be quite the same again when the baby was born. An entirely new and unpredictable stage of our lives had begun, which was to bring difficulties, decisions, heartaches and great joy. This new presence in our lives would, from this day forward, be with us in every moment, waking and sleeping, and would change our lives irreversibly. You, too, come silently into our hearts when the time is right, changing us at our roots. Once you have become God-with-us, we can never again be without you.

❦ Year B

> *'Know this, too: your kinswoman Elizabeth has, in her old age, herself conceived a son, and she whom people called barren is now in her sixth month, for nothing is impossible to God.'* (Luke 1:36–7)

The most barren places of our experience are often pregnant with our deepest truths, if we will only wait and watch, in patient trust, for their gestation.

❦ Year C

> *As soon as Elizabeth heard Mary's greeting, the child leapt in her womb and Elizabeth was filled with the Holy Spirit.* (Luke 1:41)

When two or more of us come together in your name, your still-unborn presence in each of us causes your still-unborn self in every other to leap for joy.

Readings

A Isaiah 7:10–14; Psalm 24(23); Romans 1:1–7; Matthew 1:18–25
B 2 Samuel 7:1–5, 8–11, 16; Psalm 89(88); Romans 16:25–7; Luke 1:26–38
C Micah 5:1–4; Psalm 80(79); Hebrews 10:5–10; Luke 1:39–44

The Feast of Christmas (25 December)

> *'Today in the town of David a saviour has been born to you; he is Christ the Lord. And here is a sign for you: you will find a baby wrapped in swaddling clothes and lying in a manger.'* (Luke 2:11–12)

We wrap our gifts in glittering paper and adorn them with ribbons, hoping to make what is really very ordinary look like something special. Your gift to us, your incarnate Word, comes barely wrapped at all. You give us that which is utterly special, but you wrap it in ordinariness, so that we won't be afraid to receive it.

The Feast of St Stephen (26 December)

> *Stephen, filled with the Holy Spirit, gazed into heaven and saw the glory of God, and Jesus standing at God's right hand. 'I can see heaven thrown open,' he said 'and the Son of Man standing at the right hand of God.' At this all the members of the Council shouted out and stopped their ears with their hands; then they all rushed at him, sent him out of the city and stoned him.* (Acts 7:55–8)

As I walked through the barracks of Auschwitz-Birkenau I felt that I was walking on holy ground. In that place there had been those who had joined their walk to death with yours. They had walked through the jaws of hell, and yet seen the gates of heaven.

For readings and reflections from 29 December onwards, see Part 2.

The Feast of St John **(27 December)**

> *Something which has existed since the beginning, that we have heard, and we have seen with our own eyes; that we have watched and touched with our hands: the Word, who is life – this is our subject.* (1 John 1:1)

He reached out to me in my distress, and my eyes met his. I saw the human friend, so completely familiar to me, but I saw, too, the mystery of the unknowable God, interpreted for me by his love.

The Feast of the Holy Innocents **(28 December)**

> *The angel of the Lord appeared to Joseph in a dream and said: 'Get up, take the child and his mother with you, and escape into Egypt, and stay there until I tell you, because Herod intends to search for the child and do away with him.'* (Matthew 2:13–14)

'Where's the baby Jesus?' little Paul asked his parents, his voice full of disbelief as he gazed at the crib in the church on Christmas morning. The day passed; dinner was over, the new games had been played, and evening came. The family watched the television news. '*There's* the baby Jesus!' exclaimed Paul with conviction, pointing to the pictures of a refugee family fleeing with their baby, the sound of gunfire at their heels.

Readings

25 December Isaiah 9:2–7; Psalm 96(95); Titus 2:11–14; Luke 2:1–14
26 December Acts 6:8–10; 7:54–9; Psalm 31(30); Matthew 10:17–22
27 December 1 John 1:1–4; Psalm 97(96); John 20:2–8
28 December 1 John 1:5 – 2:2; Psalm 124(123); Matthew 2:13–18

First Sunday after Christmas

> *Let the message of Christ, in all its richness, find a home with you.* (Colossians 3:16)

Tangled up in all the conflicting demands of our lives we forget that the richest treasure of all asks nothing more of us than a little space in our hearts where he may be at home.

1 January

> *As for Mary, she treasured all these things and pondered them in her heart.* (Luke 2:19)

I discover that I make my loudest noises about the things that matter least to me, and the things that touch my deepest levels are simply held in silence.

Epiphany (6 January)

> *Going into the house they saw the child with his mother Mary, and falling to their knees they did him homage. Then, opening their treasures, they offered him gifts of gold, frankincense and myrrh.* (Matthew 2:11)

Carol paused for a moment and rested her hand on the head of her small son sleeping in the little bed. As she did so, she remembered the day. There had been a shaft of gold, when his laughter had broken through the greyness of her anxiety. There had been a moment of true prayer, when he had held his breath in delight as a robin hopped across the window-sill. There had been a time of pain and its healing, as she had soothed his grazed knee and kissed away his tears. Gold for joy; incense for prayer; myrrh for healing. Gifts from a child. Gifts for a Child.

Second Sunday after Christmas

> *'No one has ever seen God;*
> *it is the only Son, who is nearest to the Father's heart,*
> *who has made him known.'* (John 1:18)

The closer we come to God's heart, in our living and in our prayer, the more vividly we shall make something of his nature known to those around us.

Sunday after Epiphany – Baptism of the Lord

> *I, the Lord, have called you to serve the cause of right;*
> *I have taken you by the hand and formed you;*
> *I have appointed you as covenant of the people and light of the nations.* (Isaiah 42:6)

You place us here, where our lives are lived, as a pledge and a promise to those around us that you are with your people. Will our lives break that promise and snuff out its light, or will they keep it and bring it to fulfilment?

Readings

First Sunday after Christmas	Ecclesiasticus 3:2–6, 12–14; Psalm 128(127); Colossians 3:12–21; Matthew 2:13–15, 19–23 (Year A); Luke 2:22–40 (Year B); Luke 2:41–52 (Year C)
1 January	Numbers 6:22–7; Psalm 67(66); Galatians 4:4–7; Luke 2:16–21
Second Sunday after Christmas	Sirach 24:1–4, 12–16; Psalm 147; Ephesians 1:3–6, 15–18; John 1:1–18
Epiphany	Isaiah 60:1–6; Psalm 72(71); Ephesians 3:2–3a, 5–6; Matthew 2:1–12
Baptism of the Lord	Isaiah 42:1–7; Psalm 29(28); Acts 10:34–8; Matthew 3:13–17 (Year A); Mark 1:7–11 (Year B); Luke 3:15–16, 21–2 (Year C)

First Sunday of Lent

❧ Year A

'Man does not live on bread alone,
but on every word that comes from the mouth of God.' (Matthew 4:4)

If I had to live only on what I can see and touch, what would I do for light, for warmth, for air or for power? What would I do for love?

❧ Year B

The Spirit drove Jesus out into the wilderness and he remained there for forty days, and was tempted by Satan. He was with the wild beasts, and the angels looked after him. (Mark 1:12–13)

Coming closer to you will expose the worst in ourselves and in each other. Will our hearts, at their limits, break down in fear or expand into a new level of trust?

❧ Year C

The word, that is the faith we proclaim, is very near to you, it is on your lips and in your heart. (Romans 10:8)

At the end of all our searching, and at the destination of all our journeying, we find you waiting for us where we first began – in the deepest stirrings of our own hearts. That is where we hear you say: 'The kingdom is very near to you . . .'

Readings

A Genesis 2:7–9; 3:1–7; Psalm 51(50); Romans 5:12–19; Matthew 4:1–11
B Genesis 9:8–15; Psalm 25(24); 1 Peter 3:18–22; Mark 1:12–15
C Deuteronomy 26:4–10; Psalm 91(90); Romans 10:8–13; Luke 4:1–13

Second Sunday in Lent

Year A

Peter spoke to Jesus: 'Lord', he said, 'it is wonderful for us to be here; if you wish, I will make three tents here, one for you, one for Moses and one for Elijah.' He was still speaking when suddenly a bright cloud covered them with a shadow, and from the cloud there came a voice which said: 'This is my Son, the Beloved; he enjoys my favour. Listen to him!' (Matthew 17:4–5)

There are wonderful moments in prayer when your presence embraces us with its power and its joy. Yet as soon as we try to capture and hold on to such moments, we lose them, because we have switched our focus away from your reality, to the lesser reality of our own needs and longings.

Year B

Because you have done this, because you have not refused me your son, your only son, I will shower blessings on you; I will make your descendants as many as the stars of heaven and the grains of sand on the seashore. (Genesis 22:16–17)

If I can let go of my dependency on what I most long to cling to, then my hands and heart will be free to receive an abundance of your blessing beyond my wildest dreams.

Year C

Jesus took with him Peter and John and James and went up the mountain to pray. As he prayed, the aspect of his face was changed and his clothing became brilliant as lightning. (Luke 9:28)

I watched as two people walked across the station forecourt. One was a tall, strong young man. He had his arm round the shoulder of his companion, who was stooped, frail in mind and body, chattering meaninglessly, and ageless in his suffering. As they passed me, I noticed a kind of clarity and openness in the face of the younger man. He was walking slowly, matching his pace to that of his companion. There was no sign of impatience in his face, or reluctance in his sheltering arm. He was listening to him intently, as if to a guru. They reached the escalator, and carefully descended, out of my sight. I shook myself, inwardly, and I knew that Christ had crossed my path, and that I had seen his radiance in a city station.

Readings

A Genesis 12:1–4a; Psalm 33(32); 2 Timothy 1:8–10; Matthew 17:1–9
B Genesis 22:1–2, 9–13, 15–18; Psalm 116(115); Romans 8:31–4; Mark 9:2–10
C Genesis 15:5–12, 17–18; Psalm 27(26); Philippians 3:17 – 4:1; Luke 9:28–36

Third Sunday of Lent

❧ Year A

The Lord said to Moses, 'Take with you some of the elders of Israel and move on to the forefront of the people; take in your hand the staff with which you struck the river, and go. I shall be standing with you there on the rock, at Horeb. You must strike the rock, and water will flow from it for the people to drink. (Exodus 17:5–6)

The rock face of my most intractable difficulties can become the source of your healing, life-giving stream, but only if I can stand squarely in front of it and claim its riches.

❧ Year B

Making a whip out of some cord, Jesus drove them all out of the Temple, cattle and sheep as well, scattered the money changers' coins, knocked their tables over and said to the pigeon-sellers, 'Take all this out of here and stop turning my Father's house into a market!' (John 2:14–16)

I have mortgaged my heart to the world's passing satisfactions and securities, and I can't keep up the repayments. Lord, please repossess me!

❧ Year C

God called to him from the middle of the bush, 'Moses, Moses!' he said. 'Here I am' he answered. 'Come no nearer,' he said. 'Take off your shoes, for the place on which you stand is holy ground.' (Exodus 3:4–5)

When heart speaks to heart, go barefoot and respect the sacred space that lies open and revealed between you. For you stand on holy ground.

Readings

A Exodus 17:3–7; Psalm 95(94); Romans 5:1–2, 5–8; John 4:5–42

B Exodus 20:1–17; Psalm 19(18); 1 Corinthians 1:22–5; John 2:13–25

C Exodus 3:1–8, 13–15; Psalm 103(102); 1 Corinthians 10:1–6, 10–12; Luke 13:1–9

Fourth Sunday of Lent

☙ Year A

Surely goodness and kindness shall follow me all the days of my life. (Psalm 23:6)

The insurance assessor was unexpectedly generous and considerate. The girl at the check-out helped me pack the shopping, and a friendly driver let me out of the side road into the flow of traffic. *Your* goodness and kindness in *theirs*, like a gold thread running through my day.

☙ Year B

For God sent his Son into the world
not to condemn the world,
but so that through him the world might be saved. (John 3:17)

Your Son, the Word from whom we are created, is not a word of accusation or a sentence of death, but an invitation into Life and re-creation

☙ Year C

And for anyone who is in Christ, there is a new creation; the old creation has gone, and now the new one is here. (2 Corinthians 5:17–18)

Peter's hobby is wood-turning. He can pick up a piece of rough timber from the wood yard and know with his fingertips the new thing that his skill can draw out of it. He has a vision of the grain and the colour and the shape that only his heart's eyes can see, as he clamps the block to the lathe. Would that he could realise that what he does for the wood, you are doing for him.

Readings

A 1 Samuel 16:1, 6–7, 10–13; Psalm 23(22); Ephesians 5:8–14; John 9:1–41

B 2 Chronicles 36:14–16, 19–23; Psalm 137(136); Ephesians 2:4–10; John 3:14–21

C Joshua 5:9–12; Psalm 34(33); 2 Corinthians 5:17–21; Luke 15:1–3, 11–32

Fifth Sunday of Lent

❦ Year A

> *Jesus cried in a loud voice: 'Lazarus, here! Come out!' The dead man came out, his feet and hands bound with bands of stuff and a cloth round his face. Jesus said to them: 'Unbind him, let him go free.'* (John 11:43–4)

Jo was seldom out of prison for more than a few months at a time. The magistrates got used to his continual reappearances for minor offences. The truth was that he found captivity a safer and more comfortable state of life than freedom, and no one could free him from his reluctance to free himself.

❦ Year B

> *Deep within them I will plant my Law, writing it on their hearts. Then I will be their God and they shall be my people.* (Jeremiah 31:33)

As long as your Word remains locked in the pages of our Bibles and hymn-books, we can get on with our lives in our own way, undisturbed. But when it takes root in our hearts, it becomes a living seed, growing us into your new creation.

❦ Year C

> *He looked up and said 'Woman, where are they? Has no one condemned you?' 'No one sir,' she replied. 'Neither do I condemn you,' said Jesus. 'Go away and don't sin any more.'* (John 8:10–11)

After you had sent them all away, we stood there alone, face to face. My accusers had no more power over me. Only one thing remained to obstruct the healing flow of your forgiveness: my obstinate reluctance to forgive myself and to redirect my gaze away from me and towards you, my healer.

Readings

A Ezekiel 37:12–14; Psalm 130(129); Romans 8:8–11; John 11:1–45
B Jeremiah 31:31–4; Psalm 51(50); Hebrews 5:7–9; John 12:20–33
C Isaiah 43:16–21; Psalm 126(125); Philippians 3:8–14; John 8:1–11

The Feast of Easter

> *'They have taken the Lord out of the tomb,' she said, 'and we don't know where they have put him.'* (John 20:2)

We search for you, like orphaned children. But you are not where we had placed you. All we can find is the space in which we had tried to contain you. 'You are looking for me in places of death,' you tell us. 'But I am Life. The Life you can never contain within a fixed idea.'

> *Then Peter and the other disciple went to the tomb. The two of them were running, but the other disciple ran faster than Peter and reached the tomb first. He bent over and saw the linen wrappings, but he did not go in. Behind him came Simon Peter, and he went straight into the tomb. He saw the linen wrappings lying there and the cloth which had been round Jesus' head. It was not lying with the linen wrappings but was rolled up by itself. Then the other disciple, who had reached the tomb first, also went in; he saw, and he believed.* (John 20:8)

Our world seems like a dark tomb too, Lord, and all we can find of you are the wrappings and the trappings of how you might have been.

Yet . . . **We have seen!**

We have seen your resurrection *energy* in a teenager paralysed in a road accident, who perseveres her way back to mobility.

We have seen your resurrection *strength* in the companion who stays alongside us through our darkest hours and carries the hope for us, when our own resources fail.

We have seen your resurrection *joy* in a child's delight over the first bluebells of spring.

We have seen your resurrection *hope* in the amazing ability of our earth to regenerate life year after year in spite of our negligence.

We have seen your resurrection *love* in the eyes of the friend who bothers to reach into our dark tomb with a gleam of caring and understanding.

Lord, we see, and we believe!

May we become, ourselves, the carriers of your resurrection light into our world's darkness.

Readings

Acts 10:34, 37–43; Psalm 118(117); Colossians 3:1–4; John 20:1–9

Second Sunday of Easter

Year A

This day was made by the Lord,
we rejoice and are glad! (Psalm 118:24)

It was the worst day Jim had ever experienced. Every hour had pitched him more deeply into despair. Nothing and nobody seemed to be on his side. At bedtime his little daughter came to say Goodnight, her eyes sad and uncomprehending. Something in her gaze opened the floodgates of his grief. The tears rose. He held the child close. She had torn aside the veil of darkness and he had caught a glimpse of starlight. It had become, after all, a day with a crack in it, through which God's love might find entrance.

Year B

The doors were closed, but Jesus came in and stood among them. 'Peace be with you,' he said. Then he spoke to Thomas, 'Put your finger here; look, here are my hands. Give me your hand; put it into my side. Doubt no longer, but believe.' (John 20:19–20, 27–8)

I remember closed doors along my own life's journey, and I remember moments when you were suddenly there, in spite of all my defences; moments when you took my hand and brought me face to face with my wounded Healer and left me no more room for doubt.

Year C

After saying this he breathed on them and said: 'Receive the Holy Spirit. For those whose sins you forgive, they are forgiven; for those whose sins you retain, they are retained.' (John 20:22–3)

It was like climbing a rock-face, trying to earn her forgiveness and her trust. And every time he reached the top, she pushed him off again, reminding him of how he had betrayed her. She held the keys of his heaven or his hell in her hands, and she chose to keep him captive in her unforgiveness.

Readings

A Acts 2:42–7; Psalm 118(117); 1 Peter 1:3–9; John 20:19–31

B Acts 4:32–5; Psalm 118(117); John 5:1–6; John 20:19–31

C Acts 5:12–16; Psalm 118(117):2–4, 22–7; Revelation 1:9–13, 17–19; John 20:19–31

Third Sunday of Easter

✠ Year A

> *Now while he was with them at table, he took the bread and said the blessing; then he broke it and handed it to them. And their eyes were opened and they recognised him; but he had vanished from their sight. Then they said to each other, 'Did not our hearts burn within us as he talked to us on the road and explained the scriptures to us?'* (Luke 24:30–2)

Amid all our blind wandering and searching, there are moments of vision and clarity when we know that we have met you along the roads of our lives. The flame that you kindle in our hearts in such moments becomes the beacon which leads us onwards.

✠ Year B

> *The disciples told their story of what had happened on the road and how they had recognised Jesus at the breaking of bread. They were still talking about all this when Jesus himself stood among them.* (Luke 24:35–6)

When we share our journeys in faith, trustfully, with each other, then we shall meet you, standing among us.

✠ Year C

> *It was light by now and there stood Jesus on the shore, though the disciples did not realise that it was Jesus. Jesus called out, 'Have you caught anything, friends?' And when they answered, 'No', he said, 'Throw the net out to starboard and you'll find something.' So they dropped the net, and there were so many fish that they could not haul it in.'* (John 21:4–6)

My nets seem to be empty for most of the time. Perhaps it's because I think I know so much better than you do how to manage my life, and because of my reluctance to believe in the possibility of a miracle to starboard.

Readings

A Acts 2:14, 22–8; Psalm 16(15); 1 Peter 1:17–21; Luke 24:13–35
B Acts 3:13–15, 17–19; Psalm 4; 1 John 2:1–5; Luke 24:35–48
C Acts 5:27–32, 40–1; Psalm 30(29); Revelation 5:11–14; John 21:1–19

Fourth Sunday of Easter

❦ Year A

'I have come so that they may have life
and have it to the full.' (John 10:10)

Twenty years ago the doctors had advised a termination. Jean and Gary gripped each other's hand as they remembered how their damaged little daughter had grown to her fullness. That growth had been wrenched out of heartbreaking hard work, but it had become a fullness for her, and for them, beyond anything they could have imagined.

❦ Year B

'I am the good shepherd; I know my own and my own know me.' (John 10:14)

I learn to know your voice, Lord, by listening to your Word within my heart. The voice of a friend who speaks into my silence. The sound of a silence that stills all my striving.

❦ Year C

'The sheep that belong to me listen to my voice;
I know them and they follow me.' (John 10:27)

Sometimes I *know* I am travelling in the right direction, however foggy the day. Those are the times when the compass of my journey exactly aligns with the true north which is planted in my soul, and when the echo of my life unmistakably recognises the voice which first gave rise to it.

Readings

A Acts 2:14, 36–41; Psalm 23(22); 1 Peter 2:20–5; John 10:1–10
B Acts 4:8–12; Psalm 118(117); 1 John 3:1–2; John 10:11–18
C Acts 13:14, 43–52; Psalm 100(99); Revelation 7:9, 14–17; John 10:27–30

Fifth Sunday of Easter

❦ Year A

The Lord is the living stone,
rejected by men but chosen by God and precious to him;
set yourselves close to him. (1 Peter 2:6)

You resisted the temptation to leap in glory from the pinnacle of the Temple; instead you consented to become its living foundation stone, to be either carelessly walked over, or trustfully built upon.

❦ Year B

'Make your home in me, as I make mine in you.' (John 15:3)

My home in you: the place where I belong, where I am safe, where I can be completely true to myself.
Your home in me: my heart, where you are the owner and the occupier, the source of all my desire and its final fulfilment.

❦ Year C

'I give you a new commandment: love one another; just as I have loved you, you also must love one another. By this love you have for one another, everyone will know that you are my disciples.' (John 13:34)

He doesn't ask us to counsel or instruct each other, to guide or to direct or solve each other's problems. He asks us only to receive each other with the open arms of love, and leave the rest to him.

Readings

A Acts 6:1–7; Psalm 33(32); 1 Peter 2:4–9; John 14:1–12
B Acts 9:26–31; Psalm 22(21); 1 John 3:18–24; John 15:1–8
C Acts 14:21–7; Psalm 145(144); Revelation 21:1–5; John 13:31–5

Sixth Sunday of Easter

✠ Year A

'I will not leave you orphans . . .
On that day
you will understand that I am in my Father
and you in me and I in you.' (John 14:18, 20)

In time and space we may feel far apart and very alone, but in the eternal reality of All-that-Is, we are one in you and one with each other

✠ Year B

'I have told you this so that my own joy may be in you and your joy may be complete.' (John 15:11)

When your Spirit flows through our hearts it transforms our anguish into peace and our mere happiness into joy.

✠ Year C

'The Holy Spirit whom the Father will send in my name will teach you everything and remind you of all I have said to you.' (John 14:26)

When you shed your light back over the landmarks of our journeys, reminding us of those sacred moments when we have been touched by your love, then we know that we are feeling the breath of your Spirit.

Readings

A Acts 8:5–8, 14–17; Psalm 66(65); 1 Peter 3:15–18; John 14:15–21
B Acts 10:25–6, 34–5, 44–8; Psalm 98(97); 1 John 4:7–10; John 15:9–17
C Acts 15:1–2, 22–9; Psalm 67(66); Revelation 21:10–14, 22–3; John 14:23–9

Seventh Sunday of Easter

❦ Year A

> *When they reached the city they went to an upper room, where they were staying . . . All joined in continuous prayer, together with several women, including Mary the mother of Jesus, and with his brothers.* (Acts 1:13–14)

And still, as the earth spins from dawn to dusk, from east to west, the never-ceasing prayer of those who seek you forms an unbroken chain of faith, encircling all creation with your love.

❦ Year B

> *No one has ever seen God;*
> *but as long as we love one another*
> *God will live in us*
> *and his love will be complete in us.* (1 John 4:12)

God becomes visible wherever love flows between us, and when love finally flows freely among us all, then God's love will be completed in us, his creation.

❦ Year C

> *Let all who are thirsty come; all who want it may have the water of life, and have it free.* (Revelation 22:17)

Water, source of life, without droughts or standpipes, without bills and without shareholders. The only qualification for receiving it is to want it.

Readings

A Acts 1:12–14; Psalm 27(26); 1 Peter 4:13–16; John 17:1–11
B Acts 1:15–17, 20–6; Psalm 103(102); 1 John 4:11–16; John 17:11–19
C Acts 7:55–60; Psalm 97(96); Revelation 22:12–14, 16–17, 20; John 17:20–6

Annunciation (*25 March*)

'I am the handmaid of the Lord,' said Mary, 'let what you have said be done to me.' (Luke 1:38)

Our response to the call of your love is not made only for ourselves, but for all creation. It matters how we choose. Our 'Yes' counts.

Readings
Isaiah 7:10–14; Psalm 40(39); Hebrews 10:4–10; Luke 1:26–38

Ascension Day

'And know that I am with you always, yes, to the end of time.' (Matthew 28:20)

With us always . . . even then, when we are walking away from you . . .
Especially then, when we are sure we can manage without you . . .
And precisely then, when we feel you have given up on us . . .
With us always, and closer to us than we are to ourselves.

Readings
Acts 1:1–11; Psalm 47(46); Ephesians 1:17–23;
Matthew 28:16–20 (Year A); Mark 16:15–20 (Year B); Luke 24:46–53 (Year C)

Pentecost Sunday

Something appeared to them that seemed like tongues of fire; these separated and came to rest on the head of each of them. They were all filled with the Holy Spirit. (Acts 2:3–4)

The flame of your Spirit is divided, to dwell in each believing heart, but in its division it is not diminished, but multiplied, so that the whole of your creation might catch your light and your fire.

Readings
Acts 2:1–11; Psalm 104(103); 1 Corinthians 12:3–7, 12–13; John 20:19–23

❦ *Trinity Sunday*

> *The grace of the Lord Jesus Christ, the love of God and the fellowship of the Holy Spirit be with you all.* (2 Corinthians 13:13)

Your trinity of communion and love encircles all we do and all we are. We are truly ourselves only when we are truly joined with one another by that circle of love, grace and fellowship.

Readings

A Exodus 34:4–6, 8–9; Daniel 3:52–6; 2 Corinthians 13:11–13; John 3:16–18

B Deuteronomy 4:32–4, 39–40; Psalm 33(32); Romans 8:14–17; Matthew 28:16–20

C Proverbs 8:22–31; Psalm 8; Romans 5:1–5; John 16:12–15

❦ *Transfiguration* *(6 August)*

> *There in their presence he was transfigured: his face shone like the sun and his clothes became as white as light.* (Matthew 17:2)

When the thick layers of our self-defence and self-importance fall away, then at last the flickering flame of faith in our hearts will shine free, transfiguring us into the carriers of your radiant love.

Readings

Daniel 7:9–10, 13–14; Psalm 97(96); 2 Peter 1:16–19
Matthew 17:1–9 (Year A); Mark 9:2–10 (Year B); Luke 9:28–36 (Year C)

❦ *All Saints* *(1 November)*

> *These are the people who have been through the great persecution and they have washed their robes white again in the blood of the lamb.* (Revelation 7:14)

Your saints, Lord, are not those who have never failed and fallen, but those who have had the honesty and courage to face their fallenness and admit their need of you, and to let your love cleanse them.

Readings

Revelation 7:2–4, 9–14; Psalm 24(23); 1 John 3:1–3; Matthew 5:1–12

Second Sunday of Ordinary Time

❦ Year A

> *Seeing Jesus coming towards him, John said, 'Look, there is the lamb of God that takes away the sin of the world.'* (John 1:29)

What a joy to discover something of the nature of God in his creation, or in music, or our work or in our human loves. But how much greater the joy in following these signposts to the destination towards which they point us.

❦ Year B

> *The Lord then came and stood by, calling as he had done before, 'Samuel! Samuel!' Samuel answered: 'Speak, Lord, your servant is listening.'* (1 Samuel 3:10)

Prayer does not flow from our lips and our minds, but from the response of our listening hearts.

❦ Year C

> *There were six stone water jars standing there, meant for the ablutions that are customary among the Jews: each could hold twenty or thirty gallons. Jesus said to the servants, 'Fill the jars with water,' and they filled them to the brim. 'Draw some out now,' he told them, 'and take it to the steward.' They did this; the steward tasted the water and it had turned into wine.* (John 2:6–9)

We believe, because it is your promise, that you will transform the water of our living and loving into the wine of your Life and Love. But the miracle is only recognised when we are poured out for others. If our wine stays in the closed jars of our hearts, it might as well be water.

Readings

A Isaiah 49:3, 5–6; Psalm 40(39); 1 Corinthians 1:1–3; John 1:29–34

B 1 Samuel 3:3–10, 19; Psalm 40(39); 1 Corinthians 6:13–15, 17–20; John 1:35–42

C Isaiah 62:1–5; Psalm 96(95); 1 Corinthians 12:4–11; John 2:1–12

Third Sunday of Ordinary Time

❧ Year A

The people that walked in darkness
has seen a great light;
on those who live in a land of deep shadow
a light has shone. (Isaiah 9:1)

When I turn my back on the Light of my life, I see only the darkness of my own shadow; but I only need to turn, and the shadow will be behind me.

❧ Year B

Remember your mercy, Lord,
and the love you have shown from of old.
In your love remember me,
because of your goodness, O Lord. (Psalm 25:5–6)

Re-member me, Lord. Re-make my dismembered heart into the image of your own. Draw my brokenness back into your wholeness.

❧ Year C

It is precisely the parts of the body that seem to be the weakest which are the indispensable ones. (1 Corinthians 12:22)

You have protected our vital organs with the strength of our bones, our flesh and our skin. Let us protect the apparently weaker members of our communities just as lovingly, and, in this way, allow their unique and vital truth, beauty and meaning to be realised.

Readings

A Isaiah 8:23 – 9:3; Psalm 27(26); 1 Corinthians 1:10–13, 17; Matthew 4:12–23
B Jonah 3:1–5, 10; Psalm 25(24); 1 Corinthians 7:29–31; Mark 1:14–20
C Nehemiah 8:2–6, 8–10; Psalm 19(18); 1 Corinthians 12:12–30; Luke 1:1–4; 4:14–21

Fourth Sunday of Ordinary Time

⁂ Year A

'How happy are the poor in spirit;
theirs is the kingdom of heaven.' (Matthew 5:3)

Susie watched delightedly as the soap bubbles rose into the air. When she tried to clasp and possess them with her small, eager hands, they burst and vanished. But when she made no claim on them and let them float freely, they reflected all the colours of the rainbow back into her shining eyes.

⁂ Year B

O that today you would listen to his voice!
Harden not your hearts. (Psalm 95:7)

The thicker the shell of my defences, the harder it will be for me to hear the call of your love, and the longer it will take for the chick of my truest being to hatch.

⁂ Year C

Now we are seeing a dim reflection in a mirror; but then we shall be seeing face to face. The knowledge that I have now is imperfect; but then I shall know as fully as I am known. (1 Corinthians 13:12–13)

Whatever we do, we can never see ourselves as we really are; the most that we can see is our mirror image, and our mirrors, made by ourselves and for ourselves, are distorted by our own illusions. But when we see you face to face, all intervening masks and mirrors will be removed. Then we will understand what it means to be loved perfectly in all our imperfection.

Readings

A Zephaniah 2:3; 3:12–13; Psalm 146(145); 1 Corinthians 1:26–31; Matthew 5:1–12

B Deutenomy 18:15–20; Psalm 95(94); 1 Corinthians 7:32–5; Mark 1:21–8

C Jeremiah 1:4–5, 17–19; Psalm 71(70); 1 Corinthians 12:31 – 13:13; Luke 4:21–30

Fifth Sunday of Ordinary Time

✠ Year A

> *'You are the salt of the earth. But if the salt becomes tasteless, what can make it salty again? It is good for nothing, and can only be thrown out to be trampled underfoot by men.'* (Matthew 5:13)

The salt of our earth comes in fine silver salt cellars, for the seasoning of our food; but it also comes in bins at the roadside, for the thawing of snow and ice. We are called to awake in those around us the appetite for God, and to melt away the barriers that hold them back.

✠ Year B

> *Lying in bed I wonder, 'When will it be day?'*
> *Risen I think, 'How slowly evening comes!'*
> *Restlessly I fret till twilight falls.* (Job 7:4)

My thoughts and fears stretch me out into an unknown tomorrow, and I live my life in the tension of a taut elastic band unless I can let go my hold and relax into the peace that only the present moment can ever offer.

✠ Year C

> *Then I heard the voice of the Lord saying:*
> *'Whom shall I send? Who will be our messenger?'*
> *I answered, 'Here I am, send me.'* (Isaiah 6:8)

Have you sent me, Lord? Or have I sent myself? Did I arrive here because I listened to you, or because I thought I could arrange my life better on my own? Am I carrying your message, or am I transmitting my own?

Readings

A Isaiah 58:7–10; Psalm 112(111); 1 Corinthians 2:1–5; Matthew 5:13–16
B Job 7:1–4, 6–7; Psalm 147(146); 1 Corinthians 9:16–19; 22–3; Mark 1:29–39
C Isaiah 6:1–8; Psalm 138(137); 1 Corinthians 15:1–11; Luke 5:1–11

Sixth Sunday of Ordinary Time

❧ Year A

If you wish, you can keep the commandments,
to behave faithfully is within your power.
He has set fire and water before you;
put out your hand to whichever you prefer.
Man has life and death before him;
whichever a man likes better will be given him. (Ecclesiasticus 15:15–18)

In every moment, every decision, every action and reaction, the choice continues, between that which tends to death and that which leads to life, and my habitual choices are making me what I shall ultimately become.

❧ Year B

Whatever you eat, whatever you drink, whatever you do at all, do it for the glory of God. (1 Corinthians 10:31)

Jane had always placed an extra chair at the table to remind her family of Jesus, 'the unseen guest at every meal'. Years later, in her final hours, she smiled across towards the empty chair beside her hospital bed, and the nurses noticed her face become radiant with a beauty not her own as she closed her eyes in death.

❧ Year C

A blessing on the man who puts his trust in the Lord, with the Lord for his hope.
He is like a tree by the waterside that thrusts its roots to the stream:
When the heat comes it feels no alarm, its foliage stays green;
it has no worries in a year of drought, and never ceases to bear fruit. (Jeremiah 17:7–8)

What feels like an aching, unfulfilled desire is just the growing pain of our own deepest roots, penetrating the dark soil of our experience to find the water of their life in you. The deeper the root-darkness, the greener the foliage, and the more life-giving the fruit.

Readings

A Ecclesiasticus 15:15–20; Psalm 119(118); 1 Corinthians 2:6–10; Matthew 5:17–37
B Leviticus 13:1–2, 45–6; Psalm 32(31); 1 Corinthians 10:31 – 11:1; Mark 1:40–5
C Jeremiah 17:5–8; Psalm 1; 1 Corinthians 15:12, 16–20; Luke 6:17, 20–6

Seventh Sunday of Ordinary Time

✠ Year A

> *Didn't you realise that you were God's temple and that the Spirit of God was living among you? If anybody should destroy the temple of God, God will destroy him, because the temple of God is sacred and you are that temple.* (1 Corinthians 3:16–17)

Christine had angel's hands, the doctors used to say. No one knew quite why she was so much finer a nurse than her colleagues. They all treated their charges as fellow human beings. Except Christine. She handled every patient as if she were touching God.

✠ Year B

> *I am making a road in the wilderness,*
> *paths in the wilds.*
> *The people I have formed for myself*
> *will sing my praises.* (Isaiah 43:19, 21)

We may have to lose our own sense of direction before we can discover your guiding, Lord. You are composing the music of our heart's song in the wilderness of our experience.

✠ Year C

> *Jesus said to his disciples: 'But I say this to you who are listening: love your enemies, do good to those who hate you, bless those who curse you, pray for those who treat you badly.'* (Luke 6:27)

'Lord, that I might love you,' I prayed.
'You will come to love me', you answered, 'when you come to love the person who has caused you the most pain in your life.'

Readings

A Leviticus 19:1–2, 17–18; Psalm 103(102); 1 Corinthians 3:16–23; Matthew 5:38–48

B Isaiah 43:18–19, 21–2, 24–5; Psalm 41(40); 2 Corinthians 1:18–22; Mark 2:1–12

C 1 Samuel 26:2, 7–9, 12–13, 22–3; Psalm 103(102); 1 Corinthians 15:45–9; Luke 6:27–38

Eighth Sunday of Ordinary Time

❦ Year A

In God alone is my soul at rest . . .
he alone is my rock, my stronghold
my fortress: I stand firm. (Psalm 62:1–2)

Sometimes it is in the still centre where we are immobilised by weakness that we find God. Sometimes it is on the hard rock of failure that we find our strength in him.

❦ Year B

Unlike other people, we need no letter of recommendation, either to you or from you, because you are yourselves our letter, written in our hearts, that anybody can see and read, and it is plain that you are a letter from Christ . . . written on the tablets of your living hearts. (2 Corinthians 3:1–3)

We come to our brothers and sisters as personally signed letters of the Lord, bringing them his love and his invitation. When they read our eyes and our hearts what message will they find? Will they read his love there, or will it be wrapped up in too many envelopes of our own making?

❦ Year C

It is good to proclaim your love in the morning
and your truth in the watches of the night. (Psalm 92:1–2)

As long as the earth spins, gentle hands will wake the child from his sleep, strong arms will lift the burden from a neighbour's shoulders, warm words will soothe the friend in distress, and a loving smile will fall like a blessing upon the sleepless. Your hands, your arms, your words, your smile, Lord, in ours.

Readings

A Isaiah 49:14–15; Psalm 62(61); 1 Corinthians 4:1–5; Matthew 6:24–34
B Hosea 2:16–17, 21–2; Psalm 103(102); 2 Corinthians 3:1–6; Mark 2:18–22
C Ecclesiasticus 27:4–7; Psalm 92(91); 1 Corinthians 15:54–8; Luke 6:39–45

Ninth Sunday of Ordinary Time

❦ Year A

> *Moses said to the people: 'Let these words of mine remain in your heart and in your soul; fasten them on your hands as a sign and on your forehead as a circlet.'* (Deuteronomy 11:18)

The Word you speak to our hearts, Lord, must be translated into every deed of our hands and every thought in our minds.

❦ Year B

> *He went again into the synagogue and there was a man there who had a withered hand . . . He said to the man, 'Stretch out your hand.' He stretched it out and his hand was better.* (Mark 3:1, 5)

As long as we sit nursing our brokenness, nothing will change, but when we stretch it out to you the way to wholeness will be opened up.

❦ Year C

> *From Paul, an apostle who does not owe his authority to men or his appointment to any human being, but who has been appointed by Jesus Christ and by God the Father who raised Jesus from the dead.* (Galatians 1:1–2)

The only authority that any of us can claim with integrity is that granted to us by the author of our being.

Readings

A Deuteronomy 11:18, 26–8; Psalm 31(30); Romans 3:21–5, 28; Matthew 7:21–7
B Deuteronomy 5:12–15, Psalm 81(80); 2 Corinthians 4:6–11; Mark 2:23 – 3:6
C 1 Kings 8:41–3; Psalm 117(116); Galatians 1:1–2, 6–10; Luke 7:1–10

Tenth Sunday of Ordinary Time

Year A

He will come to us as showers come,
like spring rains watering the earth. (Hosea 6:3)

Through all the clamour of my spoken prayers and pleadings, Lord, how easily I forget that underneath it all you are constantly nourishing those longings that my heart cannot speak, nor my words express.

Year B

The Lord God called to the man: 'Where are you?' he asked. 'I heard the sound of you in the garden,' he replied. 'I was afraid because I was naked, so I hid.' (Genesis 3:9–11)

The first sin, and perhaps the only sin, is to alienate ourselves from you, and hide from your presence. To sin is to separate ourselves from you, our living source.

Year C

Jesus went to a town called Nain . . . When he was near the gate of the town it happened that a dead man was being carried out for burial, the only son of his mother, and she was a widow . . . When the Lord saw her he felt sorry for her. 'Do not cry,' he said. Then he went up and put his hand on the bier and the bearers stood still, and he said: 'Young man, I tell you to get up.' And the dead man sat up and began to talk, and Jesus gave him to his mother. (Luke 7:11–16)

Resurrection begins with compassion. We may not be able to raise each other to new life, but we can reach out to each other with that first step of compassion. A first step on the road that leads to eternal life.

Readings

A Hosea 6:3–6, Psalm 50(49); Romans 4:18–25; Matthew 9:9–13
B Genesis 3:9–15; Psalm 130(129); 2 Corinthians 4:13 – 5:1; Mark 3:20–35
C 1 Kings 17:17–24; Psalm 30(29); Galatians 1:11–19; Luke 7:11–17

Eleventh Sunday of Ordinary Time

❦ Year A

> *'Cure the sick, raise the dead, cleanse the lepers, cast out devils. You received without charge, give without charge.'* (Matthew 10:8)

A gentle touch on a fevered forehead.
A warm greeting to raise dead spirits back to hope.
An embrace of acceptance for the unlovely.
A word of affirmation to cast out fear.
All freely given, and asking nothing more of us but that we freely pass them on.

❦ Year B

> *Jesus said: 'This is what the kingdom of God is like. A man throws seed on the land. Night and day, while he sleeps, when he is awake, the seed is sprouting and growing; how, he does not know.'* (Mark 4:26–8)

The seed of your kingdom lives and grows more freely in the heart of a sleeping child, than in all the collected works of the world's theologians. Let us not ask to know how. Let us simply be the soil for your seeding.

❦ Year C

> *Jesus said [to Simon the Pharisee]: 'There was once a creditor who had two men in his debt; one owed him five hundred denarii, the other fifty. They were unable to pay, so he pardoned them both. Which of them will love him more?' 'The one who was pardoned more, I suppose,' answered Simon. Jesus said, 'You are right.'* (Luke 7:40–3)

My most dearly loved friends are those who have been with me in the painful, shameful moments of my life. They have known my worst and given me of their best. My love for them is my response to that giving and forgiving.

Readings

A Exodus 19:2–6; Psalm 100(99); Romans 5:6–11; Matthew 9:36; 10:8
B Ezekiel 17:22–4; Psalm 92(91); 2 Corinthians 5:6–10; Mark 4:26–34
C 2 Samuel 12:7–10, 13; Psalm 32(31); Galatians 2:16, 19–21; Luke 7:36 – 8:3

Twelfth Sunday of Ordinary Time

❦ Year A

> *'Why, every hair on your head has been counted. So there is no need to be afraid.'* (Matthew 10:31)

Joan held her newborn daughter in her arms, stroking each toe and finger and caressing the tiny eyebrows with a love that would spend itself gladly in the years to come for the one who had come to birth. Do you not hold us, too, in tenderness, Lord, and spend yourself in love for us? You, who are the source and wellspring of all our loving.

❦ Year B

> *It began to blow a gale and the waves were breaking into the boat so that it was almost swamped. But Jesus was in the stern, his head on the cushion, asleep.* (Mark 4:37–9)

The deepest part of us, that dwells in you, remains at peace whatever storms are raging in our lives. Help us, Lord, to find that deep centre of stillness in you where we draw the strength and the courage to master our storms.

❦ Year C

> *One day when Jesus was praying alone in the presence of his disciples he put this question to them, 'Who do the crowds say I am?' And they answered, 'John the Baptist; others Elijah; and others say one of the ancient prophets come back to life.' 'But you,' he said, 'Who do you say I am?'* (Luke 9:18–20)

My life unfolds itself like a play on a stage. Sometimes I think I can see you in some of the characters and plot, and feel your absence in other parts. I might even try to name your parts in my life's drama. But who are you *really*? You are the play. You are the playwright.

Readings

A Jeremiah 20:10–13; Psalm 69(68); Romans 5:12–15; Matthew 10:26–33

B Job 38:1, 8–11; Psalm 107(106); 2 Corinthians 5:14–17; Mark 4:35–41

C Zechariah 12:10–11; Psalm 63(62); Galatians 3:26–9; Luke 9:18–24

Thirteenth Sunday of Ordinary Time

✠ Year A

'Anyone who finds his life will lose it; anyone who loses his life for my sake will find it.' (Matthew 10:39)

When I settle down, comfortable in my own certainties, I am sovereign of my own little domain, but if I embrace the challenge of my *un*certainties, the whole of creation is mine to discover and rejoice in.

✠ Year B

Death was not God's doing,
he takes no pleasure in the extinction of the living.
To be – for this he created all. (Wisdom 1:13)

It was never your desire that we should die. Yet you turn our dying into a means of grace, by leading us, through death, to that complete emptying of ourselves which makes space for the eternity of your own life in us – the life for which you created us.

✠ Year C

When Christ freed us, he meant us to remain free. Stand firm, therefore, and do not submit again to the yoke of slavery. (Galatians 5:1)

The vets at the Animal Shelter worked tirelessly to free the seabirds from the paralysing tar of the oil slick. There would be further disasters, they knew. But their hearts soared with hope as they watched the cleansed birds fly free and high, away above the polluted waters.

Readings

A 2 Kings 4:8–11, 14–16; Psalm 89(88); Romans 6:3–4, 8–11; Matthew 10:37–42
B Wisdom 1:13–15; 2:23–4; Psalm 30(29); 2 Corinthians 8:7, 9, 13–15; Mark 5:21–43
C 1 Kings 19:16, 19–21; Psalm 16(15); Galatians 5:1, 13–18; Luke 9:51–62

Fourteenth Sunday of Ordinary Time

❧ Year A

'Come to me, all you who labour and are overburdened, and I will give you rest. Shoulder my yoke and learn from me, for I am gentle and humble in heart and you will find rest for your souls. Yes, my yoke is easy and my burden light.' (Matthew 11:28–30)

We find your promised rest, not by evading the burdens of our lives, but by carrying them on your strength. We find our deepest freedom when we are yoked to you.

❧ Year B

Jesus said to them: 'A prophet is only despised in his own country, among his own relatives and in his own house,' and he could work no miracles there, though he cured a few sick people by laying his hands on them. He was amazed at their lack of faith. (Mark 6:4–6)

Suppose, Lord, that you were to walk among us now, among those who call themselves your own friends, brothers and sisters, and suppose you were to walk through your own house here in our town today . . . would you find among us the faith that would open the path of your transforming power to our world, or would you shake your head and sadly walk away?

❧ Year C

'I am sending you out like lambs among wolves. Carry no purse, no haversack, no sandals. Salute no one on the road. Whatever house you go into, let your first words be: "Peace on this house!" And if a man of peace lives there, your peace will go and rest on him.' (Luke 10:4–7)

The market place is milling with Saturday shoppers. Occasionally I look into the face of a passing stranger and her glance meets mine. For a second or two a shaft of recognition passes between us, and we know we have met momentarily in our shared humanity and been enriched by that meeting as we pass on our separate ways. Our peace has rested upon each other and been received.

Readings

A Zechariah 9:9–10; Psalm 145(144); Romans 8:9, 11–13; Matthew 11:25–30

B Ezekiel 2:2–5; Psalm 123(122); 2 Corinthians 12:7–10; Mark 6:1–6

C Isaiah 66:10–14; Psalm 66(65); Galatians 6:14–18; Luke 10:1–12, 17–20

Fifteenth Sunday of Ordinary Time

Year A

Thus you provide for the earth;
you drench its furrows,
you level it, soften it with showers,
you bless its growth. (Psalm 65:10)

The tears that flow through the dark and lonely hours are the rains that soften our hearts with the compassion that can respond to the darkness and the loneliness of each other.

Year B

And Jesus said to them: 'If you enter a house anywhere, stay there until you leave the district. And if any place does not welcome you and people refuse to listen to you, as you walk away, shake off the dust from under your feet as a sign to them.' (Mark 6:10–12)

You have come to us, Lord, to our hearts and our homes, and you have promised never to leave us – unless we refuse to welcome you and listen to your Spirit in our hearts. You will live in us for as long as we desire to live in you.

Year C

'But a Samaritan traveller who came upon him was moved with compassion when he saw him. He went up and bandaged his wounds, pouring oil and wine on them. He then lifted him onto his own mount, carried him to the inn and looked after him.' (Luke 10:33–5)

Jane was the black sheep of the third form, with a very dubious reputation. The teachers cold-shouldered her and her classmates' parents wished she went to some other school. Not many people knew that it was Jane who stopped every evening in the underpass on her way home to share a few words and a sandwich with the homeless people down there.

Readings

A Isaiah 55:10–11; Psalm 65(64); Romans 8:18–23; Matthew 13:1–23
B Amos 7:12–15; Psalm 85(84); Ephesians 1:3–14; Mark 6:7–13
C Deuteronomy 30:10–14; Psalm 69(68); Colossians 1:15–20; Luke 10:25–37

Sixteenth Sunday of Ordinary Time

Year A

'The kingdom of heaven is like a mustard seed which a man took and sowed in his field. It is the smallest of all the seeds, but when it has grown it is the biggest shrub of all and becomes a tree so that the birds of the air come and shelter in its branches.' (Matthew 13:31–2)

Our faith springs from the tiniest beginnings. Its growth is your gift to us, given not just for ourselves, but so that others might find a home in your love, made visible through ours.

Year B

In Christ Jesus, you that used to be so far apart from us have been brought very close, by the blood of Christ. For he is the peace between us, and he has made the two into one and broken down the barrier which used to keep them apart. (Ephesians 2:13–14)

Like distant, separated points around the edge of a circle, we discover, as you draw each of us closer to you, our centre, so we are drawn closer to each other, until we shall all be One in you.

Year C

Martha, who was distracted with all the serving, said: 'Lord, do you not care that my sister is leaving me to do the serving all by myself? Please tell her to help me!' But the Lord answered: 'Martha, Martha,' he said. 'You worry and fret about so many things, and yet few are needed, indeed only one. It is Mary who has chosen the better part; it is not to be taken from her.' (Luke 10:40–2)

The church porch was full of notices: a garden party, a cleaning rota, coffee mornings and discussion groups, hospital visiting and mother-and-toddler groups. A lively church. And in a small side chapel there was the most important notice of all: 'Reserved for quiet prayer.'

Readings

A Wisdom 12:13, 16–19; Psalm 86(85); Romans 8:26–7; Matthew 13:24–43

B Jeremiah 23:1–6; Psalm 23(22); Ephesians 2:13–18; Mark 6:30–4

C Genesis 18:1–10; Psalm 15(14); Colossians 1:24–8; Luke 10:38–42

Seventeenth Sunday of Ordinary Time

❧ Year A

> *Give your servant a heart to understand how to discern between good and evil.* (1 Kings 3:9)

Decisions may be made in my head, but discernment can only happen in my heart.

❧ Year B

> *There is one Body, one Spirit, just as you were all called into one and the same hope when you were called. There is one Lord, one faith, one baptism, and one God who is Father of all, through all and within all.* (Ephesians 4:4–6)

Our divisions are like the fences we might erect to mark the boundaries of our human territories. Below the fences lies the soil in which all our hearts are rooted, and below the soil is the rock upon which all our faith is founded.

❧ Year C

> *'What father among you would hand his son a stone when he asked for bread? Or hand him a snake instead of a fish? Or hand him a scorpion if he asked for an egg? If you, who are evil, know how to give your children what is good, how much more will the heavenly Father give the Holy Spirit to those who ask him?'* (Luke 11:11–13)

Alice was dying before her time, in a makeshift hospital ward at the end of the war. A minor operation had gone wrong because she was so seriously under-nourished and weak. Yet there was joy in her eyes as she held her little grandson in her arms. Then she pressed a small paper bag into his hands – her month's sugar ration and her only source of energy. Small token of immeasurable love.

Readings

A 1 Kings 3:5, 7–12; Psalm 119(118); Romans 8:28–30; Matthew 13:44–52
B 2 Kings 4:42–4; Psalm 145(144); Ephesians 4:1–6; John 6:1–15
C Genesis 18:20–32; Psalm 138(137); Colossians 2:12–24; Luke 11:1–13

Eighteenth Sunday of Ordinary Time

Year A

Come to the water all you who are thirsty;
though you have no money, come! (Isaiah 55:1)

It was quite a culture shock for Jim and Maura, moving from an affluent suburb to a depressed industrial town. In their old home they had been able to buy everything except companionship. Here in their new home, companionship was what they craved above all else, and they discovered with joy that it was given freely and abundantly by their hard-pressed and often unemployed neighbours.

Year B

'I am the bread of life. He who comes to me will never be hungry.' (John 6:35)

How shall your bread be baked for us today? Out of the flour of our lived experience, and the water of our tears, and the yeast of your Spirit in our hearts. So that we might bring it to your hungry world.

Year C

Then Jesus said to them, 'A man's life is not made secure by what he owns, even when he has far more than he needs.' (Luke 12:15)

The Neighbourhood Watch meeting had just heard the police talk on household security systems. Next morning Joe noticed that May hadn't taken in her milk and he went round to check on her. It was then that he found her lying helpless after her fall. And it was then that he learned that neighbourly watchfulness is about a different kind of security.

Readings

A Isaiah 55:1–3; Psalm 145(144); Romans 8:35, 37–9; Matthew 14:13–21
B Exodus 16:2–4, 12–15; Psalm 78(77); Ephesians 4:17, 20–4; John 6:24–35
C Ecclesiastes 1:2; 2:21–3; Psalm 95(94); Colossians 3:1–5, 9–11; Luke 12:13–21

Nineteenth Sunday of Ordinary Time

☙ Year A

After sending the crowds away, Jesus went up into the hills by himself to pray. When evening came, he was there alone, while the boat, now far out on the lake, was battling with a heavy sea, for there was a head wind. In the fourth watch of the night he went towards them, walking on the lake. (Matthew 14:23–5)

I battle with my heavy seas, Lord, and where are you? You are with the Father, drawing the strength for both of us before coming to me with your saving grip.

☙ Year B

Elijah went into the wilderness, a day's journey, and sitting under a furze bush wished he were dead. 'Lord,' he said, 'I have had enough. Take my life; I am no better than my ancestors.' Then he lay down and went to sleep. But an angel touched him and said: 'Get up and eat.' He looked round, and there at his head was a scone baked on hot stones, and a jar of water. (1 Kings 19:4–6)

Sometimes it seems that it is when we are 'running on empty' that you come, so unexpectedly, to refill us with hope and trust, and when we fall into the exhaustion of despair that you bring us, so unhoped-for, the means to keep us going.

☙ Year C

Jesus said to his disciples: 'There is no need to be afraid, little flock, for it has pleased your Father to give you the kingdom.' (Luke 12:32)

Julie flopped into the chair, so thankful for the relaxing acceptance of her friend's home, after a gruelling day trying to make a good impression at the job interview. Here there was nothing to fear. Her friend gave her freely the love and affirmation that she had been striving so hard and so fruitlessly to earn for herself in the workplace.

Readings

A 1 Kings 19:9, 11–13; Psalm 85(84); Romans 9:1–5; Matthew 14:22–33
B 1 Kings 19:4–8; Psalm 34(33); Ephesians 4:30 – 5:2; John 6:41–51
C Wisdom 18:6–9; Psalm 33(32); Hebrews 11:1–2, 8–19; Luke 12:32–48

Twentieth Sunday of Ordinary Time

✠ Year A

God never takes back his gifts or revokes his choice. (Romans 11:29)

It is our own unfaithfulness, Lord, not yours that makes us set aside your gifts and falter in our choosing of your way.

✠ Year B

Go on singing and chanting to the Lord in your hearts, so that always and everywhere you are giving thanks to God who is our Father in the name of our Lord Jesus Christ. (Ephesians 5:19–20)

The joyful awareness of you that we have in the depths of our being is like a living stream that can penetrate the deepest cracks and hollows of our broken world, though we may never realise where our heart's song flows or with what life-giving power.

✠ Year C

With so many witnesses in a great cloud on every side of us, we, too, then, should throw off everything that hinders us, especially the sin that clings so easily, and keep running steadily in the race we have started. Let us not lose sight of Jesus, who leads us in our faith and brings it to perfection. (Hebrews 12:1–2)

I stand in line, waiting to receive communion. For a moment I see myself standing in another, longer line. In front of me all those who have gone before, in faith. Behind me all who will follow after. And, at our head, the source and destination of our journey, the Christ who leads and waits to be received.

Readings

A Isaiah 56:1, 6–7; Psalm 67(66); Romans 11:13–15, 29–32; Matthew 15:21–8
B Proverbs 9:1–6; Psalm 34(33); Ephesians 5:15–20; John 6:51–8
C Jeremiah 38:4–6, 8–10; Psalm 40(39); Hebrews 12:1–4; Luke 12:49–53

Twenty-first Sunday of Ordinary Time

❦ Year A

> *Then Simon Peter spoke up: 'You are the Christ,' he said, 'the Son of the living God.' Jesus replied 'Simon, son of Jonah, you are a happy man; because it was not flesh and blood that revealed this to you but my Father in heaven.'* (Matthew 16:15–17)

We spend years of our lives gathering knowledge and understanding from our learning and experience, but the inner certainties of true wisdom come to us unbidden in timeless moments of revealed clarity.

❦ Year B

> *Then Jesus said to the Twelve, 'What about you, do you want to go away too?' Simon Peter answered, 'Lord, who shall we go to? You have the message of eternal life and we believe.'* (John 6:67–8)

To go away from you is to try to tear my own life out from its roots. An impossibility: you are everything I am and I have no being except in you.

❦ Year C

> *'People from east and west, from north and south, will come to take their places at the feast in the kingdom of God. Yes, there are those now last who will be first, and those now first who will be last.'* (Luke 13:29)

When I finally stopped walking away from you and turned round to face you, I discovered that all my values turned with me and my life was back to front.

Readings

A Isaiah 22:19–23; Psalm 138(137); Romans 11:33–6; Matthew 16:13–20
B Joshua 24:1–2, 15–18; Psalm 34(33); Ephesians 5:21–32; John 6:60–9
C Isaiah 66:18–21; Psalm 117(116); Hebrews 12:5–7, 11–13; Luke 13:22–30

Twenty-second Sunday of Ordinary Time

❦ Year A

Do not model yourselves on the behaviour of the world around you, but let your behaviour change, modelled by your new mind. (Romans 12:2)

Our true shape is not the one imposed from the pressures around us, but the one that emerges from within us, where you dwell, as a flower emerges from a seed.

❦ Year B

Jesus called the people to him again and said, 'Listen to me, all of you, and understand. Nothing that goes into a man from outside can make him unclean; it is the things that come out of a man that make him unclean. For it is from within, from men's hearts, that evil intentions emerge.' (Mark 7:14–16, 21)

Help me to see, Lord, that it isn't the pressures of my circumstances that lead me away from you, but my way of reacting to them.

❦ Year C

Father of orphans, defender of the widow,
such is God in his holy place.
God gives the lonely a home to live in,
he leads the prisoners forth into freedom. (Psalm 68:5–6)

First we discover in you everything we truly are. And then the even greater discoveries begin, as we find in you everything we lack and long for.

Readings

A Jeremiah 20:7–9; Psalm 63(62); Romans 12:1–2; Matthew 16:21–7

B Deuteronomy 4:1–2, 6–8; Psalm 15(14); James 1:17–18, 21–2, 27; Mark 7:1–8, 14–15, 21–3

C Ecclesiasticus 3:17–20, 28–9; Psalm 68(67); Hebrews 12:18–19, 22–4; Luke 14:1, 7–14

Twenty-third Sunday of Ordinary Time

❦ Year A

'Where two or three meet in my name,
I shall be there with them.' (Matthew 18:20)

Where your love flows through our human circles, they become mirrors of your Trinity, where each is bound to all and all to each, and every circle is centred on you.

❦ Year B

They brought Jesus a deaf man who had an impediment in his speech; and they asked him to lay his hand on him . . . and Jesus said to the man 'Ephphatha', that is, 'Be opened.' And his ears were opened, and the ligament of his tongue was loosened and he spoke clearly. (Mark 7:32–5)

Until you open our hearts to hear your truth, our lips will remain incapable of speaking it to others. Lord, that we might hear!

❦ Year C

You sweep men away like a dream,
like grass which springs up in the morning.
In the morning it springs up and flowers:
by evening it withers and fades. (Psalm 90:5–6)

As we watch the chicks of May take flight on their autumn migrations – hatched yesterday and flown tomorrow – we remember our own springing and fading, and we trust you for the unseen harvest.

Readings

A Ezekiel 33:7–9; Psalm 95(94); Romans 13:8–10; Matthew 18:15–20
B Isaiah 35:4–7; Psalm 146(145); James 2:1–5; Mark 7:31–7
C Wisdom 9:13–18; Psalm 90(89); Philemon 9–10, 12–17; Luke 14:25–33

Twenty-fourth Sunday of Ordinary Time

❦ Year A

Peter went up to Jesus and said, 'Lord, how often must I forgive my brother if he wrongs me? As often as seven times?' Jesus answered, 'Not seven, I tell you, but seventy-seven times.' (Matthew 18:21–2)

Just when I thought I had finally forgiven him, a chance remark awakened all my old resentments. How deep must my forgiveness go, Lord? From the quiver on my lips through the tears in my eyes, right down to the gash in my heart!

❦ Year B

You say that you have faith and I have good deeds; I will prove to you that I have faith by showing you my good deeds – now you prove to me that you have faith without any good deeds to show. (James 2:18)

When I pick a ripe, healthy apple, I know that the apple tree has sound, deep roots, but if there are no apples on the tree, how can I know that the tree is alive at all?

❦ Year C

The Lord spoke to Moses, 'Go down now, because your people whom you brought out of Egypt have apostasised . . . They have made themselves a calf of molten metal and have worshipped it . . . Leave me now, my wrath shall blaze out against them and devour them; of you, however, I will make a great nation . . .' But Moses pleaded with the Lord his God. 'Lord,' he said, 'why should your wrath blaze out against this people of yours . . .?' So the Lord relented. (Exodus 32:7–11, 14)

Janet and Jean sat huddled together, both equally terrified by their mother's fury, even though the damage was entirely Jean's fault. Eventually Janet had to break the deadlock. She went to their mother and begged her not to punish Jean. Her mother looked at them both and her eyes softened. In Janet's eyes she saw a depth of love for her sister that took her completely by surprise. It was more than strong enough to overcome her rage. It was strong enough to heal the relationship between the three of them.

Readings

A Ecclesiasticus 27:30 – 28:7; Psalm 103(102); Romans 14:7–9; Matthew 18:21–35
B Isaiah 50:5–9; Psalm 115(114); James 2:14–18; Mark 8:27–35
C Exodus 32:7–11, 13–14; Psalm 51(50); 1 Timothy 1:12–17; Luke 15:1–32

Twenty-fifth Sunday of Ordinary Time

✠ Year A

My thoughts are not your thoughts, my ways are not your ways – it is the Lord who speaks. Yes, the heavens are as high above the earth as my thoughts above your thoughts. (Isaiah 55:8–9)

My image of you is as far removed from your reality as a pinpoint of starlight in the night sky is removed from the fiery sun that is its source – yet both shine with the same light and it is only my distance from you that makes the difference.

✠ Year B

Peacemakers, when they work for peace, sow the seeds which will bear fruit in holiness. (James 3:18)

Making peace, whether in the everyday of family life or in the arena of international affairs, can feel like ploughing through a muddy, unyielding field, yet without that heartbreaking, backbreaking toil, you will have nowhere to scatter the seeds of love.

✠ Year C

Then by lowering the bushel, raising the shekel,
by swindling and tampering with the scales,
we can buy up the poor for money,
and the needy for a pair of sandals. (Amos 8:5–6)

Whenever I make use of another person's good nature to achieve my own ends or to bolster my comfort and ease, I offend against your love as surely and as seriously as the most scheming of politicians.

Readings

A Isaiah 55:6–9; Psalm 145(144); Philippians 1:20–4, 27; Matthew 20:1–16
B Wisdom 2:12, 17–20; Psalm 54(53); James 3:16 – 4:3; Mark 9:30–7
C Amos 8:4–7; Psalm 113(112); 1 Timothy 2:1–8; Luke 16:1–13

Twenty-sixth Sunday of Ordinary Time

✠ Year A

> *'A man had two sons. He went and said to the first: "My boy, you go and work in the vineyard today." He answered, "I will not go," but afterwards thought better of it and went. The man then went and said the same thing to the second son, who answered, "Certainly, sir," but did not go. Which of the two did the father's will?'* (Matthew 21:28–31)

Janet worried and fretted over her rebellious daughter, who adamantly refused to go to church with the rest of the family. Years later, when her obedient children had long since strayed from their faith, she recognised her daughter's deep abiding love of God and her commitment to those in need around her.

✠ Year B

> *John said to Jesus, 'Master, we saw a man who is not one of us casting out devils in your name; and because he was not one of us we tried to stop him.' But Jesus said, 'You must not stop him: no one who works a miracle in my name is likely to speak evil of me. Anyone who is not against us is for us.'* (Mark 9:38–40)

The good news of your love is all-inclusive, Lord. Any exclusions are of our own making, not of yours.

✠ Year C

> *Woe to those ensconced so snugly in Zion*
> *and to those who feel so safe on the mountain of Samaria . . .*
> *they will be the first to be exiled;*
> *the sprawlers' revelry is over.* (Amos 6:1, 7)

Just as I begin to feel safe and sure in your presence, something happens to rekindle some forgotten fear or some unhelpful distraction. I lose my footing and fall victim to the landslip, only to tumble, bruised and tearful, to the foot of the mountain, and there to find myself received into your waiting arms again.

Readings

A Ezekiel 18:25–8; Psalm 25(24); Philippians 2:1–11; Matthew 21:28–32
B Numbers 11:25–9; Psalm 19(18); James 5:1–6; Mark 9:38–43, 45, 47–8
C Amos 6:1, 4–7; Psalm 146(145); 1 Timothy 6:11–16; Luke 16:19–31

Twenty-seventh Sunday of Ordinary Time

❦ Year A

> *There is no need to worry; but if there is anything you need, pray for it, asking God for it with prayer and thanksgiving, and that peace of God, which is so much greater than we can understand, will guard your hearts and your thoughts, in Christ Jesus.* (Philippians 4:6–7)

We try to cling to *our* ways of peace by staying on the outer edges of life's confrontations, but *your* peace is right at their centre. It is the axis around which our whole being spins, with all its needs and sorrows.

❦ Year B

> *Jesus said, 'I tell you solemnly, anyone who does not welcome the kingdom of God like a little child will never enter it.'* (Mark 10:15)

A child's passport to life is her thrill of joy at all its wonders and her intense desire to engage in its mystery. Let these same gifts be our passport to your kingdom-life.

❦ Year C

> *The apostles said to the Lord, 'Increase our faith.' The Lord replied, 'Were your faith the size of a mustard seed you could say to this mulberry tree, "Be uprooted and planted in the sea," and it would obey you.'* (Luke 17:5–6)

A tiny grain of faith can be enough to uproot the weeds of fear and doubt that choke our hearts. And a tiny mustard seed can flavour the whole pot of soup in which our lives are lived.

Readings

A Isaiah 5:1–7; Psalm 80(79); Philippians 4:6–9; Matthew 21:33–43
B Genesis 2:18–24; Psalm 128(127); Hebrews 2:9–11; Mark 10:2–16
C Habakkuk 1:2–3; 2:2–4; Psalm 95(94); 2 Timothy 1:6–8, 13–14; Luke 17:5–10

Twenty-eighth Sunday of Ordinary Time

Year A

> *'The king said to his servants, "The wedding is ready; but as those who were invited proved to be unworthy, go to the crossroads in the town and invite everyone you can find to the wedding." So these servants went out onto the roads and collected together everyone they could find, bad and good alike, and the wedding hall was filled with guests.'* (Matthew 22:8–10)

We may be very surprised when we see some of the unlikely people you have invited to your wedding feast – but they may be even more surprised if they find *us* there!

Year B

> *The word of God is something alive and active: it cuts like any double-edged sword but more finely . . . No created thing can hide from him; everything is uncovered and open to the eyes of the one to whom we must give account of ourselves.* (Hebrews 4:12–13)

When my friend looked deep into my eyes, I knew that he was reading my soul. He was knowing me, just for that moment, as you know me always, Lord, yet loving me with your unconditional love. To be fully known, yet to be wholly loved – these are the two edges of the sword of your word.

Year C

> *Naaman the leper went down and immersed himself seven times in the Jordan, as Elisha had told him to do. And his flesh became clean once more like the flesh of a child. Returning to Elisha, he said 'Now I know that there is no God in all the earth except in Israel. Now please accept a present from your servant.' But Elisha replied, 'As the Lord lives, whom I serve, I will accept nothing.'* (2 Kings 5:14–16)

There is nothing we can give you in gratitude for our healing, except to live out the fullness of lives made whole again, as reflections of your love.

Readings

A Isaiah 25:6–10; Psalm 23(22); Philippians 4:12–14, 19–20; Matthew 22:1–14

B Wisdom 7:7–11; Psalm 90(89); Hebrews 4:12–13; Mark 10:17–30

C 2 Kings 5:14–17; Psalm 98(97); 2 Timothy 2:8–13; Luke 17:11–19

Twenty-ninth Sunday of Ordinary Time

Year A

When we brought the Good News to you, it came to you not only as words, but as power and as the Holy Spirit and as utter conviction. (1 Thessalonians 1:4–5)

Janice rarely speaks directly of her faith. But in the quiet authority of the life she lives in you, those who know her know that they are touching one who is in touch with you, one through whom the currents of your love are flowing.

Year B

The Lord has been pleased to crush him with suffering.
If he offers his life in atonement,
he shall see his heirs, he shall have a long life
and through him what the Lord wishes will be done.
His soul's anguish over
he shall see the light and be content. (Isaiah 53:10–11)

When we feel crushed by life's weight we can choose whether to let it press us down into ourselves, or whether to join our brokenness to yours, and become, like you, carriers of grace to others.

Year C

The Lord is your guard and your shade;
at your right side he stands.
By day the sun shall not smite you,
nor the moon in the night. (Psalm 121:5–6)

In those parts of our life that seem like empty deserts, we feel the extremes of the desert climate: the burning pain of anger or disappointment; the cold darkness of despair. But you, who made both sun and moon, hold us in the far greater orbit of your unchanging love.

Readings

A Isaiah 45:1, 4–6; Psalm 96(95); 1 Thessalonians 1:1–5; Matthew 22:15–21
B Isaiah 53:10–11; Psalm 33(32); Hebrews 4:14–16; Mark 10:35–45
C Exodus 17:8–13; Psalm 121(120); 2 Timothy 3:14 – 4:2; Luke 18:1–8

Thirtieth Sunday of Ordinary Time

❦ Year A

'You must love the Lord your God with all your heart, with all your soul, and with all your mind. This is the greatest and the first commandment. The second resembles it: you must love your neighbour as yourself. On these two commandments hang the whole Law, and the Prophets also.' (Matthew 22:37–40)

Love is not an optional extra, to warm and soften our ways of living and relating; it is the very energy of life holding all creation in being and relationship.

❦ Year B

See, I will bring them back from the land of the North
and gather them from the far ends of the earth;
all of them: the blind and the lame,
women with child, women in labour:
a great company returning here.
They had left in tears,
I will comfort them as I lead them back. (Jeremiah 31:8–9)

The sight of the Lord's people returning home is full of surprises. They look more like a casualty ward on a Saturday night, but we know who they are: we can recognise them by their tear-stained, life-soiled faces, transfigured now with joy.

❦ Year C

'Two men went up to the Temple to pray, one a Pharisee, the other a tax collector. The Pharisee stood there and said this prayer to himself: "I thank you, God, that I am not grasping, unjust, adulterous, like the rest of mankind, and particularly that I am not like this tax collector here. I fast twice a week; I pay tithes on all I get." The tax collector stood some distance away, not daring even to raise his eyes to heaven; but he beat his breast and said, "God, be merciful to me, a sinner." ' (Luke 18:9–13)

When I think of the things that I do best in life, and feel the satisfaction of doing them better than my friends or colleagues, then I meet my inner Pharisee, who points her finger at me with the words 'And *you* thought you were a tax collector!'

Readings

A Exodus 22:20–6; Psalm 18(17); 1 Thessalonians 1:5–10; Matthew 22:34–40
B Jeremiah 31:7–9; Psalm 126(125); Hebrews 5:1–6; Mark 10:46–52
C Ecclesiasticus 35:12–14, 16–19; Psalm 34(33); 2 Timothy 4:6–8, 16–18; Luke 18:9–14

Thirty-first Sunday of Ordinary Time

❧ Year A

Truly I have set my soul
in silence and peace.
A weaned child on its mother's breast,
even so is my soul. (Psalm 131:2)

She was only three months old; she was incontinent and inarticulate and utterly dependent on me. Yet, as I held her in my arms, she taught me more about trust and faith than I could ever begin to understand, let alone teach *her.*

❧ Year B

Listen, Israel: the Lord our God is the one Lord. You shall love the Lord your God with all your heart, with all your soul, with all your strength. Let these words I urge on you today be written on your heart. (Deuteronomy 6:5–7)

The words of our lips vanish into thin air, unless they are embodied in the way we live our lives. May our listening lead us into loving, and may our loving become one with our living.

❧ Year C

The Lord is faithful in all his words
and loving in all his deeds.
The Lord supports all who fall
and raises all who are bowed down. (Psalm 145:13–14)

Jake was getting old and feeling the strain in his back. But his garden was his pride and joy. After the storm he put on his boots and went out to tend his plants. Lovingly, he bound up those that had been flattened by the wind and supported them with canes and twine. Those that had snapped completely, he brought into the house, put the broken flowers in a vase and took new cuttings from the shattered plants. It was his sacrament of faith, of hope, and of love.

Readings

A Malachi 1:14 – 2:2, 8–10; Psalm 131(130); 1 Thessalonians 2:7–9, 13; Matthew 23:1–12

B Denteronomy 6:2–6; Psalm 17; Hebrews 7:23–8; Mark 12:28–34

C Wisdom 11:22 – 12;2; Psalm 145(144); 2 Thessalonians 1:11 – 2:2; Luke 19:1–10

Thirty-second Sunday of Ordinary Time

✠ Year A

> *'The bridegroom was late and the bridesmaids all grew drowsy and fell asleep. But at midnight there was a cry, "The bridegroom is coming! Go out and meet him!" '* (Matthew 25:4–6)

In all our doing and arranging, let us not forget your deeper call to live in grace-filled and expectant waiting.

✠ Year B

> *Jar of meal shall not be spent,*
> *jug of oil shall not be emptied,*
> *before the day when the Lord sends rain on the face of the earth.* (1 Kings 17:14)

When we come to the last remnants of our own resources, we are standing close to the brink of your saving grace.

✠ Year C

> *'He is God, not of the dead, but of the living, for to him all people are in fact alive.'* (Luke 20:38)

In a garden there is no death, but only the falling of seed to the waiting earth. Lord, holder of our dead darkness, and of the seeds you have planted there, let our gardens live!

Readings

A Wisdom 6:12–16; Psalm 63(62); 1 Thessalonians 4:13–18; Matthew 25:1–13
B 1 Kings 17:10–16; Psalm 146(145); Hebrews 9:24–8, Mark 12:38–44
C 2 Maccabees 7:1–2, 9–14; Psalm 17(16); 2 Thessalonians 2:16 – 3:5; Luke 20:27–38

Thirty-third Sunday of Ordinary Time

✠ Year A

> *'You have shown you can be faithful in small things, I will trust you with greater; come and join in your master's happiness.'* (Matthew 25:21)

Ruth had been hurt that day in the office, many years ago, by the unjust reprimand, and Elaine had helped to ease the hurt by resting her hand on her colleague's arm in a gesture of understanding. Today, as Ruth reeled under the shock of the diagnosis of her terminal illness, she remembered that gesture of love, and suddenly she knew who to turn to in her need and her loneliness.

✠ Year B

> *The learned will shine as brightly as the vault of heaven, and those who have instructed many in virtue, as bright as stars for all eternity.* (Daniel 12:3)

When we hold our children in our arms, gently pointing out the consequences of hurting others, the light we kindle in their minds casts its glow over all the human family.

✠ Year C

> *The day is coming now, burning like a furnace; and all the arrogant and evil-doers will be like stubble. The day that is coming is going to burn them up, says the Lord of hosts, leaving them neither root nor stalk. But for you who fear my name, the sun of righteousness will shine out with healing in its rays.* (Malachi 3:19–20)

Out of the harvest of our lives, the stubble of our failure. Out of the stubble of failure, the smoke of our shame. Out of the smoke of shame, the ashes of hope, and out of the ashes the nutrients for the new life, waiting for the healing rays of the sun, and a new beginning.

Readings

A Proverbs 31:10–13, 19–20, 30–1; Psalm 128(127); 1 Thessalonians 5:1–6; Matthew 25:14–30

B Daniel 12:1–3; Psalm 16(15); Hebrews 10:1–14, 18; Mark 13:24–32

C Malachi 3:19–20; Psalm 98(97); 2 Thessalonians 3:7–12; Luke 21:5–19

Christ the King *(Last Sunday of the Year)*

☙ Year A

> *The Lord says this: I am going to look after my flock myself and keep all of it in view . . . I rescue them from wherever they have been scattered during the mist and darkness.* (Ezekiel 34:11–12)

When you seem far away and high above us, Shepherd-Friend, let us know that it is only so that you might the more clearly see where we have strayed to and come to carry us home.

☙ Year B

> *Jesus answered [Pilate], 'Yes, I am a king. I was born for this, I came into the world for this: to bear witness to the truth; and all who are on the side of truth listen to my voice.'* (John 18:37)

A king who lives by truth and a kingdom founded on love. We were born for this: to serve such a King, and to grow such a Kingdom.

☙ Year C

> *The people stayed there watching Jesus. As for the leaders, they jeered at him. 'He saved us,' they said, 'let him save himself if he is the Christ of God, the Chosen One.'* (Luke 23:35–6)

It was hard for Mark to imagine, as he watched his father dying in agonising pain and disfigurement, that he had lived out his life as a surgeon whose touch had saved so many others. Then the end came, and as the stricken doctor gave back his life-breath to God, his face relaxed into a peace beyond understanding. It was in that moment that Mark understood the difference between truly healing and merely curing.

Readings

A Ezekiel 34:11–12, 15–17; Psalm 23(22); 1 Corinthians 15:20–6, 28; Matthew 25:31–46

B Daniel 7:13–14; Psalm 93(92); Revelation 1:5–8; John 18:33–7

C 2 Samuel 5:1–3; Psalm 122(121); Colossians 1:11–20; Luke 23:35–43